"Ia Eradze's book represents a milestone in the study of the dollarization of a transition economy. She has demonstrated that dollarization cannot be derived solely from the calculations of utility-maximizing individuals, but that its dynamics must be understood in terms of the interplay of modes of accumulation, institutional structure, social power relations and prevailing ideas. Ms. Eradze has presented a political-economic work in the truest sense."

Prof. Dr. Christoph Scherrer *Director, International Center for Development and Decent Work, University Kassel, Kassel*

Unravelling the Persistence of Dollarization

This volume engages with the roots, dimensions, and implications of foreign currency domination in states with a national currency. Referred to as unofficial dollarization in literature, this is a worldwide phenomenon among developing countries and has a long history.

This monograph provides a political economic analysis of dollarization in Georgia and is structured around three themes: the genesis of dollarization (1991–2003), the persistence of dollarization (2003–12) and the politicization of dollarization (2012–19). The case of Georgia is especially representative of the post-socialist transition states, but also has wider applicability.

A high level of dollarization is a significant barrier to economic growth, macroeconomic and political stability, functional monetary policy, as well as social welfare. The Covid-19 crisis and the increasing debt of developing countries in foreign currency exacerbate dollarization-related vulnerabilities for these economies.

This book will be of interest to postgraduate students in global/comparative political economy, development economics or transition economies, researchers in monetary sovereignty, central banking, exchange rate policies, currency hierarchy, money, financialization, and policy makers in dollarized countries and global institutions.

Ia Eradze is a researcher at the Institute for Social and Cultural Studies, Ilia State University, Tbilisi. She is also a fellow in the Legacies of Communism research network, which was initiated by the Leibniz Centre for Contemporary History in Potsdam (ZZF). Her area of research is political economy and historical evolution of finance in the post-socialist space. Her most recent pieces include *Financialization of Monetary Policy in a Dollarized Economy: The case of Georgia*, https://doi.org/10.1093/cje/beac019 Cambridge Journal of Economics and *Taming Dollarization Hysteresis: Evidence from Post-socialist States*, which will appear in an edited volume (Edward Elgar Publishing).

Europa Economic Perspectives

Providing in-depth analysis with a global reach, this series from Europa examines a wide range of contemporary economic issues from areas around the world. Intended to complement the *Europa Regional Surveys of the World* series, *Europa Economic Perspectives* will be a valuable resource for academics, students, researchers, policymakers, business people and anyone with an interest in current world economic affairs.

While the *Europa World Year Book* and its associated *Regional Surveys* inform on and analyse contemporary economic, political and social developments, the Editors considered the need for more in-depth volumes written and/or edited by specialists in their field, in order to delve into a country's or a region's particular economic situation, or to examine economic theories in the context of current global economic affairs. Volumes in the series are not constrained by any particular template, but may explore any aspect of a country's recent economic issues in order to increase knowledge.

Advances in Geoeconomics
Edited by J. Mark Munoz

The Economic Crisis and its Aftermath in the Nordic and Baltic Countries
Do As We Say and Not As We Do
Hilmar Þór Hilmarsson

Deficit Politics in the United States
Taxes, Spending and Fiscal Disconnect
Dennis S. Ippolito

The Japanese Economy
Strategies to Cope with a Shrinking and Ageing Population
Randall S. Jones

Unravelling the Persistence of Dollarization
The Case of Georgia
Ia Eradze

For more information about this series, please visit: www.routledge.com/Europa-Economic-Perspectives/book-series/EEP.

Unravelling the Persistence of Dollarization

The Case of Georgia

Ia Eradze

Routledge
Taylor & Francis Group
LONDON AND NEW YORK

Cover image: © Shutterstock

First published 2023
by Routledge
4 Park Square, Milton Park, Abingdon, Oxon OX14 4RN

and by Routledge
605 Third Avenue, New York, NY 10158

Routledge is an imprint of the Taylor & Francis Group, an informa business

British Library Cataloguing in Publication Data
A catalogue record for this book is available from the British Library

Library of Congress Cataloging-in-Publication Data
A catalog record has been requested for this book

ISBN: 978-1-032-14584-6 (hbk)
ISBN: 978-1-032-14615-7 (pbk)
ISBN: 978-1-003-24017-4 (ebk)

DOI: 10.4324/9781003240174

Typeset in Times New Roman
by Taylor & Francis Books

To my parents and their generation, who had to carry the heaviest burden of post-Soviet transition.

Contents

Illustrations

Figures

Tables

Abbreviations

CB	Central Bank
CBR	Central Bank of Russia
CEE	Central and Eastern Europe
CIS	Commonwealth of Independent States
CUG	Civil Union Georgia
FTA	Free Trade Agreement
DEG	Deutsche Investitions- und Entwicklungsgesellschaft
EBRD	European Bank for Reconstruction and Development
EC	European Commission
EFF	Extended Fund Facility
EPRC	Economic Policy Research Centre
EU	European Union
FC	Foreign Currency
FED	Federal Reserve System
FMO	Dutch Entrepreneurial Development Bank
FSU	Former Soviet Union
FX	Foreign Exchange
GATT	The General Agreement on Tariffs and Trade
GDP	Gross Domestic Product
GEL	Georgian Lari
GYLA	Georgian Young Lawyers Association
HI	Historical Institutionalism
IDP	Internally Displaced Person
IFC	International Finance Corporation
IFI	International Financial Institution
IMF	International Monetary Fund
IO	International Organization
ISFED	International Society for Fair Elections and Democracy
JEC	Joint Economic Committee
KfW	Kreditanstalt für Wiederaufbau
NATO	North Atlantic Treaty Organization
NC	National Currency
NBG	National Bank of Georgia

NGO	Non-governmental Organisation
OECD	Organisation for Economic Cooperation and Development
OSGF	Open Society Georgia Foundation
OSI	Open Society Institute
PTI	Payment to Income
RA	Regulation Approach
ROA	Return on Assets
ROE	Return on Equity
SBFIC	Savings Banks Foundation for International Cooperation
SDR	Special Drawing Right
SME	Small and Medium Enterprise
TI	Transparency International
UNDP	United Nations Development Programme
UNICEF	United Nations Children's Fund
UNM	United National Movement
US	United States
USAID	United States Agency for International Development
USD	United States Dollar
PTL	Payment to Loan
VAT	Valued Added Tax
WB	World Bank
WTO	World Trade Organisation
WWII	World War II

The author

Ia Eradze is a researcher at the Institute for Social and Cultural Studies, Ilia State University, Tbilisi. She is also a fellow in the research network Legacies of Communism, which was initiated by the Leibniz Centre for Contemporary History in Potsdam (ZZF). Her area of research is political economy and historical evolution of finance in the post-socialist space. Her most recent pieces – 'Financialization of Monetary Policy in a Dollarized Economy: The Case of Georgia' https://doi.org/10.1093/cje/beac019 in the *Cambridge Journal of Economics* and 'Taming Dollarization Hysteresis: Evidence from Post-socialist States' will appear in an edited volume (Edward Elgar Publishing).

Acknowledgements

This book is the result of a long but exciting four years of daily work, research puzzles, and struggles. The entry point to this monograph was prompted by the 2015 protests of Georgian households, who were indebted in foreign currency and faced financial issues upon the depreciation of the Georgian lari. This is when the issue of dollarization started to haunt me as a researcher, and I asked myself how a sovereign state could let its society be indebted in a foreign currency.

This work would not have come to life without the enormous intellectual and moral support of others. My book owes a lot to many at the University of Kassel and elsewhere, who had made invaluable proposals and critique during the process. I am enormously grateful to Professor Christoph Scherrer, who introduced me to the field of political economy and has supported me intellectually throughout these years. From him I have learned to be more investigative, courageous towards innovative approaches, and critical but open to critique at the same time. My work has also gained from discussions at workshops, seminars, and conferences at different places. Among others, I would like to thank Professor Joscha Wullweber, Professor Hansjörg Herr, Anil Shah, Halyna Semenyshyn, Jorge Enrique Forero, Anna Weber, and Marcel Zeitinger for their comments and productive critique. I am thankful to Ismail Karapete for encouraging me to take on the challenge of studying a complex financial phenomenon and for his feedback on different chapters.

My fieldwork in Georgia has been possible only through the help of different people. I would like to thank my interviewees for finding the time and interest, and to others, who have opened their doors to me for these meetings. I am thankful to many in Georgia, who have kept their ears open to my research and offered me various platforms and possibilities to present different parts of this book. The constant interaction with the Georgian audience, in academia and beyond, has been an invaluable proof of the plausibility of this monograph. Writing this book would not have been possible without the financial support of the German Academic Exchange Service (DAAD).

I have enjoyed enormous support from my family while working on this book. My husband Ronny has given me courage from the beginning and lifted my spirits on difficult days. My sons, Elias and Nikoloz, have offered a perfect balance to long days spent in a library.

I hope that this book contributes not only towards academic research, but also to the policymaking agenda and inspires others to challenge prevailing hegemonic ideas.

Part I

Dollarization and its discontents

Some moneys […] are far more equal than others.

(Cohen, 2011, p. 123)*

*The quote refers to George Orwell's *Animal Farm* (1945)

DOI: 10.4324/9781003240174-1

1 Introduction

Why does dollarization matter and what is at stake?

A walk through any street of a Georgian city means an encounter with numerous currency exchange shops, often in a row close to one another, competing with profitable exchange rates. Every change in the currency value is observed anxiously by the Georgian population, as it might cause difficulties in the servicing of loans in foreign currency. Despite a decreasing trend of dollarization over recent years, the rate of loan dollarization was[1] 55% in 2020, while deposit dollarization exceeded 60% (National Bank of Georgia, 2021, p. 56). These figures[2] might appear meaningless at first glance. Yet, if dollarization is seen from the perspective of households, numbers acquire faces, projecting names and stories of unsecured lives. Consumer loans (12.8% of total loans) and mortgages (21% of total loans) have long become an inseparable part of the daily lives of Georgians (National Bank of Georgia, 2021, p. 98). Difficulties in credit repayment impose the threat of homelessness to borrowers, when home ownership is the only social and economic security for most citizens. These threats were manifested during the currency crisis of 2015–2016 as unhedged borrower households had to suffer the most severe consequences of the currency depreciation. More than 50% of retail loans were denominated in foreign currency in 2016 (National Bank of Georgia, 2016, p. 88) and more than 90% of households that were indebted in foreign currency earned money in the national currency (International Monetary Fund, 2015b, pp. 11–12). By the end of 2016 almost 50% of household loans were collateralized by housing, and the rate of dollarization in this case reached 74% (National Bank of Georgia, 2019).

Dollarization is not only connected to the indebtedness of households, but also undermines the sovereignty of the country. The level of dollarization in corporate loans is higher than in retail loans (41%), respectively 60% in SME loans and 70% in corporate loans (National Bank of Georgia, 2021, p. 101). Moreover, 80% of the public debt is denominated in foreign currency (International Monetary Fund, 2021, p. 32). Not only are most of the loans and deposits denominated in foreign currency, but also certain segments of the market, like real estate, set prices in dollars. Thus, monetary sovereignty is challenged. High levels of dollarization can lead to instabilities in the financial sector and in the case of a financial crisis, the National Bank of Georgia (NBG) cannot fully take over the role of a

DOI: 10.4324/9781003240174-2

lender of last resort. Moreover, foreign capital dominated financial systems (referring to foreign ownership of commercial banks) are neither sensitive nor responsive to dollarization issues and might even worsen the overall situation through excessive foreign currency lending. For an import-dependent country like Georgia,[3] high dollarization and vulnerability to exchange-rate fluctuations has a negative impact on prices. Depreciation of the national currency also leads to the increase of external debt. Dollarization-led issues decrease the credibility of the government and might cause a political crisis, as well.

Dollarization related issues were aggravated during the Covid-19 pandemic. The pandemic had a deteriorating impact on retail loans. The share of restructured non-performing and negative loans increased especially for foreign currency loans due to the depreciation of the Georgian lari against the USD (by 14%) and the Euro (by 25%), in 2020. Key sectors of the Georgian economy – real estate development and management, tourism, restaurants, car dealers – were hit most by the pandemic and they were exposed to the currency depreciation risk due to their high shares of foreign currency loans (National Bank of Georgia, 2021, pp. 103–106). The forceful evictions of indebted households were stopped for a short period only in 2020 (Pertaia, 2020), although housing acquired a completely different meaning during the pandemic, as it turned into a key space of security and survival. Government debt to GDP increased from 40% to 60% in 2020 due to increased borrowing (mostly in foreign currency) to meet pandemic-related challenges (International Monetary Fund, 2021, p. 19).

Thus, dollarization is a threat to the well-being of Georgians, as well as to overall economic development and political stability. Though the dollar has been a hegemonic currency since the 1990s, dollarization has not been perceived as a problem by political and economic power groups or by civil society in Georgia. It was the currency crisis, since the end of 2014, that rang alarm bells first in the pockets of households and then in the minds of politicians. Between 2015 and 2017, the Georgian lari lost 50% of its value against the US dollar (World Bank, 2018, p. 6). As the lari depreciated people started to protest in the streets, because their foreign currency loan costs had increased. Moreover, exchange-rate fluctuations contributed to household over-indebtedness through increases in the debt burden and in prices. In 2015, around 30% of retail borrowers spent more than one-half of their income on servicing loans (International Monetary Fund, 2015a, p. 18).

Dollarization was all of a sudden everywhere, from the parliament to TV screens, public transport, and living rooms. The lari crisis had a spillover effect on politics; not only was the credibility of commercial banks and the NBG decreasing, the legitimacy of the government was also drawn into question. Currency depreciation uncovered socio-economic issues that had accumulated over decades and the elephant in the room could not be ignored any more. Thus, dollarization was finally problematized and politicized in 2015; the trajectory of this process was controversial, spontaneous, and emotional, entangled with conflicts and hot-headed debates.

Expert and public discussions on dollarization have been polarized, focusing on finding scapegoats and avoiding a fundamental historical analysis of the problem. Either banks were blamed for tempting people to take credits in foreign currency (cheating them on loan conditions), or the whole responsibility was shifted towards 'financially uneducated' borrowers. Another set of polarized debates has been ongoing among and between the government, the central bank, commercial banks, and international organizations (IOs), highlighting the diversity of interests, as well as the complexity of policymaking. Discourses on the logic of markets, the 'legitimacy' of profit-making, the 'truth' of financial knowledge, social welfare, and state responsibilities have been entangled in these debates. Discussions on dollarization reflect power relations within and outside the Georgian state, as well as its peripheral positioning in the global structure – shedding light on the limitations and possibilities of the policy space for small open economies with import, capital, and currency dependencies.

The polarization of the debate about dollarization and its complexity highlight the need to explore the roots of the problem of dollarization and its persistence. Yet, the literature of dollarization offers limited answers to these questions and the gaps in the academic literature further strengthen the necessity of this book (see Chapter 2). Dollarization is usually explained as an outcome of financial and macroeconomic instabilities and is supposed to decrease with low inflation and stable macroeconomic conditions (see e.g., Ize & Yeyati, 2003). However, it is well documented by now that this is not the case. This puzzle has been referred to as 'persistence' or 'hysteresis' of dollarization and a number of authors have tried to explain it (see Aslanidi, 2008; Duffy et al., 2006; Guidotti & Rodriguez, 1992; Havrylyshyn & Beddies, 2003; Ize & Yeyati, 2003; Oomes, 2003; Rappoport, 2009; Uribe, 1997; Valev, 2007; Winkelried & Castillo, 2010). This literature treats dollarization as a purely economic phenomenon, rooted in high inflation and economic instability, ignoring the role of social and political processes at the domestic and international levels, or in institutions or civil society. Nevertheless, factors such as inflation, investor decisions, trust, or the development of the financial system are insufficient for understanding the genesis and hysteresis of this phenomenon. A comprehensive historical explanation of the persistence of dollarization is missing in the literature. Moreover, the existence of the puzzle is itself a clear manifestation of the blind spots in the studies of dollarization, offering a legitimate reason for questioning the understanding of dollarization in the aforementioned literature.

Georgia represents a classical example of dollarization hysteresis. Even though the Georgian economy has experienced growth since 2004 (after the Rose Revolution), macroeconomic indicators have improved, inflation has decreased, and institutions have developed, financial dollarization persists at high levels. Therefore, this book aims to contribute to the understanding of and theorizing on dollarization by studying the Georgian case. The main findings of the research will introduce a new perspective into the current debates around dollarization in Georgia. In response to policy issues and the academic puzzle, this book engages with the following research questions: why does dollarization persist in Georgia? How and why has dollarization come into being in Georgia? Has dollarization been problematized and why?

In order to answer these questions and overcome the economism of the existing literature, the first part of this monograph analyses dollarization applying a state-theory approach (Chapter 2). The analytical linkage between dollarization and the state draws on the historical interconnectedness of nation states and national currencies, as well as on the responsibility of the state for monetary affairs and the socio-economic welfare of society. Dollarization is not just a monetary issue, it is entangled with socio-economic and political developments, therefore, it requires broad analysis, embedded in history, culture, politics, daily life, institutions, and decision-making structures. Moreover, the historical parallelism between the emergence of dollarization and the independent post-Soviet Georgian state (since 1991) offers fruitful ground for understanding the genesis and persistence of the hegemony of a foreign currency alongside the process of state-building. Thus, the state is both the structure and agent in this research.

The understanding of the state is rooted in the political economic state debate and takes a peripheral state approach as the starting point of analysis. A relational state approach enables the analysis of different forces within the state, including political and economic power groups, civil society, and international actors. The embeddedness of these groups in production relations and manifold power relations at the domestic and global level sheds light on the driving forces, interests, factors, and attitudes of dollarization. The regulation and Dependency School premises on the peripheral-state approach are supplemented with post-structural concepts for methodological openness (referring to structure-agency relations) to move beyond the economic focus. Moreover, the study of the peripheral positioning of the Georgian economy in the global structure introduces another level of analysis – the global context. This dimension has a crucial importance especially for issues like dollarization in small countries such as Georgia. The concept of peripheral financialization, moreover, sheds light on the persistence of dollarization by analysing the development of the financial sector and monetary policy.

Yet, the peculiarities of the Georgian state and findings from the empirical research outline the limitations in the above-mentioned theoretical frame and inspire thought of a hybrid state model, embedded in Soviet experience. A political-economic understanding of hybridity, expressed in controversial governance tactics and economic setting, is conceptualized on the verge of colonial legacies and transition imperatives in this work. Uncovering the irregularities and controversies of the Georgian state is crucial for understanding dollarization and also contributes towards theorizing the Georgian state.

The book is structured around the main questions alongside major historical political developments. The first question deals with the history of dollarization from 1991 until the Rose Revolution of 2003; the second explains the persistence of dollarization in post-revolution Georgia, where dollarization remained high despite major economic and institutional reforms; the last part focuses on the trajectory and factors of the politicization of dollarization, from the change of government in 2012 to the lari crisis of 2015–2016, including post-crisis de-dollarization efforts until 2019. Each part is based on an analysis of the Georgian state and provides answers to the genesis, hysteresis, or politicization of dollarization by embedding dollarization in political debates, government tactics, policies and institutions, economic interests, the accumulation regime, civil society attitudes, and global processes and international actors.

The second part provides a historical context for dollarization by tracing its roots to the first years of independence. Therefore, Chapter 3 deals with the history of dollar hegemony in the world, as well as its main preconditions in Georgia. The main aim is to outline the linkages of dollarization with the transition agenda enforced in Georgia since independence (1991). The process of transition marked the beginning not only of capitalist market creation, but also of Georgia's integration into the world market. Therefore, the roots of dollarization are explored in broad structural changes such as the liberalization of the capital account, the currency, and prices. Yet, as dollarization cannot be explained without socio-economic and political developments at the local level, Chapter 4 analyses the formation of political and economic groups, civil society groups, governance technologies, and the new accumulation regime. This chapter provides not only the local context, but also identifies specific channels and factors of dollarization. Moving beyond a broader context, Chapter 5 focuses on the hyperinflation of 1993–1994, the birth of the Georgian national currency, the lari, in 1995 and the Russian economic crisis of 1998. These three developments are crucial for understanding the history of dollarization. Negative experiences of the inflation in the 1990s turned out to be long lasting for the Georgian public, shaping their attitudes towards the national currency. The events around hyperinflation also decided the fate of the Russian ruble in Georgia and the final victory of the dollar over the Russian currency. Moreover, the history of the lari and its first big test – the Russian crisis – identify the key factors that strengthened the role of the dollar in Georgia. The last segment of the first part, Chapter 6, engages with the history of the Georgian financial system, embedding the roots of dollarization in the functioning of commercial banks and the central bank during the 1990s.

The third part is the core of the study, as it deals with the major question of the persistence of dollarization. It begins with the Rose Revolution (2003) and an analysis of the new Georgian state. Chapter 7 provides the explanation of dollarization hysteresis by linking it with the rhetoric of state building and development of Saakashvili's government, analysing the main foci of civil society and exploring the post-revolution accumulation regime in relation to dollar hegemony. The analysis of the Georgian state is linked with global processes, influences, narratives, and ideas. The chapter provides explanations on the peaceful coexistence of the dollar and the new Georgian state, as a top reformer and a platform for liberalism. It also answers the question of why dollarization was neither challenged nor problematized in political or public discourse. Furthermore, the persistence of dollarization is explained in relation to economic changes, despite the improvement of macroeconomic stability. Chapter 8 considers the core factors of the persistence of dollarization by analysing the major developments in the financial sector and central banking. The post-revolution period marked the beginning of the revival of the Georgian financial system by opening the doors to foreign capital and shaping commercial banks as major actors. Excessive lending to households (also in foreign currency) led to a credit boom in 2005–2006, creating systemic risks for unhedged borrowers and for overall financial stability. The loosening of the regulatory framework and the excess liquidity of banks in foreign currency further encouraged foreign currency lending. The chapter also deals with central bank policies and assesses their plausibility in terms of local context needs and challenges. It also analyses policy spaces and dilemmas of the National Bank regarding de-dollarization measures.

The fourth part (Chapter 9) describes the politicization process of dollarization by analysing the currency crisis of 2015 and household over-indebtedness. It provides a broader political and economic context of the Georgian state after the change of government in 2012 and highlights the main socio-economic issues. The currency crisis is analysed in connection with previous historical developments as a triggering cause for the problematization of dollarization. Furthermore, the chapter deals with the responses of the government and central bank to dollarization and to over-indebtedness, assessing their effectiveness and plausibility. Chapter 10 summarizes the main findings of the book and reflects on the main implication of dollarization in the times of Covid-19.

Thus, the analysis of dollarization alongside and within the Georgian state helps us to understand the structure in which dollarization could emerge and still exists. It also outlines the agency of the Georgian state in dealing with or disregarding questions of dollarization. It demonstrates the unwillingness and inability, as well as the lack of knowledge of the Georgian political elite to tackle the issue. It uncovers the entangled and inseparable interests of political elites and capital factions who saw no interest in a strong national currency. It unravels the accumulation regimes in connection with dollarization. It highlights the influence of IOs in creating legal, spatial, and practical frameworks for a foreign currency to enter the country and then to call for de-dollarization. It points out the weakness of civil society groups over economic or monetary issues that did not and could not challenge government policies or the transition agenda of IOs.

Notes

1 Until 2014 the level of loan dollarization even exceeded deposit dollarization.

2 Until 2017, the central bank of Georgia regulated only commercial banks. Consequently, the measurement of dollarization level, as well as other available data on the financial sector is derived from commercial banks. Data from micro-finance organizations, online loan platforms, and peer-to-peer lending is missing.
3 Georgia's trade deficit was -44.8% in 2019 (Geostat, 2021, p. 2).

References

Aslanidi, O. (2008). Dollarization in Transition Economies: New Evidence from Georgia (No. 366; Charles University GERGE-EI Working Paper Series).

Duffy, J., Nikitin, M., & Smith, R. T. (2006). Dollarization Traps. *Journal of Money, Credit, and Banking*, 38(8), 2073–2097.

Geostat. (2021). External Merchandise Trade in Georgia: January. www.geostat.ge.

Guidotti, P., & Rodriguez, C. A. (1992). Dollarization in Latin America: Gresham's Law in Reverse? (91/117; IMF Working Papers).

Havrylyshyn, O., & Beddies, C. H. (2003). Dollarization in the Former Soviet Union: from hysteria to hysteresis. *Comparative Economic Studies*, 45(3), 329–357.

International Monetary Fund. (2015a). Georgia: Financial Sector Assessment Programme. Macroprudential Policy Framework – Technical Note. https://www.elibrary.imf.org/view/journals/002/2015/009/002.2015.issue-009-en.xml.

International Monetary Fund. (2015b). Georgia: Financial Sector Assessment Programme. Stress Testing the Banking Sector – Technical Note. https://www.elibrary.imf.org/view/journals/002/2015/007/article-A001-en.xml.

International Monetary Fund. (2021). Eighth Review under the Extended Fund Facility Arrangement – press release; and staff report (Issue 21/79). https://www.imf.org/en/Publications/CR/Issues/2021/04/16/Georgia-Eighth-Review-Under-the-Extended-Fund-Facility-Arrangement-Press-Release-and-Staff-50358.

Ize, A., & Yeyati, E. L. (2003). Financial Dollarization. *Journal of International Economics*, 59, 323–347.

National Bank of Georgia. (2016). Ts'liuri angarishi [Annual Report]. https://nbg.gov.ge/publications/annual-reports.

National Bank of Georgia. (2019). Seskhebi uzrunvelq'opis mikhedvit [Loans across collateral types]. https://nbg.gov.ge/en/statistics/statistics-data.

National Bank of Georgia. (2021). Annual Report 2020. https://nbg.gov.ge/publications/annual-reports.

Oomes, N. (2003). Network externalities and dollarization Hysterisis: The case of Russia (03/96; IMF Working Papers).

Pertaia, L. (2020, April 9). gamosakhleba shecherda [Evictions have been stopped]. *Netgazeti*. https://netgazeti.ge/news/442078/.

Rappoport, V. (2009). Persistence of Dollarization after Price Stabilization. *Journal of Monetary Economics*, 56(7), 979–989.

Uribe, M. (1997). Hysteresis in a Simple Model of Currency Substitution. *Journal of Monetary Economics*, 40, 185–202.

Valev, N. T. (2007). The Hysteresis of Currency Substitution: currency risk vs. network externalities (No. 07–23; Andrew Young School of Policy Studies Research Paper Series).

Winkelried, D., & Castillo, P. (2010). Dollarization Persistence and Individual Heterogeneity. *Journal of International Money and Finance*, 29(8), 1596–1618.

World Bank. (2018). Georgia from Reformer to Performer. https://openknowledge.worldbank.org/handle/10986/29790.

2 The obscurities of dollarization

Dollarization as a contested phenomenon

Financial dollarization refers to the replacement of national currency functions by another currency, where dollar is used as a general term for all foreign currencies. One can differentiate between official and unofficial dollarization, where the latter can have two forms – currency and asset substitution. If in the first case, a foreign currency is used for exchange, foreign currencies are used for saving as a form of asset substitution (Levy-Yeyati, 2006, pp. 63–64). The measurement of dollarization differs across countries, but deposit dollarization is most often used as a key indicator. Priewe and Herr highlight two more aspects: foreign and government debt dollarization (Priewe & Herr, 2005, p. 163). Price dollarization can also be an important indicator in measuring dollarization. Georgia faces unofficial financial dollarization, and its rate refers to the share of foreign currency in loans and deposits.

Dollarization is not a new phenomenon, but it turned into the spotlight of academics and policymakers in the late 1990s, after the financial crises of Argentina, Asia, and Russia (Lin & Ye, 2010, p. 1124). Dollarization already existed in the nineteenth century in African countries (Egypt, Ghana, Liberia, Tunisia etc.) and became a typical characteristic for post-Soviet economies from the beginning of the 1990s (Versal & Stavytskyy, 2015, p. 21). There is relatively little known on the history of dollarization, and it has been considered to be a 'secondary phenomenon' (Priewe & Herr, 2005, p. 159). Dollarization has been mostly studied in Latin American countries (Levy-Yeyati, 2006, p. 66). Relatively little research has been done on post-Soviet economies (see exceptions, e.g., Aslanidi, 2008; Brown et al., 2017; Havrylyshyn & Beddies, 2003), even though these states still demonstrate high levels of dollarization.

Dollarization is a major challenge for economic development, but it can also have some advantages. Under full dollarization the missing role of a central bank as the lender of last resort would remove a safety net from banks and encourage them to function without it. Thus, dollarization would support the development of domestic financial markets. It can also

DOI: 10.4324/9781003240174-3

encourage consolidation of fiscal reforms as interest rates would decrease with the disappearance of inflation and debt service costs would diminish (Eichengreen, 2001, pp. 269–272). Full dollarization can be a way of avoiding inflation and a balance of payment crisis, and it can encourage integration into the world economy (because of stable prices in the dollar) (Arellano & Heathcote, 2010, p. 945). Furthermore, dollarization gives households an opportunity to make deposits in a safe currency; budget deficits cannot be financed by central bank credits, which can avoid problems in the monetary system and full dollarization enables one to save the costs of having one's own currency (Priewe & Herr, 2005, pp. 170–171). Moreover, dollarization can encourage trade between dollarized countries and the USA (Lin & Ye, 2010, p. 1125).

Nevertheless, dollarization has disadvantages for developing countries and scholars urge for de-dollarization in most cases (Aslanidi, 2008; de Nicoló et al., 2003; Levy-Yeyati, 2006; Mecagni et al., 2015). Dollarization limits the independence of monetary policy (Priewe & Herr, 2005, p. 160) and restrains a central bank from being a lender of last resort (Mecagni et al., 2015, p. 1). It causes higher financial fragility as banks bear higher deposit volatility and insolvency risks. Dollarization might also lead to a financial crisis during depreciation due to currency mismatches (de Nicoló et al., 2003, p. 2). Furthermore, dollarization affects output volatility negatively and hinders economic growth (Levy-Yeyati, 2006, pp. 108–109). A high rate of dollarization disables control on exchange rates and inflation reduction strategies, which can support the functioning of shadow economy (Aslanidi, 2008, p. 2; Kakulia & Aslamazishvili, 2000, p. 41). Dollarized countries practically lose exchange rate as a policy tool. If normally currency depreciation could increase international competitiveness of exports goods and services, dollarization and high vulnerability to currency depreciation challenges this norm (Priewe & Herr, 2005, pp. 175–176). Developing countries usually take foreign debt in foreign currency, and as these countries usually cannot demonstrate high liquidity rates, they have to accept high interest rates or increase the national wealth in foreign currency. This phenomenon is referred as an 'original sin' by Eichengreen and Hausmann (Priewe & Herr, 2005, pp. 167–168) (see on original sin: Eichengreen & Hausmann, 1999; Hausmann & Panizza, 2003).

Therefore, de-dollarization is of high relevance for dollarized countries, but the attempts to get away from foreign currency domination are not always successful. After the financial crisis of 2008, Central and Eastern European countries tried to tackle dollarization through limiting the supply of foreign currency loans, empowering borrowers (financial education, right to information on risks, payment to income, and loan to value ratios) and developing national currency markets (Eradze, 2022b). These policies have been implemented in line with dominant theoretical approaches to dollarization. Prohibition of foreign currency loans and deposits, macroeconomic and financial stability, financial deepening, prudential regulation, confidence building in national currency have been widely discussed as de-dollarization policies in the academic debate (Aslanidi, 2008; Havrylyshyn & Beddies, 2003; Levy-Yeyati, 2006; Naceur et al., 2015). However, these measures have not turned out to be very effective for several reasons. These de-dollarization policies were developed as a reaction to the crisis and not as a logical outcome of rethinking such structural factors as the functioning of the state, accumulation regime or central banks. As dollarization of household loans especially is directly related to the retreat of neoliberal states from their social responsibilities (such as provision of housing, education or health) (see Kolasa, 2021), rethinking of the state is crucial. Moreover, a global solution was not discussed in line with changes on local levels. Yet, dollarization is a global issue which is embedded in asymmetrical global power relations (see Ongena et al., 2020) and it cannot be solved within particular countries only (see Eradze, 2022b).

Dollarization is rather under-theorized. Most scholarships focus on economic dimensions, which could partially be explained by the fact that most of the dollarization literature is written by economists (see for example Koji, 2017) and political scientists who have not paid too much attention to it so far (see Eradze, 2022b). The portfolio view by Ize and Yeyati (2003) explains dollarization through the portfolio decisions of investors, who choose a currency composition of their portfolios according to risk-return calculations of their investments in national and foreign currencies. Different from the portfolio model, the market failure view unravels dollarization through market imperfections, externalities, and improper regulation (Levy-Yeyati, 2006, pp. 78–79). However, the institutional view raises the importance of the quality of institutions. This model argues that if countries have a good institutional record, their repudiation costs are low, which will result into low interest rates and no inflation bias (Levy-Yeyati, 2006, pp. 82–83). The impact of institutions on the level of dollarization is manifold. Monetary policy that does not consider long-term consequences might encourage inflation for the sake of growth. Persistence of such a process may lead to the diminishing value of national currency and dollarization (Kishor & Neanidis, 2015, p. 817). Trust in the national currency is one more crucial aspect in understanding dollarization, where political and economic stability plays a significant role (Priewe & Herr, 2005, pp. 167–168) (see Kakulia & Aslamazishvili, 2000, pp. 37–40, for the Georgian case). Moreover, foreign ownership of banks and lending in foreign currency can encourage dollarization, especially in developing countries (see Basso et al., 2011). Differences in foreign and national currency loan interest rates play an important role in encouraging foreign currency loans, as they are usually cheaper (see on foreign-owned banks Barisitz, 2005; Beck & Brown, 2015; Detragiache et al., 2006; Luca & Petrova, 2008). Banks in foreign ownership might get involved in the so-called carry trade, lending money in foreign currency to local firms and households. This not only increases the level of loan dollarization but can also lead to liquidity and a banking crisis, especially when national currencies devaluate (Priewe & Herr, 2005, p. 172).

Thus, dollarization is mostly discussed through purely economic lenses in the literature, and it appears as though these approaches are trying to squeeze a giant genie into a tiny bottle. These explanations are in line with neoclassical economics, assuming that agents are rational, self-interested, and that they make rational choices. This assumption is mostly accompanied by a supposition of perfect information and efficient markets. However, economization of the academic discussion makes it difficult to explain why dollarization persists after macroeconomic and financial stability is achieved. Examples of developing countries have shown that despite a significant improvement in inflation rates and financial indicators, dollarization rates remain high. This phenomenon has been referred to as hysteresis (see Duffy et al., 2006; Guidotti & Rodriguez, 1992; Havrylyshyn & Beddies, 2003; Ize & Levy-Yeyati, 2005; Oomes, 2003; Rappoport, 2009; Uribe, 1997; Valev, 2007; Winkelried & Castillo, 2010). Theoretical approaches to dollarization persistence, which analyse currency or asset substitution, as well as dollarization of transactions, try to solve the persistence puzzle either through models where inflation rate or its volatility plays a key role (Duffy et al., 2006; Guidotti & Rodriguez, 1992; Ize & Yeyati, 2003) and or by network externalities (Feige et al., 2003; Oomes, 2003; Uribe, 1997; Valev, 2007). Yet, these models also remain trapped in narrow economistic explanations (see Eradze, 2022b).

The nation state – national currency nexus

Weakness of currencies (in terms of losing its functions) cannot be explained without understanding the state (as argued in Eradze, 2022b). Yet, the state is usually missing in economic models of dollarization and if it enters the debate, it does so only in terms of a prudential regulation. Three main reasons can be identified for supporting the linkage between dollarization and the state. First, it is a matter of the state to deal with currency issues, as dollarization makes households, firms, the overall economy, and the financial system vulnerable to exchange-rate volatilities. Second, dollarization directly limits state capacities in terms of monetary policy and countercyclical fiscal policy mechanisms. Third, governments lose tools of communication with a society with a weak national currency. Moreover, in terms of neoliberal states, the rise of foreign currency loans is directly linked with and caused by the retreat of governments from providing affordable housing, health, and education (see Eradze, 2022b). However, states are not outsider actors that need to fix the problem, but are a vessel of these relations and serve as an important actor at the same time. Thus, how can dollarization be contextualized in a post-Soviet state such as Georgia?

There are two ways of thinking about currencies in relation with states: analytical and historical. The analytical linkage is connected with the understanding of currencies in terms of a hegemonic project, which is embedded within the state. Yet, the creation of money and of a national currency does not occur on the state level and with state actors only, rather this process is embedded in global struggles with the involvement of the global state and non-state actors. The second linkage is historical and further strengthens the validity of the first link. It comes out of linkages between national currencies and nation states and highlights the importance of national money in nation and state building.

National currencies have always been related to the idea of the nation state and national identity. Authors like Anthony Giddens (1985), Gianfranco Poggi (1978), Eric Hobsbawm (1992) have pointed at the historical parallelism between the emergence of a nation state and national currency (Gilbert & Helleiner, 2011, pp. 3–4). The introduction of national banknotes in the nineteenth century and the removal of different forms of money from the system was connected to the increasing role of the state in the everyday economic life of its citizens. Increasing trust in national currency was important which indicated the 'introduction of more representative forms of government, as well as [...] emerging nationalist sentiments' (Gilbert & Helleiner, 2011, p. 5). With the development of industrial capitalism, the importance of money and national currency increased. Issues of exchange rates became obvious and the idea of creating central banks arose in the early 1920s to build a certain mechanism of macroeconomic control (Gilbert & Helleiner, 2011, p. 6). After the collapse of industrial capitalism in the 1930s and the introduction of Keynesian economics, 'the state came to harness money as a way of linking itself to the inhabitants of the territory it governed' (Gilbert & Helleiner, 2011, p. 7). Though dollarization literature considers money as a means of exchange, payment, and store of value, this does not explain why some monies are preferred over others. Money needs to be explained with the use of geographical, political, historical, and cultural perspectives (Gilbert & Helleiner, 2011, p. 1). Money can also be understood as a tool of communication, which in the context of a nation state gives people a feeling of belonging to a community (Gilbert & Helleiner, 2011, p. 7). Thus, functions of national currency go beyond the well-known five functions of money and includes such features as: communication, trust, and belonging to a national community (Cooper, 2009, p. 10), shaping and strengthening national identities (Helleiner, 1998).

Even though there is an extensive literature on state building in transition context, it has predominantly focused on analysing institutions and measuring the success of these states with the standards of western nation states (see Rekhviashvili & Polese, 2017, pp. 4–5, for the discussion on this strand of literature). This literature is rather silent about state-capital relations or the role of national currencies in state-building. Changes in post-Soviet and Central and Eastern European (CEE) countries since the 1990s are mostly discussed in the transition framework, which has not been developed into a proper theory. Post-socialist space has been regarded as a 'deviation from capitalism' (Papava, 2005, p. 14), and not much attention has been paid to the development of its theory. As Müller correctly points out, the *East* remains disconnected from the rest of the world and the major concepts like ex-Soviet, post-socialist, or old Eastern bloc highlights 'this condition of being stuck in time [...] as though after almost 30 years, the communist East has not found its way in the present yet' (Müller, 2020, p. 741).

In contrast with most transition approaches, the Regulation School puts an emphasis on the role of the state in transition, looking at production and consumption, economic regulation, labour, and power (Pavlinek, 2003, pp. 100–102). However, in the early application of the theory to post-communist countries, state socialism was often equated with Fordism (e.g. Altvater, 1993), though later attempts to analyse post-communist transformation were more successful (Pavlinek, 2003, pp. 105–106; Pickles & Smith, 1998; Smith & Swain, 1998), relations between national and global economies and the analysis of other actors as regulators besides the states were missing (Pickles & Smith, 1998, p. 29).

Transition literature falls short on explaining political economy of state building, as well. Scholars have either focused on markets or states in their analysis of transition. Market transition theorists have mostly ignored the importance of the state in the transition process (Rona-Tas & Guseva, 2014, p. 29). The little attention paid to the state can be explained by the fact that the state was discredited, and societies preferred a market economy, without acknowledging the consequences (Brabant, 1998, p. 359). The main aim throughout the 1990s was to weaken the state apparatus and create political pluralism. Reforming the economic sphere enjoyed primacy over the political aim of achieving democracy within the transition agenda (Cheterian, 2008, p. 689).

Thus, the theoretical debate on post-Soviet states and markets is rather limited for understanding why political society in Georgia allowed foreign currency domination, how dollarization fitted in the state-building narrative and in dominant discourses of the Georgian civil society, which social groups and actors gained from dollarization in Georgia and who lost. Moreover, dollarization would be embedded within the accumulation regime which emerged in independent Georgia and where foreign capital has played a significant role.

Dollarization in a hybrid state

Various labels have been used to describe the pre-2003 revolution Georgian state, such as pseudo democracy (see Diamond, 2002), or façade democracy (see Carothers, 2002), while post-revolution Georgia has been framed as authoritarian liberal (Jobelius, 2011), competitive authoritarian (Lazarus, 2010), or state-managed capitalism (Timm, 2013). The Georgian state has indeed emerged as a hybrid state on the crossroads of the Soviet past and transition. Post-socialist states cannot be measured or analysed within a western state model, but differences from this model do not necessarily indicate that the state is abnormal or failed. A failure of such states is mostly explained through domestic issues and weaknesses in academic debates. Foreign governments and international organization (IOs) usually pick up the role of a saviour and try to build western states. Simultaneously, they gain enormous power in internal affairs. This provides a perfect ground for imposing numerous directives, recommendations, or adjustment programmes.

Hybridity is understood in political economic terms in this book. Its core idea is not about measuring the level of democratization, as it is usually conceptualized in the academic debate (see Aprasidze, 2004; Cheterian, 2008; Wheatley & Zürcher, 2008). Hybridity is about understanding divergences between the official rhetoric and actual policies, which usually rest on informal governance tactics. It is a way of coping with contrasting differences between the past and present. It is also the result of trying to put a new skin on an old body, which does not fully fit. Even though one tries to demonstrate the good new skin, it remains a façade and cover up of the old body. It takes a much longer time to grow into a new skin. The hybridity of the Georgian state is thus analysed along the following axes: political and civil societies, accumulation regime, governance tactics, and positioning of the state in the global structure. It was exactly due to the hybrid character of the Georgian state that the emergence and persistence of foreign currency domination was possible.

Hybridity has a time dimension as well (Figure 2.1). New political and economic imperatives of marketization and democratization did not develop on an empty page, but rather clashed with the pre-existing historical and cultural conditions that were not necessarily compatible with the new way of life. Exactly this set of contradictions and the time pressure on implicating new transition reforms resulted into divergences between rhetoric and practice. Informalities kept providing a stabilization mechanism for the state, as a way of disobeying and coping with the transition paradigm (see on informalities Aliyev, 2014, p. 22). Therefore, in Georgia new institutions, constitution, etc. have often been used as a façade to cover up the structures of informal governance (Aprasidze, 2004, p. 45). Moreover, state intervention and market competition appear to be coexisting in Georgia in favour of the power of the ruling class (Christophe, 2005, pp. 24–25). Thus, selectivity and stability are key characters of hybridity in Georgia.

Patterns of hybridity are not static; they change across different governments (Table 2.1). Even though the 2003 Rose Revolution meant the birth of the new Georgian state, it did not change everything. Path dependency on informalities, authoritarian practices, as well as patrimonialism or market interventions proved to be lasting patterns of statehood. Most importantly, Georgia kept its façade character, although in a different way. Whereas Shevardnadze mostly tried to fool IOs that his government was implementing reforms, Saakashvili was reforming the country, but fooling the population and the international community over the actual practices and means of these reforms. While Shevardnadze's government was primarily concerned with rent seeking, Saakashvili had the ambition of building a new state,

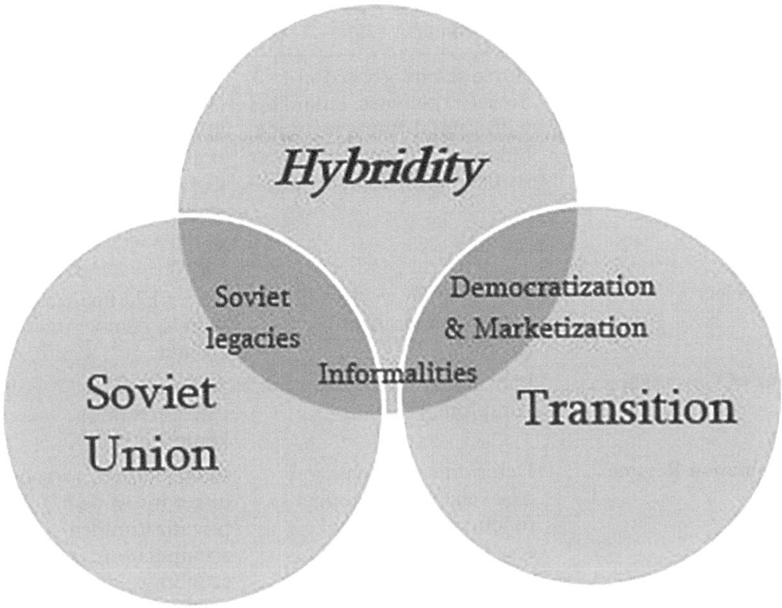

Figure 2.1 The time dimension of hybridity
Source: Author's illustration.

though personal gains were not fully forgotten. Furthermore, if Shevardnadze's government rested on the patronage system, where corruption and kompromat (a Russian word for compromising material) represented most important governance tools, Saakashvili's power was rather based on the police, though corruption remained at the elite level and kompromat was still utilized in governance.

Though Georgian state acquired different types of hybridity during Shevardnadze's and Saakashvili's presidencies, in both cases it represented a strong state (Figures 2.2 and 2.3). Thus, there was no retreat of the state, as often argued for in transition literature (see for e.g. Brabant, 1998; Cornia, 2012, pp. 294–295; Rona-Tas & Guseva, 2014, pp. 28–29). In this context a question of the agency of the Georgian state in relation to dollarization becomes even more plausible. Why did the Georgian state not avoid foreign currency domination?

The Georgian governments succeeded in freeing themselves from socio-economic responsibilities towards the public but remained the most important actor throughout the transition process. None of the major changes, reforms, or redistribution of political and economic power happened without the direct involvement of the government that was in a protective relationships with businesses and market actors. Moreover, Georgian state demonstrated strong agency

Table 2.1 Patterns of hybridity during Shevardnadze's and Saakashvili's presidencies

	Shevardnadze (1995–2003)	*Saakashvili (2003–2012)*
Political Society	Bureaucratic, rooted in Soviet experience, entangled with capital fractions, weak linkage with the public, rent seeking aims, façade values	Western-oriented, modernization and libertarian ideas, state-building aim, rent seeking (not primarily), control over public and civil society, façade values
Civil Society	Emerging on western liberal ideas, democratization agenda	US or EU financed NGOs, democratization agenda
Means of Governance	Patrimonialism, corruption, kompromat	Authoritarianism, police, elite corruption, kompromat
Accumulation Regime	Deteriorated production base, chaotic economic functioning, informal economy (with criminal elements), speculative finance, dependency on imports, foreign capital and foreign currency, liberalization reforms,	Financialized, foreign direct investment/ privatization-led accumulation, service economy, very weak production, high share of informal economy, de-regulated finance, dependency on imports, foreign capital and foreign currency, neoliberal reforms
Positioning in the Global Structure	Peripheral, not well integrated into the global economy	Peripheral, better integrated into the global economy, increased dependencies on the goods and capital from the core

Source: Author's visualization.

not only vis-à-vis the market, but also in relation to international actors. However, currency related issues and the importance of a strong national currency remained beyond the scope of the political agenda.

Dollarization did not turn into the spotlight within the new, post-revolution state building project either. The process of marketization and the integration of Georgia into global capitalism was intensified after the 2003 Rose Revolution. The post-revolution government demonstrated such key characteristics of statehood as authoritarian governance combined with a libertarian understanding of state and economic policies, achieving success in a neoliberal understanding of good governance. Libertarian ideas on monetary policy, deregulation of the financial sector and liberalization policies to attract foreign capital further supported the persistence of dollarization albeit alongside economic growth and stability. The dominant political discourse on economic development, in line with modernization, was not opposed by any significant forces of civil society at that time. Democracy remained in the official rhetoric but disappeared from practice. A shift of focus of IOs from democracy to good governance enabled the Georgian government to gain their hearts through its attainment of high rankings for good governance (see Lazarus, 2013). As Lazarus demonstrates, a good governance narrative not only enabled the WB and the IMF to interfere in the political sphere of developing countries, but also successfully served the purpose of implementing neoliberal economic policies in these states, in favour of capital freedoms and the technocratization of the decision-making process (Lazarus, 2013, pp. 6–7). Thus, Georgia emerged into an authoritarian neoliberal state after the revolution, which was primarily demonstrated in the changing character of the state as less democratic, becoming a state that was deploying legal and constitutional measures instead of democratic participation (see Bruff, 2014). Even though Saakashvili's government built a police state, authoritarianism is not reduced to coercion, as it can be traced 'in the reconfiguring of state and institutional power' (Bruff, 2014, p. 115). Neoliberal projects deploy legal, administrative, and coercive tools of governance to justify their politics (Bruff & Tansel, 2019, p. 239). These tactics were constantly used by the post-Rose Revolution government, as well as constitutional changes to strengthen executive power, the prohibition of

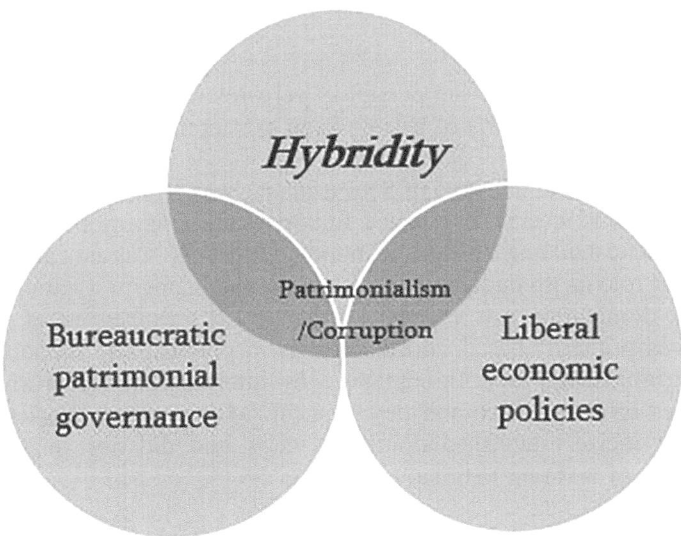

Figure 2.2 Hybridity under Shevardnadze
Source: Author's illustration.

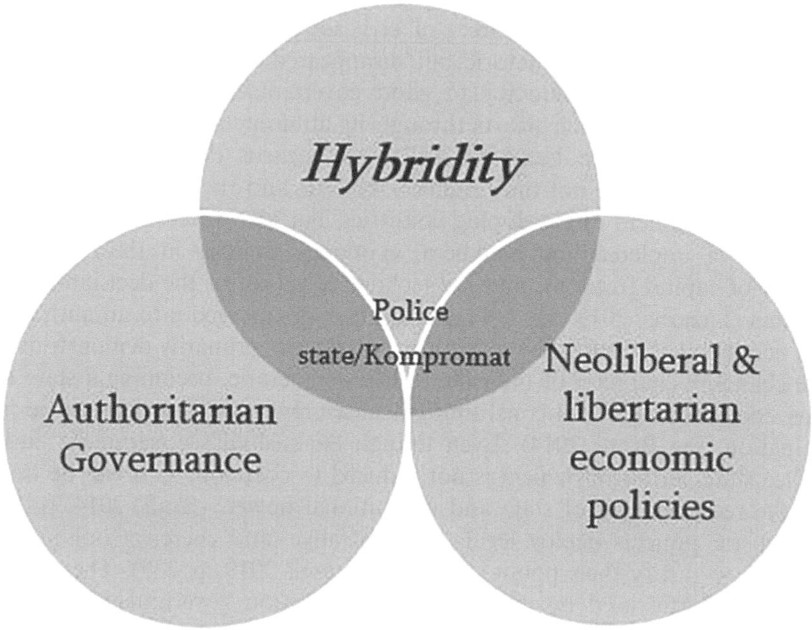

Figure 2.3 Hybridity under Saakashvili
Source: Author's illustration.

strikes to weaken labour, the pursuit of zero tolerance politics, and tax terrorism or the blackmailing of businesses to extract money and property from them (see Eradze, 2020).

Thus, the patrimonial state of Shevardnadze was replaced by Saakashvili's authoritarian neoliberal governance. In both cases dollarization could coexist with the state building agenda, as national currency was not attributed an important role in strengthening the feeling of belonging to a nation. Foreign currency domination was enabled by the hybrid arrangement of the state, which was primarily based on the interests of political and economic elites. These arrangements were strengthened by international actors and global discourses on governance and development. Moreover, civil society groups did not criticize established dominant views and did not emphasize the importance of a strong national currency.

Dollarization and peripheral financialization

The state is a social power relation, which is embedded in production relations, and is characterized through coercion to capital accumulation and wage labour.[1] The state is also responsible for structural inequalities within the production relations. Accumulation strategies need the support of the state, which is also dependent materially on the proper functioning of businesses. This is where the structural political dominance of capital is manifested, although the interests of capital can also differ (Becker, 2008, p. 10).

A regime of accumulation refers to a means of the stable reproduction of socio-economic relations, whereas a mode of regulations explains how this regime has been enabled and established (Lipietz & Jenson, 1987). Here, 'Each *regime of accumulation* represents a distinct pattern of economic evolution which, [...], is relatively stable. [....] Each *mode of regulation* is constituted by a historically developed, relatively integrated network of institutions', [that] 'governs the accumulation process' (Brenner & Glick, 1991, pp. 47–48; italics original). Forms of accumulation (Table 2.2) or reproduction are influenced by an institutional configuration of structural forms of regulation. In regulation the basic forms of social relations and structural forms of regulation can be identified in a capitalist society. Under the basic forms, commodity and state forms are meant, whereas structural forms are loan and competition relations, ecological and money restrictions (Becker, 2002, pp. 271–273).

Currency relations are embedded in the relations between state apparatus and capital accumulation (Figure 2.4). Moreover, they are directly linked with political and civil societies, the unity of which makes up the state and where hegemony is 'protected by the armored coercion' (Gramsci, 2000, p. 235). An important terrain for these relations, according to Gramsci, is a civil society, where 'struggle[s] over social norms and over the pre-formation of legal norms and forms of state intervention that sustain specific forms of accumulation and social reproduction' (Becker et al., 2010, pp. 226–227). Different institutions – the family, the church, the media, etc. – make up civil society. A political society consists of the government, the parliament, the police, the military, the bureaucracy, and the law (Wullweber, 2012, p. 32). Hegemonic struggles within civil society not only define the fate of political leadership or economic domination, but they also reflect the attitudes and

Table 2.2 Types of Accumulation

Productive	*Investments in productive sphere*
Fictive	Investments in finance
Extensive	Surplus value achieved through organizational changes and spreading to new areas of activity, competitive regulation
Intensive	Surplus value achieved through existing capitalist activities, monopolistic regulation, mass consumption
Extrovert	Strengthening exports (active) – countries of the core, or import dependency (passive) – peripheral countries
Introvert	Focus on domestic markets

Source: Author's table based on Becker, 2002; Becker et al., 2010.

interests of different social groups towards the importance of a strong national currency. Thus, a successful regulation or governance is not intentionally created by capital or the state, but through a process of struggle for hegemony, which is neither independent nor completely determined by societal structures (Brand, 2005, pp. 31–34).

Hegemony can be established only when the universalization of particular interests in the ethic-political stage takes place. This act of universalization is a political moment which is a result of negotiations and does not necessarily express interests of the society (Wullweber, 2012, p. 33). Accordingly, the hegemony of a foreign currency can be established if it is accepted by the key capital fractions and social groups, without necessarily expressing broader social interests. Yet, a consensus is not the only precondition for hegemony, as it is also backed up by coercion. However, it should be noted that the relation between the economic base and the superstructure goes both ways as they each influence one other (Scherrer, 2001, p. 4; see also Demirović, 2007, p. 31). The role of global actors and foreign capital is especially important for hegemonic struggles in peripheral economies, where external dominance might turn into the internalization of external interests – local classes might find a common interest with international capital and create alliances (Becker, 2008, p. 16). Therefore, the interests of global capital may have a strong influence on the establishment of dollar hegemony in peripheral states like Georgia.

Acknowledging a very valid critique about Regulation School (see theories Dzudzek et al., 2012, p. 14; Scherrer, 1995, p. 466), this research goes beyond economism and functionalism in the analysis and puts societal struggles and dynamics in the spotlight. Therefore, a Foucaldian concept of dispositive is introduced (instead of mode of regulation) as 'a thoroughly heterogeneous ensemble consisting of discourses, institutions, architectural forms, regulatory decisions, laws, administrative measures, scientific statements, philosophical, moral and philanthropic propositions' (Foucault, 1980, p. 194).[2]

Dollarization is rooted in the process of global capital accumulation, and therefore the positioning of the Georgian economy in the global structure matters; accumulation models differ in the centre and the periphery. The understanding of statehood should not be limited to its territorial borders, especially for peripheral countries. It can be stretched to an international level in reference to other states or IOs (Table 2.3). Though IOs lack certain features of the state, they are still in a continuum with statehood forms (Becker, 2002, p. 275). Thus, the analysis of the state should occur simultaneously at national and international levels linking both dimensions. Following Poulantzas (1976), a mechanical division between internal and external factors can be broken down. The analysis of internal factors has primacy, and internal and external factors need to be analysed in connection with each other (Ataç et al., 2008, p. 5).

The concepts of periphery and core can be traced to the dependency theory that emerged in the 1960s and 1970s as a critique to the

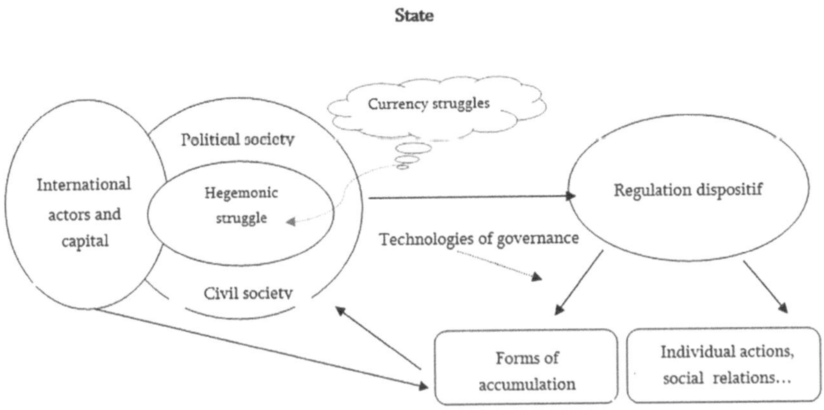

Figure 2.4 The state
Source: Author's illustration based on the literature discussed in this chapter.

Table 2.3 Levels and dimensions of foreign influence

Foreign Influence	*Level of Ideas*	*Material Level*	*Possible Influence / Outcomes*
Political Society	Policy recommendations	Government funding, debt, grants	Stabilizing impact – governments have less chance to be authoritarian; legitimacy source for policies
Civil Society	Predefinition of thematic focus for projects and grants	NGO funding	Promoting hegemonic or counterhegemonic projects, strengthening certain discourses and ignoring others
Capital Accumulation	Policy recommendations for Central Bank, choice of economic sectors for investment, impact on loan policy of banks	Foreign capital in finance and production, Central Bank funding	Strengthening economic dependencies of the country, ignoring local context and needs

Source: Literature discussed in this section and observations of this study.

modernization theory in Latin America. The pioneers of the theory emphasized the importance of global structures and the role of history (especially colonial influences in the Global South even after the end of colonialism) in the development process. Exactly these relations in favour of the Global North or core countries hindered the development of states of the Global South or periphery (Kufakurinani et al., 2017, pp. vi–vii). Capitalism has and always had a global character, and it has been linked to globalization and its implications have structurally differed in the core and periphery which are 'two sides of the same coin' (Amin & Kvangraven, 2017, p. 14). If in the countries of the capitalist centre the production tool industry and the consumption goods industry are connected and the market is expanding, this kind of accumulation does not happen in the periphery. Peripheral countries often face issues of technological dependency that hinders the development of the production of goods. These countries become dependent on imports and their trade balance worsens with time (Becker et al., 2013, pp. 35–36). These deficits are mostly financed by foreign borrowing, which does not only increase the debt burden, but also raises the level of dollarization (see Eradze, 2022a).

The accumulation regime in Georgia, which emerged especially after the 2003 revolution, can be characterized by the domination of fictive capital production in the money-commodity-money circle. Fictive capital is a very liquid form of capital investment, and it is often used in times of uncertainty and when investment in productive sectors is lacking. This type of accumulation is characterized through threats of instability (see Becker, 2002, p. 270). Moreover, the Georgian economy resembles key patterns of capital accumulation in peripheral economies – passive extraversion, where the issue of technological dependency hinders the development of production of goods and these countries become dependent on imports (Becker et al., 2013, pp. 35–36). Therefore, peripheral countries like Georgia need capital to tackle current account deficits due to trade imbalances. Import dependence becomes especially visible in the wake of fast economic growth and the rise of investment. Financing current account deficits through foreign capital often leads to the over-indebtedness of these countries and debt restructuring programmes usually appear as a door opener for creditors to implement political and economic influence (Becker, 2008, pp. 12–14). Theoretically, capital could enter these countries through productive investment or in the form of money capital. However, the export of money capital has become even more important especially in the wake of financialization as peripheral countries have become attractive for capital investment with high interest rates (Becker et al., 2013, pp. 35–36). Capital flows from the core to the periphery, in search of higher profits, has led to the process of financialization in the Global South (see for literature overview Bonizzi, 2013; Karwowski & Centurion-vicencio, 2018; Karwowski & Stockhammer, 2017) (see Karwowski & Centurion-vicencio, 2018, p. 4) (Table 2.4).

Financialization can be defined as a 'pattern of accumulation in which profit making occurs increasingly through financial channels rather than through trade and commodity production' (Krippner, 2005, p. 174) This process is mostly driven by foreign capital flows in the countries of the Global South, where foreign capital took over key sectors of economies, especially the raw material sector. In the late nineteenth and twentieth centuries infrastructure and banking became attractive for foreign investment

Table 2.4 Financialization of accumulation regime and everyday life

Increasing power of finance	*Foreign capital domination*	*Household over indebtedness*	*Issues in financing SMEs and productive sectors*
Increasing profits, consolidation of power among few actors, expansion of financial institutions towards non-financial spheres	Foreign ownership of banks, excessive liquidity in foreign currency	Rising consumer loans and mortgages, also in foreign currency, over-indebtedness of households	Expensive loans for SMEs and difficulties to access credit, barriers for the development of productive sphere

Source: Author's table, based on theoretical debates in this chapter and empirical research in this book.

(Becker, 2008, pp. 13–16). In the 1990s western European capital started to expand towards central, eastern, and south-eastern Europe. In the transformation process there was a consensus among local and international financial institutions and western governments on the scenarios of rapid privatization and shock therapy, though not everyone profited from the entrance of transnational capital (Becker, 2014). Privatization and liberalization in central, eastern, and south-eastern Europe enabled foreign banks to enter these markets. The process was largely encouraged by the International Monetary Fund (IMF) and WB, as they thought foreign banks would guarantee financial stability in these countries (Ćetkovic, 2011, p. 3). In particular, bank capital from small European countries like Austria, Sweden, and Greece has been expanding. For example, in Slovenia the accumulation model was characterized by financialization in the form of increasing household debt and increased consumption. Whereas, in the Baltic countries and southern European states financialization turned out to be the motor for economic growth. All these countries fulfilled the function of a market for capital and consumption of good exports from western Europe (Becker, 2014). Such a rapid growth in credit was driven through a significant difference between interest rates on loans and deposits, as well as by the profit orientation of bank managers. Furthermore, as some of these managers came to the region only for short terms to work, they were interested in high bonuses through credit growth (Ćetkovic, 2011, pp. 3–4). Tourism, real estate, and construction are the rentier sectors of economy in the process of financialization. Investments are being made in these sectors in the frame of trade liberalization(Becker & Weissenbacher, 2015, p. 4).

Thus, the liberalization of capital accounts in the Global South enabled foreign capital inflow without restrictions under the motto of increased efficiency and better competition. Yet, it creates a dilemma for debtor countries to ensure the inflow of foreign credit on the one hand and avoid capital flight of foreign exchange (FX) reserves on the other hand (Epstein, 2001, p. 5).

When capital mobility is free and there are no restrictions, residents of given countries have the freedom to have assets and liabilities in foreign currency (Painceira, 2009, p. 5). Yet, financialization is not imposed or predefined by processes in the core, but domestic embeddedness of these developments is also crucial (Karwowski & Centurion-vicencio, 2018, p. 15; Karwowski & Stockhammer, 2017, p. 62). Shifts in the accumulation regime cannot be analysed without studying the financialization of the state, which has often been forgotten in financialization studies (see Karwowski & Centurion-vicencio, 2018, pp. 4–5; Eradze, 2022a). State policies, laws, and regulations not only shape the accumulation regime but also the everyday life of citizens and their accessibility to finance. However, domestic political and economic processes define the extent and intensity of financialization (Becker & Weissenbacher, 2015, p. 5).

Georgia demonstrates key patterns of peripheral financialization described above. The first liberalization policies of the early 1990s paved the way for the process of financialization in the country, although this process intensified after the 2003 revolution. The rise of foreign capital inflows especially towards the banking sector not only encouraged the development of the financial system, but it also shaped the oligopolist banking market and defined bank lending policies. The radical deregulation reforms of the Georgian government enabled Georgian banks in foreign ownership to set their own rules of the game. This resulted in mass lending to households, also in foreign currency, led to a credit boom and household over-indebtedness alongside rising loan dollarization rates (see Chapters 8 and 9). Yet, intensified lending in foreign currency was not the only channel of financialization that encouraged dollarization. The financialization of monetary policy through the 2009 shift to inflation targeting by the Georgian central bank caused the subordination of exchange rate stability to price stability aims. Inflation targeting significantly weakened the central bank and empowered commercial banks, making de-dollarization even more difficult. Subsequently, foreign currency domination did not pose any threats to the FDI-led accumulation regime in Georgia, as foreign-owned banks did not oppose the libertarian ideological discourse of the political society (see Eradze, 2022a).

Conclusion

The literature of dollarization is rich, covering case studies of a wide range of dollarized countries throughout the world. Yet, while this phenomenon has been in the research spotlight of economists and political sciences, the literature of political economy has not yet paid much attention to it. Most dollarization studies have a narrow economic focus and even though they provide important empirical data analysis, a wide range of factors remain disregarded in explaining the phenomenon. The lack of plausibility of this kind of explanations is demonstrated in the puzzle of the persistence of dollarization; economic factors appear to be insufficient for understanding why dollarization persists at high levels after dollarized countries achieve certain levels of macroeconomic stability and economic growth.

Dollarization is not only an economic phenomenon, the consideration of its history, politics, culture, institutions is crucial for grasping its roots and persistence. This gap in the literature can be filled by embedding the dollarization debate into already existing political economy literature on currencies, currency hierarchy, theories of money and national currency, including nation-state relations. Therefore, dollarization is explored within a state theory in this book.

The understanding of the state in this research is based on the concept of a peripheral state, where the state is understood as a social relation. Five analytical categories guide the analysis of the state in this work: political and civil societies, accumulation regime, governance, technologies, and positioning in the global structure. Furthermore, the peripheral character of the state highlights the embeddedness and positioning of the Georgian state in global power structures, in which power is distributed asymmetrically. Georgia is referred to as a hybrid state, where the concept of hybridity helps to highlight controversial policies, informal practices, and façade politics and explains dollarization as well. Furthermore, the focus on the state's hybrid character encourages the analysis of the historical momentum of state formation not only in terms of the break-up of the Soviet Union, but also with regard to the new processes of democratization and marketization. Thus, such an approach of unfolding time, space, and power provides insights into the puzzling terrain of Georgian statehood and foreign currency domination.

Notes

1 Brief excerpts from the conceptualization of dollarization within the state theory (from this section) will be published in Eradze (2022b).

2 All these elements can make up a system that Foucault calls apparatus, which is strategic and always has a certain historical function in response to specific needs. However, even though each apparatus has a function, it can also produce effects that were not intended or wanted (Foucault, 1980, pp. 194–195). Becker uses the concept of Regulationsdispositiv, based on Foucault's dispositive.

References

Aliyev, H. (2014). The Effects of the Saakashvili Era Reforms on Informal Practices in the Republic of Georgia. *Studies of Transition States and Societies*, 6(1), 19–33.

Altvater, E. (1993) *The Future of the Market: An Essay on the Regulation of Money and Nature after the Collapse of 'Actually Existing Socialism'*. Verso.

Amin, S., & Kvangraven, I. H. (2017). A Dependency Theory. In U. Kufakuriani, I. H. Kvangraven, F. Santana, & M. D. Styve (Eds.), *Dialogues on Development Volume I: on Dependency* (pp. 12–17). Online Book.

Aprasidze, D. (2004). The Bureaucratic-Patrimonial State in Georgia: Has the 'Roses Revolution' Given It a New Lease of Life? *Central Asia and the Caucasus*, 1(25), 42–48.

Arellano, C., & Heathcote, J. (2010). Dollarization and Financial Integration. *Journal of Economic Theory*, 145(3), 944–973.

Aslanidi, O. (2008). Dollarization in Transition Economies: New Evidence from Georgia (No. 366; Charles University GERGE-EI Working Paper Series).

Ataç, I., Lenner, K., & Schaffar, W. (2008). Kritische Staatsanalyse(n) des globalen Südens. *Journal Für Entwicklungspolitik*, XXIV(2), 4–9.

Barisitz, S. (2005). Banking in Central and Eastern Europe since the Turn of the Millennium – An Overview of Structural Modernization in Ten Countries. *OeNB Focus on European Economic Integration*, 2(05), 58–82.

Basso, H. S., Calvo-Gonzalez, O., & Jurgilas, M. (2011). Financial Dollarization: The role of foreign-owned banks and interest rates. *Journal of Banking and Finance*, 35, 794–806.

Beck, T., & Brown, M. (2015). Foreign Bank Ownership and Household Credit. *Journal of Financial Intermediation*, 24(4), 466–486.

Becker, J. (2002). *Akkumulation, Regulation, Territorium: Zur kritischen Rekonstruktion der französischen Regulationstheorie.* Metropolis Verlag.

Becker, J. (2008). Der Kapitalistische Staat in der Peripherie: polit-ökonomische Perpektiven. *Journal Für Entwicklungspolitik*, XXIV(2), 10–32.

Becker, J. (2014). Muster kapitalistischer Transformation in Osteuropa. *Zeitschrift Marxistische Erneuerung*, 99.

Becker, J., Jäger, J., Leubolt, B., & Weissenbacher, R. (2010). Peripheral Financialization and Vulnerability to Crisis: A Regulationist Perspective. *Competition & Change*, 14(3), 225–247.

Becker, J., Jäger, J., & Weissenbacher, R. (2013). Abhängige Finanzialisierung und ungleiche Entwicklung: Zentrum und Peripherie im europäischen Integrationsprozess. *Journal Für Entwicklungspolitik*, XXIX(3), 34–55.

Becker, J., & Weissenbacher, R. (2015). Changing Development Models: Dependency School Meets Regulation Theory. Colloque International Recherche & Regulation 2015 'La Theorie de La Regulation a l'epreuve Des Crises', 10–12 June 2015.

Bonizzi, B. (2013). Financialization in Developing and Emerging Countries. *International Journal of Political Economy*, 42(4), 83–107.

Brabant, J. M. van. (1998). *The Political Economy of Transition: Coming to grips with history and methodology.* Routledge.

Brand, U. (2005). *Gegen-Hegemonie: Perspektiven globalisierungskritischer Strategien.* VSA-Verlag Hamburg.

Brenner, R., & Glick, M. (1991). The Regulation Approach: Theory and History. *New Left Review*, 188, 45–120.

Brown, M., De Haas, R., & Sokolov, V. (2017). Regional Inflation, Banking Integration, and Dollarization. *Review of Finance*, 22(6), 2073–2108.

Bruff, I. (2014). The Rise of Authoritarian Neoliberalism. *Rethinking Marxism*, 26(1), 113–129.

Bruff, I., & Tansel, C. B. (2019). Authoritarian neoliberalism: trajectories of knowledge production and praxis. *Globalizations*, 16(31), 233–244. DOI: 10.1080/14747731.2018.1502497.

Carothers, T. (2002). The End of the Transition Paradigm. *Journal of Democracy*, 13 (1), 5–21.

Cetkovic, P. (2011). Credit Growth and Instability in Balkan Countries: The Role of Foreign Banks. In *Research on Money and Finance Discussion Papers* (Issue 27). Research on Money and Finance Department of Economics, SOAS.

Cheterian, V. (2008). Georgia's rose revolution: Change or repetition? Tension between state-building and modernization projects. *Nationalities Papers: The Journal of Nationalism and Ethnicity*, 36(4), 689–712.

Christophe, B. (2005). From Hybrid Regime to Hybrid Capitalism? The Political Economy of Georgia under Eduard Shevardnadze. Varieties of Capitalism in Post-Communist Countries, 23–24 September 2005, University of Paisley.

Cooper, S. (2009). Currency, Identity, and Nation-Building: National Currency Choices in the Post-Soviet States. *American Political Science Association Annual Convention*, September.

Cornia, G. A. (2012). Transition, Structural Divergence, and Performance: Eastern Europe and the Former Soviet Union during 2000–7. In G. Roland (Ed.), *Economics in Transition The Long-Run View* (pp. 293–317). Palgrave Macmillan.

de Nicoló, G., Patrick, H., & Ize, A. (2003). Dollarizing the Banking System: Good or Bad (No. 146; IMF Working Paper).

Demirović, A. (2007). Politische Gesellschaft - zivile Gesellschaft. Zur Theorie des integralen Staates bei Antonio Gramsci. In *Hegemonie gepanzert mit Zwang: Zivilgesellschaft und Politik im Staatsverständnis Antonio Gramscis* (pp. 21–40). Nomos.

Detragiache, E., Tressel, T., & Gupta, P. (2006). Foreign Banks in Poor Countries: Theory and Evidence (No. 18; IMF Working Paper).

Diamond, L. J. (2002). Thinking About Hybrid Regimes. *Journal of Democracy*, 13 (2), 21–35.

Duffy, J., Nikitin, M., & Smith, R. T. (2006). Dollarization Traps. *Journal of Money, Credit, and Banking*, 38(8), 2073–2097.

Dzudzek, I., Kunze, C., & Wullweber, J. (2012). Einleitung: Poststrukturalistische Hegemonietheorien als Gesellschaftskritik. In I. Dzudzek, C. Kunze, & J. Wullweber (Eds.), *Diskurs und Hegemonie: Geselschaftskritische Perspektiven* (pp. 7–29). transcript Verlag.

Eichengreen, B. (2001). What Problems can Dollarization Solve? *Journal of Policy Modeling*, 23(3), 267–277.

Eichengreen, B., & Hausmann, R. (1999). Exchange Rates and Financial Stability (No. 7418; NBER Working Paper Series).

Epstein, G. A. (2001). *Financialization, Rentier Interests, and Central Bank Policy* (pp. 1–43). Political Economy Research Institute.

Eradze, I. (2020). samtomop'ovebiti indust'riis socialur-ek'ologiuri k'rizisebi sakhelmts'ipos msheneblobis da ganvitarebis narat'ivebis ch'rilshi [Socio-ecological crises of the extractive industry in the prism of state building and development narratives]. In K. Eristavi & T. Qeburia (Eds.), *ekst'rast'ivist'uli gadak'vetebi: p'olit'ik'a, ek'ologia da sotsialuri samartlianoba* [Extractivist Intersections: politics, ecology, and social justice] (pp. 146–171). Social Justice Center, Heinrich Böll Foundation South Caucasus.

Eradze, I. (2022a). Financialization of Monetary Policy in a Dollarized Economy: the case of Georgia. *Cambridge Journal of Economics*. https://doi.org/10.1093/cje/beac019.

Eradze, I. (2022b). Taming Dollarization Hysteresis: Evidence from Post-socialist Countries. In C. Scherrer, A. Garcia, & J. Wullweber (Eds.), *Handbook on Critical Political Economy and Public Policy*. Edward Elgar Publishing Ltd.

Feige, E. L., Šošiæ, V., Faulend, M., & Šonje, V. (2003). Unofficial Dollarization in Latin America: Currency Substitution, Network Externalities and Irreversibility. In D. Salvatore, J. W. Dean, & T. D. Wilnett (Eds.), *The Dollarization Debate* (pp. 46–72). Oxford University Press.

Foucault, M. (1980). The Confession of the Flesh. In C. Gordon (Ed.), *Power/Knowledge: Selected Interviews and Other Writings 1972–1977* (pp. 194–229). Pantheon Books.

Giddens, A. (1985). *The Nation-State and Violence.* Polity.

Gilbert, E., & Helleiner, E. (2011). Introduction: nation-states and money: historical contexts, interdisciplinary perspectives. In E. Gilbert & E. Helleiner (Eds.), *Nation-States and Money: The past, present and future of national currencies* (pp. 1–23). Routledge.

Gramsci, A. (2000). The Gramsci Reader: Selected Writings 1916–1935. In D. Forgacs (Ed.), *New York University Press.* New York University Press.

Guidotti, P., & Rodriguez, C. A. (1992). Dollarization in Latin America: Gresham's Law in Reverse? (91/117; IMF Working Papers).

Hausmann, R., & Panizza, U. (2003). On the Determinants of Original Sin: An empirical investigation. *Journal of International Money and Finance*, 22(7), 957–990.

Havrylyshyn, O., & Beddies, C. H. (2003). Dollarization in the Former Soviet Union: from hysteria to hysteresis. *Comparative Economic Studies*, 45(3), 329–357.

Helleiner, E. (1998). National Currencies and National Identities. *American Behavioral Scientist*, 41(10), 1409–1436.

Hobsbawm, E. (1993) *Nations and Nationalism since 1780*, 2nd ed. Cambridge University Press.

Ize, A., & Levy-Yeyati, E. (2005). Financial de-dollarization: Is It for Real? (No. 187; IMF Working Papers).

Ize, A., & Yeyati, E. L. (2003). Financial Dollarization. *Journal of International Economics*, 59, 323–347.

Jobelius, M. (2011). Georgia's authoritarian liberalism. In *South Caucasus 20 Years of Independence* (pp. 77–92). Friedrich Ebert Stiftung South Caucasus.

Kakulia, M., & Aslamazishvili, N. (2000). *dolarizatsia sakartveloshi: massht'abebi, pakt'orebi, daz'levis gzebi* [Dollariztion in Georgia: Dimensions, Factors, Solutions] (J. Meskhia, Ed.). Institute of Economy of the Georgian Science Academy.

Karwowski, E., & Centurion-vicencio, M. (2018). Financialising the State: Recent developments in fiscal and monetary policy (No. 11; Financial Geography Working Papers).

Karwowski, E., & Stockhammer, E. (2017). Financialisation in emerging economies: a systematic overview and comparison with Anglo-Saxon economies. *Economic and Political Studies*, 5(1), 60–86.

Kishor, N. K., & Neanidis, K. C. (2015). What Is Driving Financial Dollarization in Transition Economies? A Dynamic Factor Analysis. *Macroeconomic Dynamics*, 19 (04), 816–835.

Koji, K. (2017). *Dollarization and De-dollarization in Transitional Economies of Southeast Asia* (K. Kubo, Ed.). Palgrave Macmillan.

Kolasa, M. (2021). Equilibrium Foreign Currency Mortgages (21/XX; IMF Working Paper Series).

Krippner, G. R. (2005). The financialization of the American economy. *Socio-Economic Review*, 3, 173–208.

Kufakurinani, U., Kvangraven, I. H., Santana, F., & Styve, M. D. (2017). Introduction: Why Should We Discuss Dependency Theory Today? In U. Kufakurinani, I. H. Kvangraven, F. Santana, & M. D. Styve (Eds.), *Dialogues on Development Volume I: on Dependency* (pp. vi–12). Online Book.

Lazarus, J. (2010). Neo-liberal State Building and Western 'Democracy Promotion': the case of Georgia. SGIR 7th Pan-European Conference on International Relations.

Lazarus, J. (2013). Democracy or Good Governance? Globalization, Transnational Capital, and Georgia's Neo-liberal Revolution. *Journal of Intervention and Statebuilding*, August, 1–28.

Levy-Yeyati, E. (2006). Financial dollarization: evaluating the consequences. *Economic Policy*, January, 61–118.

Lin, S., & Ye, H. (2010). Dollarization does promote trade. *Journal of International Money and Finance*, 29(6), 1124–1130.

Lipietz, A., & Jenson, J. (1987). *Rebel sons: the Regulation*. lipietz.net.

Luca, A., & Petrova, I. (2008). What drives credit dollarization in transition economies? *Journal of Banking and Finance*, 32(5), 858–869.

Mecagni, M., Corrales, J. S., Garcia-verdu, R., Imam, P., Macario, C., & et.al. (2015). *Dollarization in Sub-Saharan Africa Experience and Lessons* (Issue May). International Monetary Fund.

Müller, M. (2020). In Search of the Global East: Thinking between North and South, *Geopolitics*, 25(3), 734–755. doi:10.1080/14650045.2018.1477757.

Naceur, S.ben, Hosny, A., & Hadjian, G. (2015). How to De-Dollarize Financial Systems in the Caucasus and Central Asia? (No. 203; IMF Working Paper).

Ongena, S., Schindele, I., & Vonnák, D. (2020). In Lands of Foreign Currency Credit, Bank Lending Channels Run Through? (No. 474; CFS Working Paper).

Oomes, N. (2003). Network externalities and dollarization Hysterisis: The case of Russia (03/96; IMF Working Papers).

Painceira, J. P. (2009). Developing Countries in the Era of Financialisation: From Deficit Accumulation to Reserve Accumulation (No. 4; Research on Money and Finance Discussion Papers, Issue 4).

Papava, V. (2005). *Necroeconomics: The Political Economy of Post-Communist Capitalism (Lessons from Georgia)*. iUniverse Inc.

Pavlinek, P. (2003). Alternative Theoretical Approaches to Post-Communist Transformations in Central and Eastern Europe (No. 46; Geography and Geology Faculty Publications).

Pickles, J., & Smith, A. (1998). Introduction: Theorising transition and the political economy of trasnformation. In J. Pickles & A. Smith (Eds.), *Theorising Transition: The Political Economy of Post-Communist Transformations* (pp. 1–22). Routledge.

Poggi, G. (1978) *The Development of the Modern State*. Stanford University Press.

Poulantzas, N. (1976) *The Crisis of the Dictatorships: Portugal, Greece, Spain*. Humanities Press.

Priewe, J., & Herr, H. (2005). *The Macroeconomics of Development and Poverty Reduction: Strategies beyond Washington Consensus*. Nomos.

Rappoport, V. (2009). Persistence of Dollarization after Price Stabilization. *Journal of Monetary Economics*, 56(7), 979–989.

Rekhviashvili, L., & Polese, A. (2017). Liberalism and shadow interventionism in Liberalism and shadow interventionism in post-revolutionary Georgia (2003–2012). *Caucasus Survey*, 1–24.

Rona-Tas, A., & Guseva, A. (2014). *Plastic Money: Constructing Markets for Credit Cards in Eight Postcommunist Countries*. Stanford University Press.

Scherrer, C. (1995). Eine diskursanalytische Kritik der Regulationstheorie. *Prokla*, 25 (3), 457–482.

Scherrer, C. (2001). 'Double Hegemony'? State and Class in American Foreign Economic Policymaking. *Amerikastudien*, 46(4), 573–591.

Smith, A., & Swain, A. (1998). Regulating and Institutionalising Capitalisms: The micro-foundations of transformation in Eastern and Central Europe. In J. Pickles & A. Smith (Eds.), *Theorising Transition The Political Economy of Post-Communist Transformations* (pp. 25–53). Routledge.

Timm, C. (2013). Economic Regulation and State Interventions: Georgia's Move from Neoliberalilsm to State Managed Capitalism (2013/03; PFH Research Papers).

Uribe, M. (1997). Hysteresis in a Simple Model of Currency Substitution. *Journal of Monetary Economics*, 40, 185–202.

Valev, N. T. (2007). The Hysteresis of Currency Substitution: currency risk vs. network externalities (No. 07–23; Andrew Young School of Policy Studies Research Paper Series).

Versal, N., & Stavytskyy, A. (2015). Financial Dollarization: a Trojan Horse for Ukraine? *Ekonomika*, 94(3), 21–45.

Wheatley, J., & Zürcher, C. (2008). On the Origin and Consolidation of Hybrid Regimes: The State of Democracy in the Caucasus. *Taiwan Journal of Democracy*, 4(1), 1–31.

Winkelried, D., & Castillo, P. (2010). Dollarization Persistence and Individual Heterogeneity. *Journal of International Money and Finance*, 29(8), 1596–1618.

Wullweber, J. (2012). Konturen eines politischen Analyserahmens - Hegemonie, Diskurs und Antagonismus. In I. Dzudzek, C. Kunze, & J. W. Hg (Eds.), *Diskurs und Hegemonie: Gesellschaftskritische Perspektiven* (pp. 29–58). transcript Verlag.

Part II

The genesis of dollarization

Money without the guarantee of gold can be only backed up by the trust of the society, stability of the state, national spirit and discipline – nothing else; without all this, fiat money is a meaningless piece of paper.

(Kandelaki, 1960, p. 68) (Author's translation)*

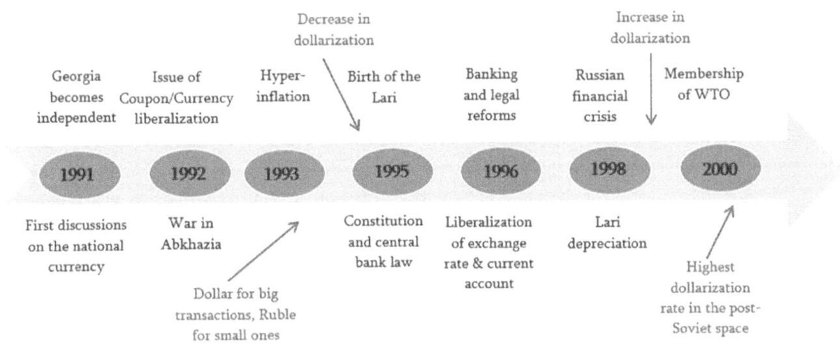

Figure T1 Timeline 1: The Origins of Dollarization
Source: Author's illustration.

*Konstantine Kandelaki was a minister of finance during the First Republic of Georgia (1918-1921).

DOI: 10.4324/9781003240174-4

3 Dollarization within the agenda of dollar diplomacy and transition

Dollar supremacy in a nutshell

The usage of the dollar outside the United States (US) has a long history. American policymakers started to support the use of the dollar in Latin America at the beginning of the twentieth century. This strategy was adopted in parallel with US military and economic expansion in the region. It was also around the same time that the supremacy of dollar diplomacy was acknowledged in comparison with the military influence, during William Howard Taft's presidency. US dollar diplomacy was not only about encouraging trade and investment, but also about strengthening the role of dollar as a currency (E. Helleiner, 2003, pp. 1–2).

Rosenberg describes how the basis of the gold standard was created in 1900–1905 along with the beginning of the US foreign financial policy. These processes strengthened the role of the dollar as an international currency, the importance of the US as a safe haven for gold reserves, and of New York as a hub for exchange transactions (Rosenberg, 1985, p. 170). These changes were backed up and carried on by a group of US economists, who had experience in US colonies and were interested in currency affairs. 'Viewing American imperialism as a benevolent carrier of science and civilization, they took seriously the "white man's burden" of rehabilitating backward economies' (Rosenberg, 1985, p. 194).

In 1915, an idea of 'pan American monetary unity' was pushed by Kemmerer, a US financial advisor to Latin America. The idea was that all countries of the American continent should have a shared monetary unit which would be equivalent to the US gold dollar. However, this kind of promotion of the dollar ended in the 1920s. Later, after World War II (WWII), during the 1940s and 1950s, US policymakers started to encourage the process of de-dollarization. Several factors contributed towards bringing an end to dollarization diplomacy: growing nationalism in Latin American countries and changes in policymaking in terms of monetary policy, opposition to dollar diplomacy within the US, and the weakening of the elite that supported this policy after Roosevelt's election, as well as revisiting the foreign policy in Latin America (E. Helleiner, 2003, pp. 4–6).

DOI: 10.4324/9781003240174-5

The change in dollar diplomacy in the 1940s was largely influenced by an ideological shift in the Federal Reserve towards embedded liberalism under the leadership of Robert Triffin. He promoted different policies than had his predecessors – capital control, an adjustable exchange rate and an activist monetary policy to achieve growth and employment instead of focusing on price stability. There was also a strategic reason behind this shift – it was more advantageous for the US to follow economic nationalism in monetary affairs in the wake of the Cold War. These changes were supported by major businesses in the country at that time (E. Helleiner, 2003, pp. 7–10).

In the post WWII period, the US was busy setting up and institutionalizing the international monetary system. If the international monetary system was based on national rules despite the existence of the gold standard before 1944 (Simmons, 2000, p. 575), the establishment of the International Monetary Fund (IMF) at the 1944 Bretton Woods Conference institutionalized universal rules for the global monetary system and thus highlighted the importance of exchange rates as a global issue (Simmons, 2000, p. 579). The IMF was supposed to create international monetary cooperation, encourage international trade, and establish exchange stability and a multilateral payment system upon the abolishment of foreign exchange (FX) restrictions (International Monetary Fund, 2016, p. 2) (Article I). However, the Fund was never free from influences of power hierarchies. By the 1960s, France was already actively engaged with a critique of the gold exchange standard and the key role of the dollar in the international monetary system. Jacques Rueff, De Gaulle's chief economic advisor at that time referred to the US balance of payment deficit as one 'without tears' (Rueff, 1972, p. 78, cited in Kirshner, 2008, p. 422), because the US printed the international reserve currency. In addition, the US had the largest voting power at the IMF (Babb & Kentikelenis, 2018, p. 18).

The break-up of the Bretton Woods system by President Richard Nixon in 1971 marked the beginning of a new era of floating exchange rates that further strengthened the role of the dollar, and 'Americans shed the costs of serving as the world's currency without significantly reducing the benefits' (Kirshner, 2008, p. 423). Thus, the US was freed from pressure, obligations, and accusations of misusing its power, while the dollar maintained its position in the international monetary system. Susan Strange referred to this change as 'a progression from exorbitant privilege to super-exorbitant privilege' (Strange,, 1987, p. 569 in (Kirshner, 2008, p. 424) of the United States. Yet, the end of the Bretton Woods system changed the role of the IMF. It was no longer responsible for supervising exchange rates that used to be pegged. Nevertheless, the Fund maintained its function of providing money for member countries in cases of issues in balance of payments (Babb & Kentikelenis, 2018, p. 17).

In line with a turn to neoliberal policies in the 1970s activist monetary policies were criticized. It was considered irrelevant for monetary policy to aim at growth and employment; instead, price stability became the core aim of monetary politics. This shift was largely supported by global financial markets. The financial crises at the end of the 1990s played a role in the promotion of dollarization. The US interest in dollarization was revitalized again in the 1990s, when dollarization debates were centred on Latin and Central American countries. Interest in dollarization was also backed up by US economic interests in Latin American countries (E. Helleiner, 2003, pp. 10–12). One of the advocators for dollarization and free banking Kurt Schuler (senior staff economist for the Joint Economic Committee (JEC) and later, a senior fellow in the Office of International Affairs, US Treasury) criticized central banks and did not believe in their role of maintaining the value of money. Schuler supported Hayek's ideas on free competitive banking, which was assumed to have the ability to eliminate the need for a central bank. However, he soon acknowledged that national governments would not support the idea of free banking. In his later work with Steve Hanke, he shifted the focus to currency boards to '[outsource] monetary policy to a more reliable foreign authority' (Cohen, 2003, p. 9).

At this time the dollar was a key international currency, which was manifested in its key economic positions in the financial and economic markets. In 2002, 90% of all transactions on the global FX markets were conducted in dollars. In 1988 the dollar was also used for almost one-half of the international trade invoices of world exports. Furthermore, almost three-fifths of foreign currency deposits and two-fifths of international bonds were in dollars. The physical circulation of the US 100-dollar bill outside the country was also increasing. Almost 90% of these bills were used abroad by the end of the 1990s (Cohen, 2004, pp. 289–291). Unofficial dollarization provided additional benefits for the US in terms of trade-related international seigniorage (advantages of doing trade in dollars) and debt-related international seigniorage (privilege of repaying a debt in low currency) (Carchedi, 2002, pp. 160–161).

The sudden revival of interest in dollarization in 1999 can be explained by the initiative of the Argentinian president Carlos Memem to accept the dollar as a foreign currency (see Barro, 1999). This idea was backed by the supporters of free banking and dollarization like Kurt Schuler and JEC Chairman Connie Mack (Cohen, 2003, pp. 8–10). Mack claimed that dollarization would be beneficial for financial stability and economic growth both in the US and in unofficially dollarized countries. He believed that through complete dollarization, risks of currency devaluation and of balance of payments crises would disappear and inflation rates decrease, thereby fostering economic growth. As for the costs of dollarization, Mack referred to the need for dollar assets for the full conversion of a circulated domestic currency, as well as the faster synchronization of business cycles with the US than would be the case without dollarization (Mack, 1999). Even though Mack and Schuler managed to place the promotion of dollarization on the political agenda of the USA, this sudden popularity of dollarization soon disappeared and Senator Mack also retired in 2001 (Cohen, 2003, pp. 8–10).

Official dollarization would not necessarily have brought any additional benefits to the US other than what it already had with unofficial dollarization. The official use of the dollar in other countries could have even caused risks for the US such as technical issues in managing a large amount of dollar flow outside the US, the possible influence of lobby interests from dollarized countries on the Federal Reserve, and tensions in foreign policy relations with dollarized countries as the dollar would increase US soft and coercive powers (Cohen, 2003, pp. 11–15). Official dollarization might cause problems for the US (along with advantages), as the Federal Reserve might be obliged to take into consideration the needs of important trade partner countries. Also, this might trigger anti-dollarization waves in these countries. Therefore, it is preferable from the US perspective to assign dollarization-related issues to the IMF (Carchedi, 2002, p. 161).

This brief history of US dollar diplomacy and the debates on the benefits and disadvantages of official or unofficial dollarization for the US demonstrate the complexity of the phenomenon and the politics behind it. Dollar policies have never been related to monetary issues only, but have always been entangled with political, geopolitical, or broad economic interests. Yet, dollarization cannot be explained only through dollar diplomacy, merely as an externally imposed phenomenon on developing countries. Such complex processes do not occur through a one-way domination and the agency of various interest groups within dollarized countries should not be undervalued. Therefore, the explanation of dollarization from a dollarized country's perspective is important. It can shed light on historical conditionalities, socio-political and economic processes, cultural acceptance or resistance to dollarization.

Back to the beginnings: the chaos and euphoria of independence

The collapse of the Soviet Union in 1991 marked, on the one hand, the independence of Georgia and, on the other hand, the beginning of chaos, uncertainties, economic hardships, social insecurity, political conflicts, and the search for a way of becoming a state. These beginnings were not easy, Georgia had to pay a high price for its independence, which resulted in one of the most severe stagnations in the post-Soviet space.

There are numerous books, articles, and reports which are replete with dense paragraphs revealing statistics that give a reader an idea of the scale and fierceness of the disastrous consequences of the break-up of the Soviet Union. These statistics offer indeed the shortest and most effective way of describing millions of lives in a few sentences. Yet, lives behind these statistics often remain beyond the sophisticated academic language. Being a part of the generation of the 1990s myself, the decade of red beans;[1] of candle lights; of water scarcity; of the selling off of heating radiators (there was no use for them except selling them as scrap); of cold classrooms and of slightly warm flats; of unemployed and then self-employed parents who were the lost generation of their times; of bribed political and economic elites; yet to solidary society – the process of transition meant more than numbers. Not just the data on Gross Domestic Product (GDP) per capita or Gini coefficient matters, but specifically how these changes affected daily lives, which strategies of survival appeared to cope with the transition and how should we understand the form of the state that emerged within and out of this context.

The Georgian economy was shrinking continuously in the first five years of independence. Economic hardships were worsened by political conflicts and wars. From 1990 to 1993, the Georgian GDP was declining by 28% per year and income per capita decreased from 4,433 US dollar (USD) to 1,437 USD. In 1995, production had decreased by 78% in comparison to 1990. This was three times more than the decline of production in the USA during the Great Depression. The economy of Georgia was gradually shifting towards a shadow economy (Tsikhelashvili et al., 2012, p. 9). Already in 1991, Georgia's agricultural production had declined by 50% and its trade volume with other countries by 59%. In 2002–2003, the ratio of the shadow economy to GDP reached 64% (Jones, 2013, p. 254). If tax revenues to GDP were 22% in 1991, in 1993 they constituted only 2% (Wang, 1999, p. 6). The consolidated fiscal deficit (without grants) amounted to 3% of GDP in 1991, whereas by 1993 this figure had increased to 26%. Georgia was fully dependent on external funding at this time, '80 percent of the [budget] deficit was financed by external loans and grants, and the remainder by the central bank' (Wang, 1999, p. 7). Furthermore, national income decreased by 34% in 1992 in comparison with 1985 (Gursoy & Chitadze, 2012, pp. 37–38). Despite economic growth, in 1996, Georgian GDP was only 26% of that in 1988. Industrial production experienced hardly any growth in difference with construction, communication, and transport sectors (National Bank of Georgia, 1997, p. 5). In 1993–1994, Georgia was still missing a national budget and a constitution. Even though there was a parliament, the legislative process did not function and 'extensive tax privileges to a wide range of organizations (such as churches, theatre, etc.) made it impossible to raise fiscal revenues even to a minimum level' (Papava, 2005, p. 139).

Political turmoil and economic disaster triggered social issues; especially, the education and healthcare systems suffered (Christophe, 2005, pp. 4–5) and income inequality was deepening. Expenditure on health as a share of total public expenditures decreased from 9.5% to 5.1% respectively in 1990 and 1995 (World Bank, 1996, p. 25), while the same indicators for education declined from 20% in 1990 to 6.7% in 1995 (World Bank, 1996, p. 28).[2] Georgia had one of the highest income inequality indicators (Gini coefficient) among transition countries throughout the 1990s (European Bank for Reconstruction and Development, 1999, p. 16). By the late 1990s, almost one-half of the income in Georgia was distributed among the 10% of the population. According to Kakulia and Aslamazishvili, it was exactly this part of the population that used the dollar as a means of payment and encouraged the process of dollarization. They note the importance of the dollar in such sectors as real estate trading, the automobile market, as well as in the trading of furniture and other imported goods. These segments functioned mostly undocumented (Kakulia & Aslamazishvili, 2000, p. 32).

The political situation was not any better: there was rivalry among newly established political parties, a radical nationalist president, powerful warlords, and paramilitary groups. Tensions in Abkhazia, Adjara, and South Ossetia,[3] civil wars, and high rates of crime made the overall situation in Georgia highly vulnerable and unstable (Wheatley, 2005, pp. 46–62). As Wheatley notes,

> By mid-1993, the dichotomy [...] between the state [...] and society [...], had more or less completely broken down. [...]. [B]oth state and society had ceased to exist; all that remained were scattered fragments that could be said to belong to both.
>
> (Wheatley, 2005, p. 80)

Therefore, the above-described economic chaos was a logical and inevitable outcome of the given political setting. The question is rather what kind of state could have possibly emerged out of this situation and whether it would be right to assess such a state with western perceptions of a nation state. The turmoil of the beginnings gave birth to a state which was neither ready for independence, nor had the knowledge or resources to deal with the challenges of sovereignty. More importantly, it had also no time for planning or constructing the present and the future. Shock therapy was knocking at the door as if it were the only real means of survival.

New beginnings: will shock therapy heal the wounds?!

> They [US economists] were explaining to hungry locals how to prepare and consume the beans once the cans were open. That the cans were sealed soon became obvious, but there was a deep conviction that cooking and eating right would open the cans. They did not.
>
> (Rona-Tas & Guseva, 2014, p. xiv)

The Georgian state was locked in a transition frame rather soon after independence. The transition agenda provided a guideline for economic and political reforms and created a legitimate context for international organizations (IOs) to interfere, shape, and influence the post-Soviet states. Early transition policies paved the way towards the integration of Georgia into global capitalism. Therefore, the analysis of transition policies is one of the best mirrors for sketching out state formation and tracing the roots of dollarization.

Transition policies were not initially meant for post-socialist countries without market economies. They can be traced to the end of the 1980s, when

Washington Consensus was designed by the IMF, WB, and the US Treasury in response to the Latin American experiences of that time (Kolodko, 2000, pp. 120–121). The Washington Consensus was based on ten policy pillars – fiscal discipline, the prioritization of public expenditure areas, tax reform, the liberalization of interest rates, competitive exchange rates, the liberalization of trade and inward foreign direct investments (FDIs), privatization, deregulation, and property rights. The author of these well-known policies, John Williamson, claims that his concept has often been misused as he had never included capital account liberalization, monetarism, supply-side economics, or minimal state among his suggestions (Williamson, 2002). Elsewhere, Williamson claimed that with deregulation he had not referred to the avoidance of state responsibilities in health, consumer rights, or environmental issues (Williamson, 2004, p. 10). The Washington Consensus has been criticized for overlooking the importance of institutions, as economic fundamentals could not have made a difference without solid institutions (Kolodko, 2000, pp. 123–124).

The Washington Consensus has provided a basis for transition policies. Most of the transition economies went through similar changes: 'de-agrarization', 'deindustrialization', expansion in services (including banks), '[the] liberalization of labour market, [...] transfer of labour across sectors, informal employment, fast job turnover, [...] mass emigration' (Cornia, 2012, pp. 302–305). It was believed that the transition process had to be implemented fast, so that communists and anti-market forces could not regain power. However, there was no will to give power to states in setting the preconditions for market creation (Rona-Tas & Guseva, 2014, pp. 28–29).

Two dominant approaches of transition are represented by shock therapy and gradualism. The first approach comes from Poland and the former Czechoslovakia and is widely used by Russian economists (Papava, 2005, p. 18). Shock therapy is based on six main reforms: 'macroeconomic stabilization; price liberalization; trade liberalization and current account convertibility; enterprise reform (especially privatization); the creation of social safety; and the development of the institutional and legal framework for a market economy' (Fischer et al., 1996, pp. 45–46). Gradualists did not call for different reforms from those demanded by proponents of shock therapy but rather argued for a slower transformation. Thus, the difference between shock therapy and gradualism is rather technical, meaning that there has been no debate on the content of transition reforms. A strong belief in the rich and free 'West' and amid support for 'the "three zatsias" *(privatizatsia, demokratizatsia, liberalizatsia)*, anti-communist sentiment left little room for articulating alternative paths for transformation' (Pickles & Smith, 1998, p. 4).

Ronas-Tas and Guseva describe the irony and sadness of the transition process in a joke about how a physicist, chemist, and economist try to open a can of beans on a remote island. While the first two try to come up with ideas on how to deal with the problem, the economist assumes that there is a can opener.

> All products are like beans in a can; they need to be made accessible and drawn into the world of economic exchange. To unlock a product a market has to be built. The market is a can opener that delivers beans, bread, cars, shoe repair [....] and government bonds.
>
> (Rona-Tas & Guseva, 2014, p. xiii)

Kolodko rightly referred to the process of transition as a: 'A shoulder-numbing shot of good anti-distorted-developing-market-economy vaccine [...] to the wrong patient' (Kolodko, 2000, p. 281).

Already in the 1990s, the crises in Russia, East Asia, and Latin American countries provided a good basis for questioning the success of Washington Consensus policies. However, the scapegoat of the failure of these policies turned out to be bad governance and not the policies themselves. Here the second generation of reforms took off (Babb & Kentikelenis, 2018, p. 20). Defenders of shock therapy blamed post-Soviet countries and a too limited implementation of shock therapy policies instead of questioning the reforms (Stiglitz, 1999, p. 3). A 2005 World Bank (WB) report documents the words of the WB Vice-president Gobind Nankani on the need for more social, institutional, country-specific analysis of economic systems instead of one-size-fits-all policy: 'there is no unique universal set of rules. [...] [W]e need to get away from formulae and the search for elusive "best practices", and rely on deeper economic analysis to identify the binding constraints on growth' (World Bank, 2005, p. xiii).

It would be one-sided to shift all the blame onto the ideologists of the reforms. As the case of Georgia demonstrates, the means of implementing these reforms also had a huge influence on their results. The failure of shock therapy was due to a mixture of poorly thought-through reforms and their failed implementation. Furthermore, the lack of cooperation and coordination among post-socialist states also played a role in the misfortunes of transition. The neoliberal bias did not acknowledge the necessity of regional coordination and the role of coordination at the regional level was instead taken over by the European Bank for Reconstruction and Development (EBRD) and the Bretton Woods institutions (Kolodko, 2000, pp. 270–271). Institutions like the IMF enjoyed great power in this process, because for most of the transition countries they provided the sole option for borrowing money (as they lacked access to international capital markets). Good recommendations from the IMF were a door opener to capital markets (Kolodko, 2000, p. 282) and transition countries competed against each other to receive more money. These states had very limited bargaining power with the IMF regarding borrowing, conditionalities, or the content of reforms. Moreover, it was easier to borrow money to develop the financial sector than fighting poverty or other social issues (Kolodko, 2000, pp. 301–304).

The transition process did not go smoothly and was not welcomed by all interest groups within the countries. The middle and upper classes usually supported the liberalization and privatization processes, forgetting the 'needs at the other end of the social rainbow' (Kolodko, 2000, p. 271). Industrialists and managers of enterprises presented a very powerful interest group in the former Soviet Union that opposed IMF reforms, privatization, and deindustrialization. They wanted to keep access to cheap credits and state subsidies without conditionalities (White et al., 1993, pp. 165–166). Yet, entrepreneurs supported market-oriented policies, representing cooperatives, private enterprises, commercial banks, etc. They were in favour of privatization as it would give them the possibility of investing their liquid assets. Both industrialists and entrepreneurs had been creating networks across the Soviet republics since the end of the 1980s to promote their ideas. Also, they were founding their own parties in Russia and trying to engage with politics (White et al., 1993, pp. 170–172).

The transition process rapidly turned out to be disappointing for the broader public , as their expectations were not met. People were told that they would become as rich as their counterparts in developed market economies, but this did not happen (Kolodko, 2000, pp. 44–46). Svetlana Alexievich's book *Second-hand Time: The Last of the Soviets* demonstrates the lives of people after the break-up of the Soviet Union. A wonderful collection of talks and interviews from the 1990s tell similar stories of hope, disappointment, radical changes, confusion, and struggles on the verges of new life with new values, authorities, and life goals. As one of the characters from her book sums it up: 'In the blink of an eye, everything became worthless. Instead of the bright future, they started telling us to get rich, love money…Bow down to this beast! The people were not prepared' (Alexievich & Translator Bela Shayevich, 2017, p. 154). Georgia was not ready for the changes either.

Towards the West: shock therapy in Georgia

The transition process in Georgia did not start with shock therapy. The Georgian government did not listen to the IMF in the early 1990s and attempted to reform the country by its own methods up until 1994. However, there was a lack of financial sources and even dirty money (through drug trafficking, weapon trading, etc.) was offered to the government in exchange for certain guarantees (Papava, 2005, pp. 138–140). The stenographic reports of parliament meetings of the early 1990s, as well as important newspapers of that time reveal that there were vivid and controversial debates about the transformation of the state and the economy (see Sakartvelos resp'ublik'a, 1991, p. 4, 1992, p. 2; Stenographic Report of the Parliament Meeting November 19, 1992; Stenographic Report of the Parliament Meeting November 24, 1992). However, the decision was made for policies recommended by the IMF, as this was considered the only way of becoming a civilized state. In the words of deputy prime minister in the field of economic reforms Roman Gotsiridze it was not a good idea to reject the reforms of the Fund: 'If we turn our backs on international monetary organizations, then Georgia, [....] is doomed to isolation for half a century. Today they dictate the fashion' (Stenographic Report of the Parliament Meeting November 24, 1992, p. 81) (author's translation from Georgian).

Even when the decision was made to bring in IOs and their money to the country, the first negotiations with the IMF were not smooth. The Georgian government was usually dissatisfied with the amount of time given for reforms, while businesses soon started to dislike the IMF as well. However, the government was communicating the IMF reforms as its own initiatives to the public (Papava, 2005, p. 143). It is not surprising that the IMF became a powerful actor in reforming and reshaping the Georgian state. Both the IMF and the WB are quite influential in development debates through the knowledge they produce, and the training they provide for the staff of finance ministries or central banks. Although in the first three decades of its existence, the Fund did not pursue neoliberal ideas, since the 1980s it has started to enforce policies based on conditionalities such as liberalization of markets. This change within the IMF was strongly connected with the new political leaders in the US and the United Kingdom at that time, Ronald Reagan and Margaret Thatcher. Later, the principles of the Washington Consensus provided a legitimation for IMF policies (Babb & Kentikelenis, 2018, pp. 18–19).

Thus, transition reforms in Georgia were an outcome of both – admiring the West and lacking alternatives. Yet, one recipe did not work for all countries, as shock therapy turned into a long-lasting shock rather than into a therapy. Shock therapy was implemented in Georgia more or less in line with the pillars of Washington Consensus – price formation (introducing new prices for liberalized goods), the indexation of minimum wages and social security (wages and benefits were increased but not in a proper relation with prices), the rise of interest rates on deposits (this growth was not corresponding with the inflation rate), no cut in government expenditures but a reduction in subsidies, reforms in the taxation system, the introduction of general customs tariffs (which did not trigger exports), no social assistance to low-income families, anti-monopoly decrees. The exchange rate of the national currency could not have been introduced as no national currency existed until 1995 (Papava, 2005, pp. 126–128). These reforms had drawbacks for the economic development of post-Soviet Georgia. For example, Papava identifies methodological mistakes in terms of reforms in the taxation system. Taxing agriculture on the assumption that big agricultural state enterprises existed, when there were only small farmers in the market, discouraged the expansion of agricultural companies and the growth of this sector. Complicated taxation rules encouraged bribery, corruption (Papava, 2005, pp. 145–151), and the flourishing informal economy (Jones, 2006, p. 41).

Overall, even though shock therapy triggered a fast way towards the transformation to a market economy, these reforms either remained a formality for a long time or partially hindered the development of the Georgian economy. The success of the transition process in Georgia was also challenged by donor competition. Christophe describes how different interests of the USA, Germany, or other countries shifted reforms and legislations in various directions, disregarding 'institutional homogeneity' (Christophe, 2005, p. 7).

Georgia's integration into the world market

The integration of Georgia into the world market was fast and damaging. Upon the adoption of an Enhanced Structural Adjustment Facility for Georgia in 1998, the IMF pushed the Georgian government to impose equal taxes on imports and locally produced goods, as well as to tax local agrarian production (Kochladze et al., 2002, p. 6). Moreover, trade and exchange restrictions were abolished in Georgia before 1999 (International Monetary Fund, 2004, p. 4) and according to the IMF, Georgia was 'free of restrictive requirements and quantitative restrictions on imports' (International Monetary Fund, 1998, p. 30). In this way, no encouragement was provided for the development of local production. In the same year, Georgia started negotiations with the World Trade Organization (WTO) with the encouragement of the IMF, becoming a WTO member in 2000. Thus, Georgia opened its markets with low tariffs and without safety measures under the General Agreement on Tariffs and Trade (GATT) agreement that had a negative influence on the development of local production. Membership of the WTO for an import-dependent country was also too early at that point (Kochladze et al., 2002, pp. 10–11). Such a sudden exposure to the world markets for a distressed economy could not have done any good at that time. Instead of throwing Georgia into the cold water of free trade and world markets, the creation of greenhouse conditions would have enabled the destroyed economy to come back to life.

Along with the opening up of its markets for free trade and integration into the world market, Georgia also became a part of the international monetary system. One of the important steps in this direction had already been undertaken at the beginning of the 1990s through currency liberalization in accordance with IMF regulations. Georgia adopted Article VIII of the IMF in 1992, allowing citizens to trade in any currency. This change made it easy to use foreign currencies, but created barriers for the development of the local currency market (Kakulia, 2001, pp. 55–56). According to Article VIII, restrictions on current payments should be abolished, currency practices should not be discriminatory, balances held in foreign currencies should be convertible, and countries should collaborate on reserve asset policies among other aims (International Monetary Fund, 2016, pp. 22–23). Decree No.259 of 5 March 1992, on 'The First Stage of Liberalization of Foreign Economic Activity' commands:

> (i) allow all enterprises to engage directly in foreign trade; (ii) allow all residents to acquire and hold foreign currency and engage in foreign transactions with a licensed FX dealer; and (iii) authorize banks to open FX accounts for all residents.
>
> (International Monetary Fund, 1998, pp. 57–58)

Thus, a green light was turned on for using foreign currencies in a country that did not even have its own currency yet, predestining a phenomenon like dollarization. Furthermore, joining Article VIII 'voluntarily' sent signals to markets and especially those who are engaged in international transactions (Simmons, 2000, p. 583). Though Georgia might have been in a desperate need of sending such signals to international markets, the question is whether the benefits of attracting investors could outweigh the long-lasting costs, for Georgia, of dollarization.

In 1996, the exchange-rate regime was liberalized in Georgia; it was set as on a managed floating course. Article VIII requirements were met and the lari became convertible (Jarocińsky & Jirny, 1999, p. 71; National Bank of Georgia, 1997, p. 19). The currency market in Georgia was liberal from the beginning without any mechanisms of capital control. In 1996, all restrictions on current account operations were abolished; thus, any citizen or non-resident could have a bank account anywhere and they could transfer any amount of money inside or outside the country. A new foreign investment law of 1996 'allowed unlimited repatriation of capital and profits and placed no limitation on holding foreign currency bank accounts' (International Monetary Fund, 1998, p. 36). Even though the lari was the only legal tender and the means of payment in Georgia and there were strict sanctions for its violation, almost no one was punished for using foreign currency in local transactions. This was partly connected with the overall corrupt practices (Kakulia & Aslamazishvili, 2000, pp. 53–54).

These developments encouraged the process of dollarization. Joining Article VIII in 1992 was like opening the country's doors to world currencies, even before Georgia had its own currency. It was clear which currency population and investors would choose when they were free to do so. The data on deposit dollarization from the early 1990s demonstrates that by 1994 the share of foreign currency deposits to total deposits was 66.7% in Georgia (De Nicoló et al., 2003, p. 33).

Capital account liberalization is one of the crucial topics in reference to the local financial and macroeconomic stability. The timing of capital account liberalization is important and in an ideal case it should not happen until macroeconomically stable environment was achieved and financial reforms implemented (Buiter & Taci, 2003, p. 12). The volatility of capital flows has not only been a matter of academic debate, as institutions like the IMF or the WB have also studied this topic since the mid-1990s (G. K. Helleiner, 1997, p. 3). Though the IMF is considered as a major supporter of capital account liberalization, it should be noted that the Fund's approach has been changing too. In the years 1995–1996, the IMF already acknowledged the need to control capital to a certain degree and temporarily in certain situations (G. K. Helleiner, 1997, p. 17). A 2015 IMF paper on capital account liberalization also highlights this considering individual case countries (Independent Evaluation Office of the International Monetary Fund, 2015, p. 2). Furthermore, it seems to be difficult to provide empirical proof for a strong positive correlation between capital account liberalization and economic growth. Thus, imposing controls on capital might indeed be more useful than liberalization in certain cases (Independent Evaluation Office of the International Monetary Fund, 2015, pp. 3–4), especially if 'capital flows pose risks to macroeconomic or financial system stability' (Independent Evaluation Office of the International Monetary Fund, 2015, p. 9).

Georgia demonstrated the highest dollarization levels in terms of asset substitution in the post-Soviet space in 2001, when the share of foreign currency deposits in total deposits reached almost 90% (Havrylyshyn & Beddies, 2003, p. 340). The 2001 country report of the IMF dedicated a separate chapter to dollarization (Chapter 5) and highlighted a persistently high level of dollarization despite the post-1998 crisis macroeconomic improvements. While reviewing different factors of dollarization, the Fund highlighted institutional and structural factors, as well as free trade implications (International Monetary Fund, 2001, p. 73). It is worth quoting these sections at length:

> Institutional factors play an important role in that they define the rules of the game, e.g., whether individuals are allowed to hold their savings in FX deposits, […], how foreign currency deposits are treated in reserve requirements, and transaction costs in moving among alternative assets.
>
> (International Monetary Fund, 2001, p. 74)

> Institutional and structural factors appear to also have played a role in the high level of dollarization in Georgia. […] [F]oreign currency deposits can be held by resident individuals and enterprises, and it enjoys one of the most open trade regimes among the CIS [Commonwealth of Independent States I.E] countries, with low tariffs.
>
> (International Monetary Fund, 2001, pp. 75–76)

> [T]he opening up of trade, reduction of tariffs and the removal of current and capital account restrictions, are usually associated with the increased use of foreign currency denominated assets.
>
> (International Monetary Fund, 2001, p. 75)

These paragraphs are interesting in terms of acknowledging the importance of such institutional changes as trade or currency liberalization in enhancing dollarization. Exactly these institutional and structural factors identified by the IMF made dollarization inevitable in Georgia in the early 1990s, even before the introduction of the lari as the national currency.

Despite the awareness of the role of trade and financial liberalization in causing dollarization, the IMF did not consider domination by a foreign currency to be problematic, but rather a natural outcome of the mentioned processes. According to the Fund, dollarization would only have been perceived as problematic if it had been triggered by domestic political and economic instability (International Monetary Fund, 2001, pp. 79–80). This line of argumentation and classification of dollarization as a natural process or a problem is rather puzzling. First, it is usually a combination of external and local factors that leads to dollarization (as the IMF itself argues). Second, how can one claim that a disease (dollarization) could be a problem only in relation with specific causes? Dollarization remains a disease no matter what kind of factors played the most important role in a particular circumstance. What matters in problematizing dollarization is its impacts on the economy and well-being of the population and not its driving causes. Third, the IMF's attempt to picture dollarization as a natural phenomenon if it is caused by external structural factors, while doing quite the opposite in case of domestic reasons, frees international actors from responsibility and shifts the blame towards national governments.

The IMF's main recommendation to the Georgian government in the same report further strengthens the observations above. The Fund advised the government to increase trust in the lari through sound macroeconomic policy, stating that 'direct measures are not advisable since they typically lead to capital flight and undermine confidence in the local currency' (International Monetary Fund, 2001, p. 73). Instead, it argued: 'regulatory limits on foreign currency deposits or punitive reserve requirements on dollar deposits may simply drive dollars offshore' (International Monetary Fund, 2001, p. 81). Acknowledging, on the one hand, the importance of institutional and structural factors in encouraging dollarization, and advising, on the other hand, that the problem should be solved mostly through increasing trust in the lari is contradictory. Why not tackle the very major causes of dollarization – institutional and structural factors (currency and trade liberalization)?

It is also remarkable that the Fund referred to dollarization already in 2001, as *hysteresis* (International Monetary Fund, 2001, p. 73), underlining the longer history of the phenomenon in the country and the expectation that it should have declined, but had not done so. The IMF tried to direct dollarization solutions towards the Georgian government to increase trust in the lari, implicitly shifting the main responsibility from the global economic and monetary system towards the political and economic instabilities in Georgia.

Conclusion

Alongside economic factors, (stable value, liquidity, and transactional networks), political factors also influence the international status of currencies. Governments are directly involved in the creation of wide transactional networks through expanding trade relationships, entering foreign markets, and increasing their power in monetary relations through different payment systems. Historically, political agency has played a role in the US in designing liquid financial markets with an explicit aim of encouraging the international status of the local currency (E. Helleiner, 2008, pp. 360–362). Despite the loss of US interest in official dollarization, it still profits from high levels of unofficial dollarization in developing countries in economic, as well as in political and geopolitical terms.

Yet, the emergence of unofficial dollarization in Georgia has been neither a preliminarily planned political project, nor a natural phenomenon. It was rather a logical outcome of the socio-economic chaos and early liberalization policies that existed in the context of transition. Thus, dollarization was inevitable in Georgia, in that specific historical setting and with those transition policies, discussed above. The lack of knowledge of Georgians, as well as of international actors about moving towards capitalist markets, the absence of institutions, and the overall political and economic chaos provided no good preconditions for a fundamental change to occur. However, the lack of caution and the disregard of global power structures accelerated the transition process in a harmful way and pushed Georgia into the world economy with wide open doors way too early and when it was too unprepared. The liberalization agenda in the early and mid-1990s predestined a weak economy and a powerless currency. The import and currency dependency of Georgia could have been anticipated as early as the start of the 1990s, as too little was done to encourage the revival of the economy. However, one side of the story is never enough to see a complete picture and, therefore, an analysis of the newly emerged state in the following chapter will shed more light on the origin of dollarization.

Notes

1 Kidney beans used to be one of the cheapest products in the 1990s. It is still associated with poor man's food, though beans are not cheap anymore.
2 Education spending to GDP decreased from 7.4% in 1990 to 0.9% in 1995 (World Bank, 1996, p. 28).
3 These are regions of Georgia. Abkhazia and South Ossetia are now occupied by Russia.

References

Alexievich, S., & Translator Bela Shayevich. (2017). *Second-Hand Time: The Last of the Soviets* (6th ed.). Fitzcarraldo Editions.

Babb, S., & Kentikelenis, A. (2018). International Financial Institutions as Agents of Neoliberalism. In D. Cahill, M. Cooper, M. Konings, & D. Primrose (Eds.), *The SAGE Handbook of Neoliberalism* (pp. 16–28). SAGE.

Barro, R. J. (1999, March). Let the Dollar Reign from Seattle to Santiago. *Wall Street Journal*.

Buiter, W. H., & Taci, A. (2003). Capital account liberalization and financial sector development in transition countries. In A. Bakker, F.P. & B. Chapple (Eds.), *Capital Liberalization in Transition Countries, Lessons From the Past and For the Future* (pp. 1–41). Edward Elgar.

Carchedi, G. (2002). Imperialism, dollarization and the Euro. *Socialist Register*, 153–173.

Christophe, B. (2005). From Hybrid Regime to Hybrid Capitalism? The Political Economy of Georgia under Eduard Shevardnadze. Varieties of Capitalism in Post-Communist Countries, 23–24 September 2005, University of Paisley.

Cohen, B. J. (2003). Dollarization, Rest in Peace. *International Journal of Political Economy*, 33(1), 4–20.

Cohen, B. J. (2004). America's Interest in Dollarization. In V. Alexander, J. Mélitz, & G. M. von Furstenberg (Eds.), *Monetary Unions and Hard Pegs: Effects on Trade, Financial Development, and Stability*. Oxford University Press.

Cornia, G. A. (2012). Transition, Structural Divergence, and Performance: Eastern Europe and the Former Soviet Union during 2000–7. In G. Roland (Ed.), *Economics in Transition The Long-Run View* (pp. 293–317). Palgrave Macmillan.

De Nicoló, G., Patrick, H., & Ize, A. (2003). Dollarizing the Banking System: Good or Bad (No. 146; IMF Working Paper).

European Bank for Reconstruction and Development. (1999). Transition Report 1999: Ten Years of Transition. https://www.ebrd.com/downloads/research/transition/TR99.pdf.

Fischer, S., Sahay, R., & Végh, C.A. (1996). Stabilization and Growth in Transition Economies: The Early Experience. *Journal of Economic Perspectives*, 10(2), 45–66.

Gursoy, F., & Chitadze, N. (2012). Economic and Political Environment of Georgia After the Restoration of National Independence. *European Journal of Economic and Political Studies*, 5(2), 35–54.

Havrylyshyn, O., & Beddies, C. H. (2003). Dollarization in the Former Soviet Union: from hysteria to hysteresis. *Comparative Economic Studies*, 45(3), 329–357.

Helleiner, E. (2003). Dollarization diplomacy: US policy towards Latin America coming full circle? (02/8; Trent International Political Economic Centre Working Papers).

Helleiner, E. (2008). Political determinants of international currencies: What future for the US dollar? *Review of International Political Economy*, 15(3), 354–378.

Helleiner, G. K. (1997). Capital Account Regimes and the Developing Countries. In *International Monetary and Financial Issues for the 1990s: Vol. VIII* (pp. 1–26). United Nations.

Independent Evaluation Office of the International Monetary Fund. (2015). The IMF's Approach to Capital Account Liberalization: Revisiting the 2005 IEO Evaluation.

International Monetary Fund. (1998). Georgia: Recent Economic Developments and Selected Issues. https://www.elibrary.imf.org/view/journals/002/1998/099/article-A001-en.xml.

International Monetary Fund. (2001). Georgia: Recent Economic Developments and Selected Issues. https://www.elibrary.imf.org/view/journals/002/2001/211/002.2001.issue-211-en.xml.

International Monetary Fund. (2004). Georgia: Ex Post Assessment of Georgia's Performance Under Fund-Supported Programs – Staff Report; Public Information Notice on the Executive Board Discussion; and Statement by the Executive

Director for Georgia. https://www.elibrary.imf.org/view/journals/002/2004/026/002.2004.issue-026-en.xml.

International Monetary Fund. (2016). Articles of Agreement: adopted at the United Nations Monetary and Financial Conference, Bretton Woods, 1944. https://www.imf.org/external/pubs/ft/aa/index.htm.

Jarociński, M., & Jirny, A. (1999). Monetary Policy and Inflation in Georgia 1996 98. *Russian & East European Finance and Trade*, 35(1), 68–100.

Jones, S. (2006). The Rose Revolution: A Revolution without Revolutionaries? *Cambridge Review of International Affairs*, 19(1), 33–48.

Jones, S. (2013). *sakartvelo: polit'ik'uri ist'oria damouk'ideblobis gamotskhadebis shemdeg* [Georgia: A Political history since independence] (M. Chitashvili (Ed.)). Center for Social Sciences.

Kakulia, M. (2001). *savalut'o sist'emis ganvitarebis p'roblemebi sakartveloshi* [Challenges of Currency System Development in Georgia] (J. Meskhia (Ed.)). Research Institute for economic and social issues affiliated with the Ministry of economy, industry and trade of Georgia.

Kakulia, M., & Aslamazishvili, N. (2000). *dolarizatsia sakartveloshi: massht'abebi, pakt'orebi, daz'levis gzebi* [Dollariztion in Georgia: Dimensions, Factors, Solutions] (J. Meskhia (Ed.)). Institute of Economy of the Georgian Science Academy.

Kandelaki, K. (1960). *sakartvelos erovnuli meurneoba* [Georgian national economy] (Book 2). Institute for the Study of the USSR.

Kirshner, J. (2008). Dollar primacy and American power: What's at stake? *Review of International Political Economy*, 15(3), 418–438.

Kochladze, M., Gujaraidze, L., & Tavartkiladze, L. (2002). Decade of Independence Effects of Economic liberalization in Georgia: country report. https://greenalt.org/en/library/decade-of-independence-effects-of-economic-liberalization-in-georgia/.

Kolodko, G. W. (2000). *From Shock to Therapy: The Political economy of Post-socialist Transformation*. Oxford University Press.

Mack, S. C. (1999). Encouraging Official Dollarization in Emerging Markets: Joint Economic Committee Staff Report. http://salsa.babson.edu/Pages/Articles/ClassSp00/DollarizatOfficial%20US%20Senate.

National Bank of Georgia. (1997). Tsliuri angarishi 1996 [Annual Report 1996]. https://nbg.gov.ge/publications/annual-reports.

Papava, V. (2005). *Necroeconomics: The Political Economy of Post-Communist Capitalism* (Lessons from Georgia). iUniverse Inc.

Pickles, J., & Smith, A. (1998). Introduction: Theorising transition and the political economy of transformation. In J. Pickles & A. Smith (Eds.), *Theorising Transition: The Political Economy of Post-Communist Transformations* (pp. 1–22). Routledge.

Rona-Tas, A., & Guseva, A. (2014). *Plastic Money: Constructing Markets for Credit Cards in Eight Postcommunist Countries*. Stanford University Press.

Rosenberg, E. S. (1985). Foundations of United States International Financial Power: Gold Standard Diplomacy, 1900–1905. *The Business History Review*, 59(2), 169–202.

Rueff, J. (1972). *The Monetary Sin of the West*. Macmillan.

Sakartvelos resp'ublik'a. (1991 July 1). sakartvelos resp'ublik'a. Rogri Unda Ikh'os Bank'ebi? [What Should Banks Look like?], N133.

Sakartvelos resp'ublik'a. (1992 March 26). sakartvelos resp'ublk'a. P'rivat'izatsia: Rogori Bazari Gvsurs? [Privatization: What Kind of Market Do We Want to Have?] N50.

Simmons, B. A. (2000). The Legalization of International Monetary Affairs. *International Organization*, 54(3), 573–602.

Stenographic Report of the Parliament Meeting November 19. (1992). Parliament of Georgia.

Stenographic Report of the Parliament Meeting November 24. (1992). Parliament of Georgia.

Stiglitz, J. E. (1999). Whither Reform? Ten Years of Transition. World Bank Annual Bank Conference on Development Economics.

Strange, S. (1987). The Persistent Myth of Lost Hegemony. *International Organization*, 41(4), 551–574.

Tsikhelashvili, K., Shergilashvili, T., & Tokmazashvili, M. (2012). sakartvelos ek'onomik'uri t'ranspormatsia: damouk'ideblobis 20 ts'eli shualeduri angarishi [Economic transformation of Georgia: 20 years of independence A midterm report]. European Initiative Liberal Academy Tbilisi.

Wang, J.-Y. (1999). The Georgian Hyperinflation and stabilization (WP/99/65; IMF Working Paper).

Wheatley, J. (2005). *Georgia from National Awakening to Rose Revolution: Delayed Transition in the Former Soviet Union*. Ashgate.

White, S., Gill, G., & Slider, D. (1993). *The Politics of Transition shaping a post-Soviet future*. Cambridge University Press.

Williamson, J. (2002). *Did the Washington Consensus Fail?*Peterson Institute for International Economy.

Williamson, J. (2004). The Washington Consensus as Policy Prescription for Development. In *Lecture series "Practitioners of Development"*. Institute for International Economics.

World Bank. (1996). Georgia: Public Expenditure Review (Issue 15779).

World Bank. (2005). Economic Growth in the 1990s: learning from a decade of reform. http://www1.worldbank.org/prem/lessons1990s/.

4 The Georgian state as a vessel of dollarization

> Traditionally, Georgia had been dazzling, bewildering and betraying the external observer
>
> (Christophe, 2005, p. 1)

Georgia as a post-Soviet state: lost in transition?

Dollarization emerged during the process of state building in a state where nationalist feelings were rather strong. Even though the Georgian state maintained its agency vis-à-vis markets and international pressure throughout the transition, currency issues were not prioritized. Therefore, a closer look into the Georgian state is required to understand its peculiarities and most importantly, trace the reasons, factors, and explanations for foreign currency domination. The process of transition played a key role in terms of empowering, shaping, and disempowering the state. It marks the clear dependency of the Georgian state on external money, which was usually accompanied by recipes for change. Yet, despite these dependencies, the state did not lose its agency, but rather acquired a façade character to cope with the pressure of transition. Georgia thus emerged as a hybrid state, which fully embraced foreign currency domination.

Georgia was guided by international organizations on its way towards marketization and democratization. The involvement of the International Monetary Fund (IMF) and other international actors in the transition process marked the beginning of dependency, which was expressed not only in financial terms, but also at the level of ideas. The Georgian state budget was based on donor money until 1996. The state budget amounted to only 5% of GDP in 1995 and did not exceed 12% in the following years (Tsikhelashvili et al., 2012, pp. 10–11). Georgia was also dependent on IMF credits in terms of repaying the interest of international debt (Wellisz, 1996, p. 20). In 1997, more than one-half of state expenditure was financed by donors. By the end of the 1990s, Georgia had become one of the 'champions' in receiving US-aid per capita; in 2000 more US money was spent per person in Georgia than

DOI: 10.4324/9781003240174-6

in Ukraine or Russia. The Georgian political elite had no alternative but to accept the aid conditionalities (Christophe, 2005, p. 6).

Though one could expect the diminished power of the state apparatus in policymaking in line with demonization of the state role as a nightmare from Soviet times, quite the opposite happened in Georgia. The top-down transition agenda, which was implemented through and by the government, empowered the state apparatus and enabled it to take over the resource distribution role completely. Scholars sometimes seem nostalgic about 'the end of the state' and the rise of market power. The diminishing role of the state in the transition process is explained by large scepticism about the role of the state and its co-optation (Brabant, 1998, p. 359). Liberal ideology and a limited role of the state in economic matters is one of the common characteristics of transition countries (Cornia, 2012, pp. 294–295). The involvement of the state in the creation of the market was denied, even though it could have been useful in many ways (Rona-Tas & Guseva, 2014, pp. 28–29). However, in Georgia, none of the major changes, reforms, or redistribution of political and economic power happened without the direct involvement of the government, which was entangled with businesses and market actors. The market-oriented rhetoric did free government from their social responsibilities, and they eagerly took it on. It can even be argued that the transition process and the dependence on donor money in state building empowered the state apparatus to take over the leading role in 'reforming' the country. A market, as such, had no chance of emergence and development in Georgia without the key economic elite or shadow economic forces that were in patronage relations with the government or that held government positions themselves. Stiglitz makes a point on privatization, on how it 'provided an additional instrument' (Stiglitz, 1999, p. 20) to certain groups to strengthen their power, instead of 'taming' the engagement of political forces into economic and market matters. The experience of privatization from Georgia also shows how the government directly profited from the process by taking over a big majority of assets for personal gains and keeping enterprise managers under direct control.

Christophe (2005, pp. 18–23) describes the creativity of the Georgian political elite in inventing different strategies and tools to escape the privatization pressures and directions of International Financial Institutions (IFIs), drawing into question the image of a powerless government against markets or international organizations (IOs). For a while, Shevardnadze's Georgia was gaining a good reputation in the region, which did not prove to be true (Broers, 2005, p. 334); the Georgian government managed to manipulate reforms. Even though Shevardnadze was quite successful in ensuring foreign aid for Georgia (by 1997 it made up 57% of the state budget), he did not implement democratic reforms. He was able to simulate well enough, to please the western donors and maintain his 'fragile hegemony' (Christophe, 2004, pp. 10–13) at home by distributing foreign-aid profit among various groups. However, by the beginning of the 2000s, IOs realized that

Shevardnadze was not committed to the reforms. The pressure from donors made Shevardnadze let young reformers play an important role in the governance process (for example, Saakashvili became the new Minister of Justice in 2000) (Christophe, 2004, p. 15). It took donors some time to realize that there were issues in the implementation of programmes, debt repayment, money protectionism of certain businesses and supporting the economic interests of the government and their friends. Thus, the IMF insisted on a State Anticorruption Program as a condition for further funding. By 2002, the World Bank (WB) also realized the necessity of cutting money to Georgia (Kochladze et al., 2002, p. 7).

Thus, the Georgian state not only kept its agency in the process of transition (despite external dependencies), but it also turned into a façade state. However, this agency was not translated into government actions in favour of public interests. The transition process gave the state apparatus the power to distribute donor money according to its rent-seeking aims. Therefore, if issues like dollarization did not provide threats for the rent seeking aims of the elites, the state would not interfere against foreign currency domination. Indeed, this was the case.

Nomenklatura[1] in new clothes: forgetting about the economy?

> A modern nation state is not only a political concept, but it is also an economic organism, built on the development of its production base and local markets.
>
> (Kandelaki, 1935, pp. 37–38; author's translation)[2]

The political society of independent Georgia went through turmoil. It officially started with the election of a former Soviet dissident and nationalist Zviad Gamsakhurdia as president in 1991 (Jones, 2006a, p. 257). It was not just the idea of independence and nationalism that brought Gamsakhurdia mass support, but 'Gamsakhurdia's appeal was as much about the defence of the little man, anticommunism, rejection of privilege, and support of blue collar-subsidized jobs as it was about national glory' (Jones, 2006a, p. 259). Gamsakhurdia had strong opposition, part of which joined the National Congress and military wings. The new National Guard and Mkhedrioni[3] were also against him. These groups managed to force the president to flee to west Georgia in 1992, where military war was conducted alongside the war in Abkhazia (Siroky & Aprasidze, 2011, p. 1234).

Shadow economy groups, Nomenclatura members, and the Soviet intelligentsia were united against Gamsakhurdia and successfully managed to overthrow his government. However, these groups could not find a compromise on power distribution among themselves, and the situation ended up in chaos. This is when Shevardnadze entered the political scene 'to ensure the survival of a self-destructive social order that was incapable of self-reproduction and therefore highly dependent on permanent input of external resources, but [...] without really changing its inner logic' (Christophe, 2004, p. 10).

With the election to the presidency in 1995 of Shevardnadze, the old political elite from the Soviet Union was brought back to life. Shevardnadze himself was part of the Soviet Nomenklatura. He had been minister of foreign affairs (1972–1985) and served as the first secretary of the central committee of the Communist Party in Georgia (Chiaberashvili & Tevzadze, 2005, p. 189). Shevardnadze's party, the Citizen's Union, is often referred to as a 'nomenklatura-based party' that was serving the interests of the economic elite (Chiaberashvili & Tevzadze, 2005, p. 202). It was exactly these Soviet legacies that helped Shevardnadze to establish a political network through his old contacts amongst the communist party and Komsomol[4] (he was communist party chef in Georgia in 1972–1985) (Wheatley, 2005, p. 92). His way of governing with its patrimonial character and a power pyramid had roots in the Soviet era. The process of governance was a constant strategic game of dissolving and forming new power groups and encouraging them to fight amongst themselves (Aprasidze, 2016, pp. 110–111). One more peculiarity, which is also a Soviet legacy, was the power of Shevardnadze's executive government over the legislative one (Wheatley, 2005, p. 95). Further continuities in Shevardnadze's presidency with the Soviet Union included: 'limited opportunities for political participation, personal rather than normative loyalties among officials, and, overall, the reduction of a meaningful public realm for the practice of politics' (Broers, 2005, p. 334).

Even though the majority of Shevardnadze's appointees were from the former communist party, he attempted to create a 'balanced cabinet' with members of the liberation movement (Wheatley, 2005, p. 76). The so-called reformers and the architects of the Rose Revolution were also represented in the Civic Union of Georgia (CUG) and in the government. For example, Mikheil Saakashvili had been a minister of justice under Shevardnadze, whereas Zurab Jhvania (prime minister after the Rose Revolution) tried to Europeanize the CUG as its secretary general (Wheatley, 2005, p. 89).

Shevardnadze's government did not possess exclusive authority, as he had to share power with two other important power centres – the paramilitary groups and shadow economic fractions. These groups also had origins in the Soviet Union (Wheatley, 2005, pp. 80–82; see also Kukhianidze, 2009) and sharing power with them was the only way to achieve a certain level of stability in the country in the mid-1990s (Wheatley, 2005, p. 103). A further power group was represented by `thieves in law', who played a significant role in the everyday life of Georgians. They had taken over the role of the police, 'restoring justice' in case of crimes or interpersonal conflicts; the population trusted them more than the police (World Bank, 2012, p. 14). Thieves in laws enjoyed so much respect and popularity that even children dreamt of becoming thieves in law, when they grew up (World Bank, 2012, p. 18). Thieves in law also had roots in the Soviet Union, as they were formed to establish order and control over criminals in Soviet prison camps. 'The high ranks in the law enforcement system reportedly had close ties with the thieves-in-law, protecting and conducting business with its elite' (World Bank, 2012, p. 14). Yet, this criminal elite was directly controlled and observed by the police and sometimes they even made deals with each other to establish stability in specific economic sectors (Koehler & Zürcher, 2004, pp. 88–89).

Thus, formal and informal powerful groups were busy in the 1990s with wars, conflicts, and power distribution issues. Furthermore, the ruling apparatus did not enjoy centralized power; there were other competing regional elites and the government had to constantly negotiate and find compromises with them. The Georgian state was a battlefield of various groups, fighting for material resources, prestige, and power (Koehler & Zürcher, 2004, p. 94). In addition, the government was unable to establish the rule of law via the police. Though the police worked for the political authorities, it did not necessarily serve societal needs. The police was criminalized and it remained so after the Rose Revolution (2003), as well (Koehler & Zürcher, 2004, pp. 88–89; Kukhianidze, 2009, p. 226). A WB report notes: 'many police were themselves criminals, involved in kidnapping, drug dealing, and racketeering. Officials at the highest levels were tied with the criminal network of "thieves-in-law"' (World Bank, 2012, p. 14). Moreover, the police under Shevardnadze were not completely subordinated to the state or the interior ministry and represented an important power group on its own. As the Georgian president and his administration failed to establish control over the police, the ministry of interior affairs and the police emerged as autonomous powerful bodies. Even the ministry of interior affairs did not manage to gain control over the police throughout the country. The main source of income for this apparatus was not money from the state budget but self-raised funds. They controlled income from smuggling and trade with illegal goods (Koehler & Zürcher, 2004, p. 89).

Even if the Georgian government had prioritized the currency issue and had enough authority to deal with it, there was still a significant barrier in terms of lack of knowledge. According to the former minister of economy and the president of the central bank there were hardly any economists educated in market economy in the Soviet Union and therefore there was a lack of knowledge about how to transform politics and institutions according to new rules (see Chechelashvili & Javakhishvili, 2017; Chechelashvili & Papava, 2017). The first leader of the country, Zviad Gamsakhurdia, is often criticized for his lack of knowledge in reforming the economic sphere of independent Georgia. Yet, he was against the rapid privatization process and advocated for state capitalism as a mixture of socialism and capitalism. He assigned officials to specific economic spheres upon personal ties and not because of their professionalism. Gamsakhurdia's team was 'too optimistic in its assessment of Georgia's economic potential as an independent nation' (Gurgenidze et al., 1994, pp. 263–264). Papava also refers to the first economic reforms in Georgia, started in 1989 with the idea of national independence, as the 'stage of naive comprehension' (Papava, 2005, p. 123), whereas in 1991–1994 economics was mostly forgotten and ignored (Papava,

2006, p. 658). According to a former dissident Irina Sarishvili, dissidents at that time did not have the requisite knowledge to deal with economic issues. This was important because these dissidents turned into a part of the political elite of Georgia after independence. The economic sphere was rather disregarded in the beginning of the 1990s, which she refers to as an 'unavoidable mistake' (Demokratizatsiya, 2004, p. 312). In addition, economists were not favoured for positions in the ministry of finance, economy, the tax department, state property management, or the National Bank in Georgia throughout the 1990s (Khaduri, 2005, p. 26).

A further explanatory factor for the origins of dollarization in Georgia is the alienation of the state from the needs of society. There was not much connection and communication between the political elite and society. The roots of such relations can be found in the Soviet past, where the state was perceived as something 'alien' (Wheatley, 2005, p. 107). The penetration of the state was low at the ideological, institutional, or conflict regulation levels, or with regard to matters pertaining to public goods provision. However, the public mattered to the government if any threat came from them to the monopolistic economic activities of the state (Wheatley, 2005, pp. 129–133). There was a feeling that 'everything which was outside the private realm belonged to the Soviet or post-Soviet state, i.e. to nobody' (Kukhianidze, 2009, p. 218). Most people relied on personal and family networks rather than on the state and there was nothing like a representative civil society (Wheatley, 2005, p. 92). This kind of alienation was due to the 'weak' political parties, as well. Most political parties had similar ideas, lacked a nationwide dimension, and had to struggle with financial challenges. Furthermore, the core structure and composition of these parties depended on personal networks and a changes in coalitions were frequent. A common strategy adopted by the opposition parties to tackle financial challenges was the selling off of party positions or making connection with businesses (Broers, 2005, p. 336).

Thus, in the 1990s old Soviet Nomenklatura, party leaders, and criminal groups turned out to be in charge of Georgia. In the constant power struggles and overall political instability, there was not much space left to prioritize currency issues. Furthermore, even if economic or currency matters had been in focus in the Georgian government, there was no knowledge or experience of doing things in the 'right' way. Therefore, it is understandable that the increasing importance of dollar was not questioned. A low prioritization of currency issues in the political chaos, lack of knowledge in economic affairs, weak state apparatus, and the alienation of the state apparatus from society enabled a phenomenon like dollarization to emerge in Georgia.

Dollarization in the service of political and economic elites: the shadow economic elite and thieves in law

During Shevardnadze's presidency, it was difficult to draw lines between the political and economic elites in Georgia (Wheatley, 2005, pp. 107–110), which was typical for the Soviet Union, where the state owned everything in the economy. However, the question was who would own which business. Business ownership was not possible without connections in the political elite; it was predefined that the political and economic elites would become entangled. Another aspect that shaped the attitude of the political elite to material resources was the idea of 'milking the state' (see (Kukhianidze, 2009, p. 217). Moscow could not be milked anymore, so now there was the Georgian state to be milked and this was done 'successfully' indeed.

Thus, material interests were the key motivation for the political elite. During Shevardnadze's presidency government posts were used for maximizing personal gains and a number of ministers turned out to become businessmen later (Christophe, 2004, p. 13; also see Kukhianidze, 2009). 'Under the post-Communist banners of "capitalism" and "market reform", these [*nomenklatura*] networks have transformed bureaucratic into financial power, privatizing not only the economy, but the state itself' (James Sherr, 2002, cited in (Chiaberashvili & Tevzadze, 2005, p. 206)

It was not just that some political elites had business interests, they were also related to each other. Shevardnadze's family and their close friends had control over all important economic activities – mineral oil, aircraft, the chamber of commerce, telecommunications, a non-ferrous metallurgy factory (in Zestafoni), the import of consumer goods, transport, local manufacturing, etc. Usually, the owners of private businesses were represented in the parliament through their own parties (for example, Gogi Topadze[5]) (Chiaberashvili & Tevzadze, 2005, pp. 191–192; Christophe, 2004, p. 18).

Privileged economic groups were allowed to achieve their goals at the cost of 'developmental perspectives of the society as a whole' (Christophe, 2005, p. 14). This explains the contradictory character of the Georgian political economy, where market-based practices were from time to time interfered with by the state to ensure the interests of political and economic elites (Christophe, 2005, p. 23). Certain privileged groups enjoyed access to institutions and resources and these relations were not transparent to the public. This kind of state order was socially embedded in the participation of wider public in the shadow economy. Thus, the state used informalities as a means of governance and offered a conflict-free environment within the legal framework for certain groups (Koehler & Zürcher, 2004, p. 94).

Apart from the political elite, other powerful groups were also involved in business: the shadow economic elite, the soviet intelligentsia, and members of the Nomenklatura. These groups took advantage of the emerging political and economic chaos in the country and started making profits through the liquidation of assets (Christophe, 2004, p. 10). 'Smuggling of timber from state-owned forests or the illegal sale of equipment from state-run enterprises' (Christophe, 2004, p. 12) was a common practice of making money in the 1990s in Georgia. Interestingly, the Georgian economic elite seemed to have most interests in the banking sector. In 1992–1993, a famous corruption practice was 'the credit form', where the National Bank issued credits only to a very limited number of firms with a seal and a name (Chiaberashvili & Tevzadze, 2005, pp. 192–193). This practice and oversupply of money by the central bank consequently led to hyperinflation, as described in the following chapter.

This interlacement of political and economic elites, as well as the orientation of politicians towards personal economic profits, shed light on the general attitude of the government to the country's well-being. These tight relations between elites also enabled the emergence of compromise on dollar hegemony, which would serve the interests of both the political and financial elites (described below). If the primary aim of the government is to ensure rents to themselves and their friends, how can one possibly expect such a government to worry about monetary sovereignty and a strong currency? This would happen only in three cases: if the material profits of the political and economic elite were threatened; if the civil society created pressure; or if the donors forced the government to act against dollarization. However, as described below, the material gains were not endangered by the dollar, as all the smuggling and undocumented informal economic activities needed the foreign currency. Donors also did not worry about the strength of the US currency at that point and the civil society was occupied with the process of democratization. Thus, nobody cared.

Alienation between the state and civil society within the democratization paradigm

Civil society was rather weak in Georgia throughout the 1990s and was mostly focused on democratization and foreign policy issues. Questions of monetary sovereignty or strong currency were out of the scope of civil society and therefore dollarization was not problematized by these groups either. Wheatley identifies two main discourses in Georgian civil society. The idea of Georgia as a European country was backed by dissidents from the Soviet era, who blamed the Soviet Union for separating Georgia from Europe. Isolationists condemned all of Georgia's neighbouring countries due to bad historical experiences and believed only in the power of the Georgian Orthodox Church. According to them, the West was perceived as a source of danger for Georgian culture and religion (Wheatley, 2005, p. 144).

In the mid-1990s, non-governmental organizations (NGOs) started to emerge as the key anchor of Georgian civil society. One of the first NGOs in Georgia had roots back in Perestroika times, mainly working on environmental or cultural issues. Most of these Anglophone NGOs were concentrated in the capital. However, from 1994–1995 more and more NGOs started to appear with new activists, 'challenging the traditional "intelligentsia" at universities and state-funded media outlets' (Broers, 2005, p. 338). Though the number of officially registered NGOs in Georgia reached 4,000 towards the end of 2000, only a small part of these organizations had an actual impact on policymaking and on the law-drafting process (Wheatley, 2005, p. 145). In this context, the Open Society Georgia Foundation (OSGF) and the Eurasia Foundation, which were established in the mid-1990s, are to be mentioned. Among the main donors of civil society organizations were the US embassy and the European Union (EU) (Muskhelishvili & Jorjoliani, 2009, p. 686). With the appearance of funding possibilities, the number of competing organizations also increased; a full-time NGO job was a good option at a time of mass unemployment. Yet, most of the NGOs were concerned with democratization problems. Muskhelishvili and Jhorjoliani argue that these NGOs saw their role as a leading and not as a representative one in promoting democracy. They understood society as an object and not a subject. '"[A]vant-gardist" feeling emerged within the sector, placing NGOs in the role of the "vanguard" of democratization' (Muskhelishvili & Jorjoliani, 2009, pp. 686–687) and this was mostly linked to the Soviet legacies. Democracy, good governance, elections, and the rule of law were among the main topics for which the overall western aid was spent (Jones, 2006b, p. 42).

Anti-western traditionalist and religion-oriented groups were also quite active in the civil society though they lacked coherence. Yet, these ideas were supported by politicians and law makers. Attempts at the demonization and marginalization of non-Orthodox religious groups often became the main reason of conflict between liberal NGOs and traditionalists. The Georgia's Writers' Union was also involved in anti-western discourse, warning against Americanization, and agitated for nationalism. This group was sympathetic to Shevardnadze (Wheatley, 2005, pp. 148–150). Besides NGOs, the media played an important role in the development of the Georgian civil society. The media, as a key source of information in Georgia, had good outreach (Broers, 2005, p. 338). The TV channel Rustavi 2, founded in 1994, was critical of Shevardnadze's government and had special importance (Wheatley, 2005, p. 154).

The Georgian government tried to create a negative picture of NGOs, referring to them as 'anti-state institutions' or 'Grantichamia' (Georgian word meaning 'grant swallower') organizations, emphasizing the role of foreign money in NGOs. Shortly before the Rose Revolution (2003), the government even tried to impose control on foreign funding, but did not succeed due to NGO opposition (Angley, 2013, p. 51; Broers, 2005, pp. 339–340). The government also raided the TV channel Rustavi 2 in 2001 (Angley, 2013, p. 46). The Central Electoral Commission even initiated an amendment on forbidding the public broadcast of interviews or other contents in relation with upcoming election campaign (at the elections of 2003). Yet, civic groups succeeded against this initiative. According to widspread opinion, Shevardnadze had to get along with NGOs and activists in order to receive foreign aid (Angley, 2013, pp. 51–52). Shevardnadze is often described as a semi-democratic ruler, but not an authoritarian one and his period of governance is referred to as one of 'feckless pluralism' (Carothers, 2002) or 'freewheeling kleptocracies' (Mitchell and Phillips, 2008, in Mitchell, 2009, p. 174). Here, the hybrid character of the Georgian state is clearly manifested, as the government tried to cover up its Soviet attitude towards civil society for the sake of receiving more funding.

Thus, throughout the 1990s, Georgian civil society was influenced by Soviet-style alienation of the state from society, pro-democratization, Western-funded civic groups, and anti-Western traditionalists. Even though these groups (especially Western-oriented NGOs) managed to challenge the government, they could not break the ice between society and government. Shevardnadze's government had an ambivalent relation with these NGOs – trying to demonize them as agents of foreign interests and tolerating their existence at the same time to make a good impression on the western donors. Nevertheless, in the dominant democratization discourse of civil society, there was no space for socio-economic issues. Democratization was understood in terms of civic rights and political pluralism only. Therefore, the issue of dollarization was out of scope of civic groups' activities at this point.

Technologies of governance: kompromat, corruption, and the dollar

The hybridity of the Georgian state rests on informal technologies of governance, which have also enabled and supported the process of dollarization. Informality is understood here as 'a myriad of (economic, social and cultural) practices spread on a spectrum between the legal, the extra-legal and illegal' (Polese et al., 2016, p. 16). One of the most important governance technologies in relation to dollarization is corruption, as bribes were mostly paid in US dollars. Wheatley identifies 'state capture' as a form of corruption that existed in Georgia under Shevardnadze. It meant the instrumentalization of the state apparatus by the political elite for private interests. The example of kompromat (Russian word for compromising information) is a good demonstration of these practices. The government collected information on public servants or other interesting people with the help of the police and the ministry of interior affairs and used this information as kompromat to threaten them. Thus, breaking the law was a mode of governance (Wheatley, 2005, pp. 104–107). Yet, corruption was not only a tool of governance but also a means of realizing rent-seeking aims. This was linked to another dimension of corruption in terms of 'milking the state', which was a common attitude in the Soviet Union. Corruption went hand in hand with the perception of Moscow as a 'cash cow' that had to be milked. In the beginning of the 1970s corruption got so alarming in Georgia that Shevardnadze was appointed as the first secretary of the central committee of the Georgian communist party to fight corruption and bribery (among other aims) (Kukhianidze, 2009, p. 217). Corruption and informalization of politics became one of Georgia's most important characteristics under Shevardnadze's presidency, and it turned into the main reason for suspending the IMF programmes towards the end of Shevardnadze's rule and shortly before the Rose Revolution (Broers, 2005, pp. 334–335).

A further articulation of corruption can be found in the relations between the political and economic elites. Under Shevardnadze's government, businesses simply could not function without having a patron or a supporter in the government. The legal system for businesses was also designed in a way that there was a need to break the rules on regulations. However, breaking rules went hand in hand with corruption. Such informal relations between businesses and the political elite produced a further informality. These powerful groups were taking advantage of their positions 'to privilege their own clients and [...] to entrap [...] all potential competitors' (Wheatley, 2005, pp. 106–107). Thus, during Shevardnadze's presidency, informal institutions were 'a source of illegal income for politicians' (Dadalauri, 2007, p. 157). Furthermore, the level of administrative corruption was very high, as a bribe was the main way for enterprises to avoid regulations or ensure proper regulations for their businesses (Broers, 2005, p. 334). It was common practice for the government to sell regulations to different business groups and interests (Christophe, 2005, pp. 24–25). However, not only regulations were being sold, but government positions were also available for renting, enabling politicians to become businessmen and vice versa. Material interests became one of the key motivations for different people to enter politics (Christophe, 2004, p. 13); see also (Nodia, 2016, p. 78). Thus, 'the state did not provide public goods; instead, it supplied 'network goods' whereby state goods and services were provided only to those who were part of a particular personalized network' (Wheatley, 2005, p. 131). These corruptive practices not only enabled the privileged groups to achieve their rent-seeking aims but also encouraged dollarization, as the dollar was usually used as a currency for bribing. The former minister of economy recalled in the interview that shortly after the adoption of lari, bribes were mostly given in dollars, followed by the lari and the Russian ruble (Participant 14, personal communication, 11 April 2017).

Corruptive practices in the Georgian state outline once more that the political and economic elites only cared about private rents and dollarization did not provide any threat to these practices, in fact, it was encouraged by the prevailing corrupt practices and informality of economy where the dollar was used as the main currency for bribes. Thus, as corruption became the main governance strategy, the governing elite alienated itself from societal needs and currency issues.

The dollar compromise

Georgian industry and agriculture were well developed in the Soviet Union. Food processing represented the most important part of the industry (about two-fifths in 1990). The diversity of economic activity spanned from electric engineering to producing chemicals, machinery, construction, tourism, and the production of consumer goods (e.g., textiles). Nevertheless, as was characteristic of Soviet republics, the industry in Georgia was dependent on other republics in terms of raw materials, markets, or energy. Agriculture occupied the leading role in the economy with specialization in tea, wine, and fruit production (Kochladze et al., 2002, p. 5). Georgian agriculture constituted

10% of food trade within the Soviet Union. Tourism also played an important role in the economy; Georgia was an attractive destination for the Soviet population (Baumann, 2010, p. 3).

After the break-up of the Soviet Union, every sector of the Georgian economy deteriorated. Thus, it was not only political instability that hindered the prioritization of currency relations, but chaotic production relations could also not back up the value of Georgian currency. The composition of the economy in terms of its sectors did not change much – agriculture remained dominant (21.5% of GDP), followed by industry (13.3% GDP), trade (11.8% GDP), and transport (11.5% GDP) as in 2000 (Kochladze et al., 2002, p. 21). The land reform programme, in terms of the dissolution of collective farms and making small farms accessible for private ownership, had disastrous results for agriculture, as peasants were unprepared and ill equipped for such a change. The primary aim of farmers was to produce for their own needs and agricultural export was removed from the agenda, which used to be one of the biggest advantages of the Georgian economy in the Soviet Union (Khaduri, 2005, p. 22). Because of these and other changes, 'the share of agriculture in the gross domestic product (GDP) has decreased from 33.6% in 1996 to 21.5% in 2000' (Kochladze et al., 2002, p. 21).

After the dissolution of the Soviet Union, enterprises in Georgia faced a number of problems – a lack of markets, capital, knowledge, and experience of working in a market economy, and a weak financial system. Thus, most of the enterprises stopped functioning. Even the money earned though privatization was often not invested in the firms, which worsened their financial situation (Tsikhelashvili et al., 2012, p. 14). The Soviet 'red directors' did not enjoy much power in Georgia in between wars and among other competing power groups. The situation was so out of control that one of the common strategies for enterprises was to stop production, in response to common thefts (Burduli, 2015, p. 37; Papava, 2005, p. 132). Furthermore, local production was discouraged through tax laws, which freed imports from taxes and thus put local producers under the pressure of unfair competition (Christophe, 2005, pp. 14–15). Consequently, by 2001, the Georgian export sector was dominated by scrap metal and wine (National Bank of Georgia, 2001, p. 16).

Privatization had a considerable influence on the further development of industry. Even though officially, everyone could be involved in the process through state vouchers, in fact, it was the old Soviet management that took over the factories again. Unfortunately, these people did not manage to make the enterprises function, leading to the demolition of companies and massive selling of the equipment as scrap (Khaduri, 2005, p. 25). By 1995, industry had been reduced by 78% in comparison with 1990 (Tsikhelashvili et al., 2012, p. 9). By the year 2000, more than 60% of the registered companies were not working. Furthermore, 15 divisions of national industry were inactive without any plan of operation. Smuggling, taxes, and inequity made it hard for small and medium enterprises (SMEs) to develop (Kochladze et al., 2002, p. 12).

The catastrophic economic situation could not be saved even by foreign direct investments (FDI) at that time. The level of FDI remained low until the end of 2000, in comparison with other post-Soviet countries (Kochladze et al., 2002, p. 13). A change in capital inflows occurred in 1997 due to the implementation of international energy projects; in specific the Baku-Sufsa[6] project played a significant role. FDI made up more than 8% of the GDP in 2003, due to the Baku-Ceyhan[7] oil project (Tsikhelashvili et al., 2012, p. 16). International financial organizations did not succeed in attracting capital to Georgia. Investors were not willing to invest and if they did, they adopted to the Georgian way of doing business quite fast (Christophe, 2005, p. 21).

Thus, the weak economic structure paved a way towards foreign currency domination in the first years of independence, and Georgia was doomed for import dependence. Import dependence in the early years of independence required the usage of foreign currency, as private market actors had to pay for goods in order to import them to Georgia. Therefore, it was not easy or really possible for the government or the central bank to prohibit conversion of the local currency to foreign currencies, as the country could have faced a further crisis – absence of goods at local markets (see Stenographic Report of the Parliament Meeting May 11, 1993, p. 97). Georgia still remains strongly dependent on imports today. A large trade deficit makes the issue of dollarization even more severe for the country. The currency devaluation-inflation spiral under dollarization makes the population vulnerable to exchange-rate changes. Moreover, a current account deficit (due to trade deficit) increases the need for borrowing on international markets and this debt is mostly denominated in foreign currency. Thus, import dependence encourages the dollarization of government debt.

Unsurprisingly employment suffered as a result of these dramatic changes. Almost 70% of the labour force was self-employed and by 2003, more than one-half of employment was in agriculture. This led to mass emigration waves from Georgia from the beginning of the 1990s. Though there are no official statistics, around 1 million people left Georgia in this period (Tsikhelashvili et al., 2012, pp. 16–17), which made up roughly one-fourth of the total population. The first mass outflow of the population took place in 1990–1995, triggered by wars and economic problems; the second outflow (1995–2005) was caused by unemployment and the search for better education possibilities. The common destination for Georgian emigrants at this time was post-Soviet countries, especially Russia, where more than 60% of Georgian emigrants resided in 2002 (Eradze, 2014, p. 11). According to the calculations of Kakulia and Aslamazishvili, the amount of remittances constituted around $20–30 million per month in 2000 (Kakulia & Aslamazishvili, 2000, p. 49). Remittances thus represented one of the major sources of foreign currency inflow into the country. Remittances supported national currency stability, as the exchange of transferred hard currency into

Georgian Lari increased demand for the national currency and stabilized its value against foreign currencies. However, the supply of hard currency also made transactions in foreign currency more comfortable (for example on the real estate market) and thus encouraged price dollarization. Moreover, a large share of the Georgian population had access to foreign currency through remittances and were thus also interested in free usage of the hard currency in transactions or savings. Thus, the compromise on foreign currency hegemony, which was primarily established by political and financial elites, was also indirectly supported by some parts of the public.

Dollarization was largely encouraged by shadow economic activities, as the dollar was a key currency for its cash-based transactions (Kakulia & Aslamazishvili, 2000, pp. 41–42). The rate of deposit dollarization exceeded 60% after 1997 and reached 80% by the year 2000 (Amaghlobeli et al., 2003, p. 56). Most of the economy had gone underground and functioned informally after independence, as probably the only means of survival at that time. According to Papava, 'The shadow economy uses the same resources and markets as the legal economy, with the sole distinction that it takes place without the recognition of the state, and indeed, in some cases even without its knowledge' (Papava, 2005, p. 40). Though shadow economies are often linked with criminal activities, this was not always the case in Georgia. In some circumstances, shadow economic activities might even be useful for society, therefore, it should not be understood as something negative per se (Papava, 2005, p. 40).

The shadow economy was a remnant of the Soviet Union, where shadow enterprises and shadow parasitism played the most significant role. In the first case, production and trade happened illegally. However, as shadow enterprises were not allowed to exist, their owners had to pay bribes to buy the right of existence. These and other practices made up shadow parasitism (Papava, 2005, p. 11). Feldbrugge identifies the following activities in the Soviet shadow economy that functioned outside state control but were complementary with the formal economy – the diversion of state property, the use of state property and administrative power for private interests, trading privately, and using bribes (Feldbrugge, 1984, pp. 530–531). The function of the informal economy in the Soviet Union was threefold: it compensated for supplies that were not ensured within the planned economy and for quite a few people these activities guaranteed more money. Furthermore, the informal sector offered jobs to those who would otherwise be unemployed (Turmanidze, 2003, pp. 9–10). The shadow economic elite played an important role in the Soviet Union, often acting as a bridge between the criminal underworld and the political elite (Wheatley, 2005, pp. 28–29).

The informal economy did not disappear after the break-up of the Soviet Union and got even stronger in independent Georgia, reaching 70% of GDP in 1999. Furthermore, the level of informal employment was rather high in both urban and rural areas and the reliance on networks and families was crucial throughout the 1990s (Aliyev, 2014, p. 25). It is impossible to provide accurate data on the size of the shadow economy in Georgia due to ambiguities in methodology and measurement. However, different estimations vary from 25% to almost 60% of GDP throughout the 1990s. Furthermore, nine-tenths of agricultural production occurred informally and this sector was the most important for the Georgian economy at that time, while the share of the informal economy in industry was almost 60% (Turmanidze, 2003, pp. 12–13). In the Georgian case, the informal economy had the following features—unregistered, unreported, illegal activities in production and services; smuggling; 'substituting state agencies by the private firms' (established by state officials) (Turmanidze, 2003, p. 14). Though the role of Georgia in the Soviet shadow economy is assessed as significant, complex, and sophisticated, the informal economic practices in Georgia have a longer history than the Soviet Union (Aliyev, 2014, p. 24).

One of the encouraging factors for strengthening the Georgian shadow economic elite was the process of privatization, as these elites managed to access most of the privatization vouchers meant for the broader population. Thus, these people could 'control the supply of and demand for vouchers and hence their prices' (Papava, 2005, p. 57). Thieves in law in Georgia can be considered among the shadow economic elite, as well. They exercised quite significant power throughout the presidency of Shevardnadze, making money through smuggling, theft, and protection rackets. They enjoyed good connections with government officials and had access to the state treasury (World Bank, 2012, p. 12). Enhanced and intensive corruption at the borders of Georgia encouraged and supported the process of smuggling. As the WB report notes: 'Anyone could bribe his way into the country with any kind of cargo and sell it without any record of import or payment of duty' (World Bank, 2012, p. 37). A further important group of the shadow economic elite were the former factory directors in the Soviet Union, known as *deltsy*. They were supposed to become entrepreneurs after the Soviet Union broke up, but their practices (e.g., cheating, bribery, falsifications) did not change. For example, if *deltsy* had earlier attempted to achieve lower state plans for overfilling their enterprises in the Soviet Union, now they tried to report only part of their production size in order to pay fewer taxes. Furthermore, they usually tried to make a career in politics to secure their economic gains by lobbying their business interests directly (Papava, 2005, pp. 52–53).

Thus, the dollar was used for the functioning of the new accumulation regime in Georgia and it served the rent-seeking interests of political and economic elites. A certain kind of compromise emerged around enduring foreign currency domination in return for private financial gains. Moreover, the 'death' of industry and the import dependence of the country made dollarization and exchange rate-related issues more severe in terms of price stability. Trade and current account deficits created the need for borrowing money abroad, which led to the original sin of dollarization due to the accumulation of external debt in foreign currency. Also, the mass emigration of the Georgian population and the inflow of remittances in dollars provided a supply of foreign currency and encouraged price dollarization, as well as dollar compromise. On the other hand, the shadow economy, corruption, and smuggling created more demand for dollar in the cash-based informal economic activities. Thus, the 'new' accumulation regime embraced the dollar and it served the interests of powerful economic groups throughout Shevardnadze's presidency.

Nationalism vs foreign currency domination

The origins of dollarization coincide with the process of nation-state building in Georgia. Therefore, it is puzzling how a foreign currency could become powerful alongside the nation-building rhetoric in a country where nationalist sentiments were rather strong. The answers to this question can be found in the postcolonial (especially Soviet) legacies of Georgian nationalism. Nationalism is understood here as 'a political principle or an ideological movement that may politicize and instrumentalize ethnicity and culture by using different discursive constructs or social communications' (Metreveli, 2016, p. 2).

Georgian nationalism has roots in the mid-nineteenth century, when the central idea of gaining autonomy within the Russian Empire and 'preserving the "Georgian self" (qartuli vinaoba)' emerged (Sabanadze, 2010, p. 73). As Mikhako Tsereteli[8] in his 1953 letter about Noe Jordania[9] writes, even though nationalism was strong in Georgia towards the end of the nineteenth century, it still did not manage to mobilize Georgians. Jordania and his supporters, inspired by Marxism, managed to mobilize different classes under the idea of fighting against the Russian empire and founded the social democratic party in Georgia (Tsereteli, 1953). Not everyone in the Georgian elite requested independence from Russia in the beginning of the twentieth century. For example, social democrats did not support the idea of independence until 1918. On the one hand, there was fear that other enemies would take over Georgia and, on the other hand, there was a belief that Russia should support the cultural development of Georgia. However, this does not mean that this part of intelligentsia did not care about nationalism or national rights (Jones, 2007, p. 12). For Georgian social democrats, self-determination was important, but international solidarity was also crucial (Kautsky, 2018, p. 268). Nationalism in twentieth-century Georgia was very much economy-oriented. Jordania considered that only economic unity could have created a common ground for the Georgian state to emerge (Zhordania, 1920, pp. 17–19). Furthermore, the class struggle should have been aimed not only against economic exploitation but also for achieving national freedom (Suny, 1996, pp. 145–146). Therefore, defending workers' rights meant the protection of national interests at that time (Jones, 2007, p. 35). The minister of finance of the First Republic of Georgia attributed economy a special role in the very definition of the state. He considered that the modern nation state was a political-economic entity, which primarily relied on the development of a local production base and local markets (Kandelaki, 1935, pp. 37–38). This kind of focus on economic development has been missing in Georgian nationalist rhetoric since then, as nationalism became rather ethno-centric.

If before sovietization, nationalism in Georgia was just one out of the many ideological forces, afterwards it became a sole political ideology, which was very hostile to ethnic minorities. Thus, the Soviet Union played an important role in shaping nationalist ideas in Georgia, which were not quite completed in 1921 (when Georgia was annexed and forcefully driven into the Soviet Union) (Sabanadze, 2010, p. 81). Sabanadze identifies three main aspects that shaped nationalism in the Soviet Union: 'first, the rapid industrialization of the Soviet Union [...]; second, the organization of the Soviet state according to the principle of nationality [...]; and third, folklorization of national identity' (Sabanadze, 2010, p. 82). Furthermore, ethnic cleavages played an important role within the Soviet Union, though no member country was ethnically homogenous. The importance of ethnicity was left out of the official rhetoric, but it was 'institutionalized by the Soviet authorities in many arenas of public life' (Wheatley, 2005, p. 27). Most dissidents in the Soviet Union were united around national ideas and after the collapse of the Soviet Union they made up the political elite (Wheatley, 2005, pp. 29–32).

The nationalistic rhetoric was very strong in Georgia in the first years of independence (1991). The beginning of the 1990s was marked with the appraisal of nationalism in Georgia; the first president Zviad Gamsakhurdia delivered radical nationalistic public speeches against ethnic minorities (Jones, 2006a, pp. 256–257). Thus, in contrast with the declaration of independence in 1918, people were mobilized around nationalist ideas in 1991 and not around class struggle or economic nationalism. However, after Shevardnadze took power, nationalism was replaced by 'national apathy' (see (Sabanadze, 2010, pp. 98–104)) in the mid-1990s, as there were too many other problems, especially the lost war in Abkhazia.

The Rose Revolution brought an important change in the perception and presentation of nationalism. Even though many scholars would argue that Georgian nationalism became rather civic in character after the Rose Revolution, Metreveli argues that a 'hybrid nationalism' evolved in Georgia (Metreveli, 2016). The author analyses conflicting understandings and the implementation of nationalism and nationhood by the Saakashvili's government that managed to merge its secular liberal image with increased financing of the Georgian church. '[U]nder hybrid nationalism, policies do not necessarily derive from a coherent national ideology [...] but rather accommodate complex, and at times conflicting, political and social interests in discrepant public policies' (Metreveli, 2016, p. 16).

The character of Georgian nationalism can explain the above-mentioned puzzling coexistence of dollarization and nationalism. Georgian nationalism has gone through transformations since the nineteenth century, shifting focuses from cultural and economic to ethnic and sovereignty questions, falling into an apathy towards nationalism before transforming into a hybrid nationalism after the Rose Revolution. However, economic matters have not been in the spotlight of nationalist feelings of Georgians since 1991; this can explain the nationalism-dollarization puzzle. The cultural and later the 'sovereignty-protecting' (Barrington cited in (Jones, 2006a, p. 258) focus of Georgian nationalism did not care about economy. As a dissident and later politician, Irina Sarishvili-Chanturia says, in the first years of independence not much focus was made on economics in general (Demokratizatsiya, 2004, p. 312). Furthermore, 'Gamsakhurdia seemed to be preoccupied with symbols of independence and paid only lip service to economic reform for most of his tenure of office' (Gurgenidze et al., 1994, pp. 263–264). Even though the economy is very important for political developments, 'it did not dominate people's minds, and definitely was not the central thing on the political agenda' (Nodia, 1998, p. 13) in Georgia. Nationalism and security-dominated discourse still goes on in Georgian politics and civil society, where social and economic issues hardly get any proper attention.

Another key factor in explaining the above-mentioned puzzle is related to historical relations with Russia. In the first years of independence, it was important for Georgia to avoid Russian influence and the West was not considered as a danger (Sabanadze, 2010, pp. 95–97). Gamsakhurdia even announced a self-imposed embargo with Russia in 1991 (Gurgenidze et al., 1994, p. 263) to highlight the strong will for detaching Georgia from the Russian orbit. This kind of nationalist feeling can explain the importance of having a national currency. Yet, it was somehow fine to use the dollar in everyday life.

Thus, the emergence of dollarization in the process of nation building and alongside strong nationalist rhetoric can be explained through two arguments. First, Georgian nationalism has not focused on economic matters since the early 1990s. Ethnic-centered nationalism (during Gamsakhurdia's presidency) was followed by the so-called nationalism apathy (under Shevardnadze) and later by hybrid nationalism (under Saakashvili). The experience of social democracy and economic development-oriented nationalism in the twentieth century had been successfully wiped off by Soviet colonialism and Georgian dissidents of the 1990s. Second, it was important to combat Russification and a national currency mattered for the sovereignty-oriented nationalism in Georgia, but it did not exclude the usage of the dollar, as the West was not perceived as a potential threat.

Conclusion

The analysis of the Georgian state, from independence (1991) until the Rose Revolution (2003) explains the emergence and acceptance of dollarization. First, a lack of knowledge of and experience of market economies, as well as the disregard of the economic sphere in general explains the lack of attention to currency matters. The national currency was important as a sign of sovereignty, but no measures were taken to strengthen it or avoid dollarization from the beginning. Second, the Georgian political and economic elites (that were often the same) were so occupied by rent-seeking interests that they would not care about such issues as a strong currency. Dollarization did not threaten these aims, quite the opposite as foreign currency was one of the main stabilizing factors of existing production relations. Third, the flourishing of the informal economy increased the demand for dollars. The regime of accumulation in independent Georgia further strengthened dollarization. The informal, smuggling-based economy was taking advantage of its informality and used dollars for most of the cash-based deals. Furthermore, as industry could not recover, the economy became import dependent which had long-lasting effects not only on the origins of dollarization but also on its persistence. Mass emigration created another channel of dollar inflow through remittances. Fourth, civil society was rather inexperienced and engaged with democratization issues, so the question of a strong currency was beyond the scope of their agenda. The broader public was occupied with political conflicts and economic survival. Thus, the emergence of the dollar as a dominant currency did not create any threat to national elites or international actors in the hybrid arrangement of patrimonial bureaucratic state; quite the opposite, it well served their rent-seeking aims of political and financial elites. There was a certain compromise among powerful interest groups locally and globally about the usage of foreign currency, not considering the importance of a strong national currency for the economic development of Georgia. Dollar hegemony was not challenged throughout the 1990s and early 2000s, as neither civil society nor the broader public had awareness about dollarization results in mid-term or long-term period. In addition, as a large share of the population had access to dollars through remittances and could use the hard currency for transactions or savings, they were also indirectly part of the dollar hegemony compromise.

Notes

1 Nomenklatura were people who held key positions in bureaucracy in the Soviet Union.
2 Konstantine Kandelaki was a minister of finance in the First Republic of Georgia (1918–1921).
3 Mkhedrioni was established in 1989 under the leadership of Jaba Ioseliani, who were later fighting against Zviad Gamsakhurdia.
4 Abbreviation for a communist youth organization in the Soviet Union.
5 Gogi Topadze was the head of the party 'Industry Will Save Georgia' and the founder of the beer company Khazbegi.
6 Baku-Sufsa oil pipeline construction was finished in 1998, bringing oil from Azerbaijan to Georgia.
7 Baku-Ceyhan-Tbilisi oil pipeline delivers oil from Azerbaijan to Turkey via Georgia. These pipelines have special importance in the region in terms of energy security and geopolitical leverage.
8 Mikhako Tsereteli was a famous Georgian historian, sociologist, linguist, and publicist.

9 Noe Jordania was one of the founding fathers of the First Republic of Georgia, (1918–1921) and the leader of the social-democratic party.

References

Aliyev, H. (2014). The Effects of the Saakashvili Era Reforms on Informal Practices in the Republic of Georgia. *Studies of Transition States and Societies*, 6(1), 19–33.

Amaghlobeli, D., Farrell, J., & Nielsen, J. (2003). The evolution of commercial banking in Georgia, 1991–2001. *Post-Communist Economies*, 15(1), 47–74.

Angley, R. E. (2013). Escaping the Kmara box: Reframing the role of civil society in Georgia's Rose Revolution. *Studies of Transition States and Societies*, 5(1), 42–57.

Aprasidze, D. (2016). 25 Years of Georgia's Democratization: Still Work in Progress. In G. Nodia (Ed.), *25 Years of Independent Georgia: achievements and unfinished projects* (pp. 91–130). Konrad Adenauer Stiftung, Ilia State University.

Baumann, E. (2010). Post-Soviet Georgia: the Rocky Path towards Modern Social Protection. In *ESPANET 2010: Social Policy and the Global Crisis* (Issue September, pp. 1–21). ESPANET.

Brabant, J. M.van. (1998). *The Political Economy of Transition: Coming to grips with history and methodology*. Routledge.

Broers, L. (2005). After the 'revolution': Civil society and the challenges of consolidating democracy in Georgia. *Central Asian Survey*, 24(3), 333–350.

Burduli, T. (2015). ek'onomik'uri gardakmnebi sakartveloshi: gza shok'uri terap'iidan ghrma da q'ovlismomtsvel tavisupal savach'ro zonamde [Economic transformations in Georgia: a way from shock therapy to deep and comprehensive free trade zone]. *Ek'onomik'a Da Sabank'o Sakme*, 3(2), 31–51.

Carothers, T. (2002). The End of the Transition Paradigm. *Journal of Democracy*, 13 (1), 5–21.

Chechelashvili, V., & Javakhishvili, N. (2017). *Oral History of Georgia: Interview with Nodar Javakhishvili*. GFSIS.

Chechelashvili, V., & Papava, V. (2017). *Oral History of Georgia: interview with Vladimer Papava*. GFSIS.

Chiaberashvili, Z., & Tevzadze, G. (2005). Power Elites in Georgia: Old and New. In E. Cole & P. Fluri (Eds.), *From Revolution to Reform: Georgia's Struggle with Democratic Insitution Building and Security Secoro Reform* (pp. 187–207). Austrian National Defence Academy and Bureau for Security Policy at the Austrian Federal Ministry of Defence.

Christophe, B. (2004). Understanding Politics in Georgia (No. 22; DEMSTAR Research Report).

Christophe, B. (2005). From Hybrid Regime to Hybrid Capitalism? The Political Economy of Georgia under Eduard Shevardnadze. Varieties of Capitalism in Post-Communist Countries, 23–24 September 2005, University of Paisley.

Cornia, G. A. (2012). Transition, Structural Divergence, and Performance: Eastern Europe and the Former Soviet Union during 2000–7. In G. Roland (Ed.), *Economics in Transition The Long-Run View* (pp. 293–317). Palgrave Macmillan.

Dadalauri, N. (2007). Political Corruption in Georgia. In S. Bracking (Ed.), *Corruption and Development: The Anti-Corruption Campaigns* (1st ed., pp. 155–166). Palgrave Macmillan UK.

Demokratizatsiya. (2004). Georgia, Moldova and Bulgaria: Dismantling Communist Structures Is Hardly Extremism: Interview with Irina Sarishvili-Chanturia, Iurie

Rošca, and Philip Dimitrov. *Demokratizatsiya: The Journal of Post-Soviet Democratization*, 12(2), 311–320.

Eradze, I. (2014). Costs and Benefits of Labor Mobility between European Union and Georgia (Policy Research for Sustainable Growth). https://www.kas.de/c/document_library/get_file?uuid=f7f36664-71ab-d38e-f39f-b061bcbf7d57&groupId=252038.

Feldbrugge, F. J. M. (1984). Government and Shadow Economy in the Soviet Union. *Soviet Studies*, 36(4), 528–543.

Gurgenidze, L., Lobzhanidze, M., & Onoprishvili, D. (1994). Georgia: From planning to hyperinflation. *Communist Economies and Economic Transformation*, 6(3), 259–281.

Jones, S. (2006a). Nationalism from under the Rubble. In L. W. Barrington (Ed.), *After Independence: Making and Protecting the Nation in Postcolonial and Post-communist Societies* (1st ed., pp. 248–276). The University of Michigan Press.

Jones, S. (2006b). The Rose Revolution: A Revolution without Revolutionaries? *Cambridge Review of International Affairs*, 19(1), 33–48.

Jones, S. (2007). *sotsializmi kartul perebshi* [Socialism in Georgian Colours] (Z. Abashidze & N. Chiaberashvili, Eds.). Ilia State University.

Kakulia, M., & Aslamazishvili, N. (2000). *dolarizatsia sakartveloshi: massht'abebi, pakt'orebi, daz'levis gzebi* [Dollariztion in Georgia: Dimensions, Factors, Solutions] (J. Meskhia, Ed.). Institute of Economy of the Georgian Science Academy.

Kandelaki, K. (1935). *sakartvelos erovnuli meurneoba: t'erit'oria da mosakhleoba* [National Economy of Georgia: territory and population], Book I. D. Kheladze Publishing.

Kautsky, K. (2018). *Georgia: A Social-Democratic Peasant Republic: Impressions and Observations [1921]* (Z. Gaiparashvili & I. Iremadze, Eds.). Friedrich Ebert Stiftung Georgien, Ivane Javakhishvili Tbilisi State University.

Khaduri, N. (2005). Mistakes Made in Conducting Economic Reforms in Post-communist Georgia. *Problems of Economic Transition*, 48(4), 18–29.

Kochladze, M., Gujaraidze, L., & Tavartkiladze, L. (2002). Decade of Independence Effects of Economic liberalization in Georgia: country report. https://greenalt.org/en/library/decade-of-independence-effects-of-economic-liberalization-in-georgia/.

Koehler, J., & Zürcher, C. (2004). Der Staat und sein Schatten: Zur Institutionalisierung hybrider Staatlichkeit im Süd-Kaukasus. *WeltTrends*, 45(Winter), 84–96.

Kukhianidze, A. (2009). Corruption and organized crime in Georgia before and after the 'Rose Revolution'. *Central Asian Survey*, 28(2), 215–234.

Metreveli, T. (2016). An undisclosed story of roses: church, state, and nation in contemporary Georgia. *Nationalities Papers*, 1–19.

Mitchell, L. A. (2009). Compromising democracy: State building in Saakashvili's Georgia. *Central Asian Survey*, 28(2), 171–183.

Mitchell, L. A. & Philips, D. L. (2008). Enhancing democracy assistance. *American Foreign Policy Interests*, 30(3), 156–175.

Muskhelishvili, M., & Jorjoliani, G. (2009). Georgia's ongoing struggle for a better future continued: democracy promotion through civil society development. *Democratization*, 16(4), 682–708.

National Bank of Georgia. (2001). Annual Report. https://nbg.gov.ge/publications/annual-reports.

Nodia, G. (1998). Dynamics of State-Building in Georgia. *Demokratizatsiya*, 6(1), 6–13.

Nodia, G. (2016). The Story of Georgia's State-Building: Dramatic but Closer to Completion. In G. Nodia (Ed.), *25 Years of Independent Georgia: Achievements and unfinished projects* (pp. 56–90). Konrad Adenauer Stiftung e. V, Ilia State University.

Papava, V. (2005). *Necroeconomics: The Political Economy of Post-Communist Capitalism (Lessons from Georgia)*. iUniverse Inc.

Papava, V. (2006). The Political Economy of Georgia's Rose Revolution. *East European Democratization*, Fall, 657–667.

Polese, A., Rekhviashvili, L., & Morris, J. (2016). Informal governance in urban spaces: Power, negotiation and resistance among Georgian street vendors. *Geography Research Forum*, 36(Special Issue), 15–32.

Rona-Tas, A., & Guseva, A. (2014). *Plastic Money: Constructing Markets for Credit Cards in Eight Postcommunist Countries.* Stanford University Press.

Sabanadze, N. (2010). *Globalization and Nationalism: the case of Georgia and the Basque Country.* Central European University Press.

Sherr, J. (2002). Presentation 'Ukraine's Euro-Atlantic Course', DUPI Seminar, October 19, Copenhagen.

Siroky, D. S., & Aprasidze, D. (2011). Guns, roses and democratization: Huntington's secret admirer in the Caucasus. *Democratization*, 18(6), 1227–1245.

Stenographic Report of the Parliament Meeting May 11 (1993). Parliament of Georgia.

Stiglitz, J. E. (1999). Whither Reform? Ten Years of Transition. World Bank Annual Bank Conference on Development Economics.

Suny, R. G. (1996). The Emergence of Political Society in Georgia. In *Transcaucasia, Nationalism, and Social Change Essays in the History of Armenia, Azerbaijan, and Georgia* (pp. 109–140). The University of Michigan Press.

Tsereteli, M. (1953). Mikhak'o Tsereteli noe j'ordanias shesakheb (Mikhako Tsreteli about Noe Jhordania). http://aboutguria.blogspot.com/2015/11/blog-post_30.html.

Tsikhelashvili, K., Shergilashvili, T., & Tokmazashvili, M. (2012). sakartvelos ek'onomik'uri t'ransportmatsia: damouk'ideblobis 20 ts'eli shualeduri angarishi [Economic transformation of Georgia: 20 years of independence A midterm report].

Turmanidze, K. (2003). State against the Invisible: The Case of Georgian Informal Economy. Masters thesis.

Wellisz, S. (1996). *Georgia: A brief survey of macroeconomic problems and policies.* CASE Foundation.

Wheatley, J. (2005). *Georgia from National Awakening to Rose Revolution: Delayed Transition in the Former Soviet Union.* Ashgate.

World Bank. (2012). *Fighting Corruption in Public Services: Chronicling Georgia's Reforms.* World Bank.

Zhordania, N. (1920). *Akhali gzit* [On a new way] (2nd ed.). kartuli bechdviti amkhanagoba [Georgain printing cooperation].

5 Hyperinflation

The origins of dollarization and the birth of the lari

The ruble as the last remnant of the Soviet Union

Even though the Soviet Union ceased to exist in 1991, the ruble remained as the currency in the former Soviet Union (FSU) countries. The developments in monetary affairs are well described by Aslund (see Aslund, 1995, 2007). Even though all central banks of FSU countries were allowed to issue credits and could create money, only the Central Bank of Russia (CBR) had the authority to print money. Despite having a common currency, each of the 15 countries had its own central bank, or as Aslund writes, there were 'fourteen central banks too many' (Aslund, 1995, p. 106). The Soviet State bank and the central banks of FSU countries did not understand that they were increasing money supply through new credits and creating the risk of inflation. Soon, all of these countries were short of cash (Aslund, 2007, p. 108).

Despite difficulties with the shared currency, the idea of maintaining a common currency was still debated in the post-Soviet space. Russia wanted to maintain the common currency, but it requested of holding the sole monetary authority. Furthermore, votes should have been fixed according to the gross domestic product (GDP) of each country, which would guarantee Russia most votes in the decision-making process. Other FSU countries were against such developments (Aslund, 1995, p. 109) as most of them preferred their national currencies as a sign of national sovereignty. Yet, a triggering cause for adopting national currencies was Russia's decision to no longer provide FSU countries with the ruble (White et al., 1993, p. 95).

The Baltic states insisted on issuing national currencies from the beginning, whereas Georgia, along with Ukraine, Moldova, and Azerbaijan wanted to have a national currency later, as they did not feel prepared for monetary reform. The rest of the countries decided to stick to the ruble. In Russia, there was no clear consensus on the currency matter – reformers wanted to nationalize the currency, as they were aware of the danger of hyperinflation. This group of people was advised from the West to issue their own rubles. However, officials from the Russian central bank, Soviet ministries, and state industry did not want to give up the idea of the Soviet Union and a common currency (Aslund, 2007, p. 109). Aslund remarks that the

DOI: 10.4324/9781003240174-7

choice of FSU countries to leave the ruble zone or not was not only economic and financial, but also political. 'Membership in the ruble zone was generally perceived as doing Russia a favour, and departure would be considered an affront' (Aslund, 1995, p. 116).

The international monetary fund (IMF) had a neutral position in the currency issue in the beginning. However, it assisted the Baltic states in 1992 to introduce their national currencies and officially advised Kyrgyzstan to leave the ruble zone in 1993. Yet, 'Through its neutrality, the IMF effectively supported a monetary chaos that condemned the CIS [Commonwealth of Independent States] to hyperinflation' (Aslund, 2007, p. 109). Estonia was the first country to introduce its own currency in 1992 (White et al., 1993, p. 95). The IMF and the European Commission (EC) supported the idea of maintaining the ruble zone and the Fund warned those countries that had started a currency reform that it would not help them. The EC also shared this position and the EC ambassador to Moscow, Michael Emerson, even compared the CIS with the common market in Europe. The IMF made a proposal at the CIS meeting in Tashkent, Uzbekistan, that all central banks could be allowed to issue money with certain limitations on domestic credits, while the CBR would have the special right of imposing penalties or even taking away the right of receiving credits. However, this plan was not accepted by the CBR, as Russia was afraid that it provided too much free-riding incentives for FSU countries (Aslund, 1995, pp. 110–111). Jeffrey Sachs criticized the Russian government and the CBR for not having a proper policy regarding the ruble zone. He argued, 'Ironically, part of the difficulty lay in encouragement from the IMF and the EC to maintain a ruble zone despite the obvious inability of the participating countries to manage such a zone in a responsible, non-inflationary manner' (Sachs, 1994, p. 43).

The National Bank of Georgia (NBG) discussed the introduction of a national currency at the very first meeting with the IMF and asked for support in currency reform. However, the Fund did not encourage this idea in 1992 and advised the Georgian government to stay in the ruble zone. Countries without national currencies could not apply for IMF credit. The same advice was given to all FSU countries at that time, except the Baltic states. There are different explanations of IMF's decision. Papava assumes that the Fund preferred to remain careful with Russia. He argues that it would have been easier for the IMF to work with one currency in all these countries, rather than twelve new ones. Papava also presents Aslund's (1995) claim that the IMF was cautious with the newly independent countries and their capabilities to start a currency reform. The Fund was perhaps apprehensive of the introduction of so many new currencies, especially being uncertain of their success (Papava, 2005, pp. 144–145). Moreover, the Fund was in general very careful with issuing credits to Georgia until the political stability was restored (referring to the war in Abkhazia) (see Stenographic Report of the Parliament Meeting June 10, 1993, pp. 93–94, 99). It is not within the scope of this research to find the right answer to this question, but the reasons behind IMF's decision could well comprise a combination of various factors from geopolitical caution to a lack of knowledge. Furthermore, changes in the IMF's position towards different FSU countries on currency matters within a short period of time indicate that the Fund did not have a plan at the outset; it made decisions on a case by case basis and according to ongoing developments. For example, the Fund urged the Georgian government to leave the ruble zone in 1993, once it was assured that inflation was inevitable, and promised the country assistance in issuing a national currency (Sakartvelos resp'ublik'a, 1993a, p. 2). Therefore, it is difficult to discuss IMF's intentions in this matter as it appears to have been unprepared for such changes. What is important though in this debate is the demonstration of Fund's power in currency affairs. Georgia did not have the financial means or proper experience to issue its national currency at the beginning of the 1990s. The monetary sovereignty of the country was dependent on the willingness of cooperation and recognition of external actors.

With the overall confusion regarding the ruble zone and currencies in the post-Soviet space, things were sliding in the wrong direction in policymaking. The Russian Central Bank had issued significant amount of credit and by 1992 they had reached 40% of GDP. Such levels of debt was triggering high inflation. Most of the loans were given to enterprises and credit was partially issued upon government decisions; a minor part of this credit (10% of GDP) was provided to other countries, so they could purchase Russian goods (Fischer, 1994, p. 15). Financing imports was especially important for the industrial lobby that wanted to maintain good relations with neighbouring countries (Sachs, 1994, p. 45). Thus, Russia decided to reduce the amount of ruble credit, decrease budget expenditure, and reduce the level of inflation. As the deputy minister of finance (Kazmin) and minister of finance (Fedorov) wrote, the agro-industrial lobby and conservative governors of the Central Bank were against these reforms. In particular, conflicts between the Ministry of Finance and the CBR created barriers for the implementation of this plan. Finally, the influence of the IMF on the CBR contributed to the achievement of compromise agreements between these two institutions (Fedorov & Kazmin, 1994, pp. 26–27). In 1993, the ruble zone was dissolved by Russia and the member countries were no longer provided with credit (Aslund, 2007, p. 110). Russia, Armenia, Belarus, Kazakhstan, Tajikistan, and Uzbekistan signed an agreement to create a new ruble zone a few months later (Fedorov & Kazmin, 1994, p. 31). Georgia was among the few countries, along with the Baltic states, who did not join the CIS in the beginning. Eventually, in 1993, Georgia also became a member (Aslund, 1995, p. 103). Thus, as Russia started a currency reform in 1993, the ruble stopped existing. The decision was announced on 24 July and all rubles issued before that day became valueless. The official reasoning behind this decision was Russia's aim to nationalize the ruble and establish monetary stability. There are different opinions on the motives of this decision – from a conspiracy by the CBR to weaken the government and the president to corruption or shocking the FSU counties in order to subordinate them (Aslund, 1995, pp. 129–130). According to Kakulia, Russia realized there were plans of issuing national currencies in the post-Soviet space and the ruble was losing its positions, so they 'took fairly tough measures' (M. Kakulia, 2008, p. 179).

Thus, the developments of the early 1990s in currency-related issues were controversial, unexpected, complicated, and unplanned. Interests of diverse groups on national, regional, and international levels clashed with each other. On the one hand, knowledge about monetary and credit policy was missing within the post-Soviet space and, on the other hand, the international community had too little understanding of Soviet specificities and inter republic relations. Furthermore, the rent-seeking interests of specific groups were influencing state policies. These developments significantly influenced the later developments in dollarization. The ruble practically lost its position in the currency hierarchy and Russia missed a chance of maintaining monetary influence over the FSU countries. One might question why Russia decided to nationalize the currency and ruin the idea of keeping a common currency zone; perhaps, Russia was preoccupied with its own economic and financial issues at that time, though, for certain groups, imperialistic monetary plans were still at stake. If Russia had any imperialist plans, they did not work, as most of the FSU countries issued their own currencies in response to the ruble shortage.

Hyperinflation in Georgia: the coupon as a doomed currency

The ruble remained as the currency in Georgia after the break-up of the Soviet Union, as in other FSU counties. In 1991, shortly after independence, the NBG was founded with the main function of guaranteeing national currency stability. The dissolution of the Soviet Union was negatively reflected on the national budget of Georgia as transfers from the Soviet budget were stopped. Thus, the Georgian budget suffered a deficit of 2 million rubles in the first years, reaching almost 20% GDP in 1992. In the economic recession, there were practically no possibilities of filling the budget apart from borrowing from the National Bank (Gursoy & Chitadze, 2012, pp. 37–38).

In 1992, the Russian Central Bank unexpectedly stopped issuing rubles for Georgia. Thus, a temporary currency – the coupon – was issued, which was initially supposed to coexist with the ruble (Wang, 1999, pp. 7–8). According to Papava, Moscow's decision to no longer provide Georgia with the ruble was its 'most important policy mistake' (Papava, 2005, p. 130). According to the former NBG president and economic advisor, Roman Gotsiridze, the political elite believed that this situation was temporary and Georgia would remain in the ruble zone. However, a group of politicians wanted to follow the Baltic example of having a national currency. Thus, the coupon was issued as a surrogate for the ruble; there was no other way than printing new money as Georgia was out of cash. Nevertheless, as the former Prime

Minister Sigua noted, Adjara was still receiving money from Russia but the governor of this region, Aslan Abashidze, was not allowed to share the money with the rest of Georgia (Kitia & Akhobadze, 2015). This fact is especially interesting in the context of political tensions between Aslan Abashidze and President Shevardnadze. Adjara was not just an autonomous republic at this time but Abashidze was trying to separate the region from the rest of the country (Wheatley, 2005, pp. 115–116), until Saakashvili finally managed to fully reconciliate Adjara politically and economically in 2004. Thus, the Russian ruble policy was not just about economic aims, but also very political and imperial, as it tried to trigger an interstate conflict in Georgia.

The coupon did not become the only means of legal payment in Georgia until the summer of 1993. In June the value of the coupon fell to 5 coupons: 1 ruble (Gurgenidze et al., 1994, p. 270). The coupon did not turn out to be successful as the Georgian economy was import dependent and the public did not trust a temporary currency (M. Kakulia, 2001, pp. 61–64). Even Georgian officials did not take these bank notes seriously, 'revealing contemptuous attitudes towards it' (Papava, 2005, p. 130). Thus, issuing coupons was a reaction of the Georgian government to unexpected processes in the region and the country was completely unprepared for this change.

Before the coupon was issued, the Georgian government was following an expansionary monetary policy. Imports of certain resources and consumption goods from the ruble-zone countries were financed. However, no real cash was transferred to these countries, thus the book money amount and, consequently, demand for cash was increasing. This process contributed to hyperinflation later (M. Kakulia, 2008, pp. 179–180). After the issue of the coupon, the volume of domestic currency broad money (M2) increased and as the Georgian government needed money to finance budget deficits, NBG credits to the government became the only means of doing so, until the bank was literally out of banknotes. Consequently, the coupon was losing its value in comparison with other currencies (Wang, 1999, pp. 7–8). 'A vicious circle of fiscal deficit, central bank credit emission, currency devaluation and substitution, and larger fiscal deficit' (Wang, 1999, p. 4) triggered inflation. Yet, even before the outbreak of hyperinflation, Georgia faced issues with inflation primarily due to price liberalization and this topic was discussed at government meetings (Sakartvelos resp'ublik'a, 1992a, 1992b).

The emission of the coupon caused a number of issues, as even some state agencies and state-owned shops did not want to accept it as a means of payment. Moreover, the rules of coupon circulation were not clear, and they were violated constantly, especially in terms of determining the coupon-ruble rate. The exchange rate was often set upon individual decisions of exchange shops or individuals (see Stenographic Report of the Parliament Meeting May 11, 1993, pp. 55–60). A further problem was that upon the issue of the coupon, the Russian ruble remained in circulation in Georgia. The Georgian government did not and could not withdraw the ruble from the market. One of the key reasons was the risk of diminishing imports, and Georgia was extremely dependent on imported goods, which needed to be paid for in rubles (Stenographic Report of the Parliament Meeting May 11, 1993, pp. 93–94). Furthermore, the idea of undertaking privatization in coupons was not successful, and this plan could not strengthen the new currency either (Stenographic Report of the Parliament Meeting May 11, 1993, p. 99). Hyperinflation was increasing at 60–70% monthly in 1994 and consequently people started to use the ruble instead of the coupon (Papava, 2005, p. 130). The coupon was depreciating against the US dollar. The dollar was widely used for big transactions, and the ruble for small and medium-sized transactions (Khaduri, 2005, p. 30). Also, if the ruble had a key function for transactions before the introduction of the lari, the dollar was an important currency for savings (M. Kakulia, 2008, p. 182). Even after the end of the hyperinflation and successful monetary reform, it was mostly ruble and not dollar holdings that enabled the process of remonetization (Jarocińsky & Jirny, 1999, p. 75). Before the adoption of the national currency of the lari, the level of dollarization reached almost 67% in 1994 (De Nicoló et al., 2003, p. 33).

The exchange rate of the non-cash Coupon to the USD increased from 1:1 in April 1993 to 200,000:1, by December 1993 (Gurgenidze et al., 1994, p. 271). Hyperinflation had severe impacts on standards of living, income inequality, and unemployment (see R. Kakulia & Khaburzania, 1993; Sakartvelos resp'ublik'a, 1993d, 1993e). The Georgian people were especially concerned about high prices, as they did not match with pensions and salaries. For example, meat was sold for Russian the ruble and one had to pay a month's wages in coupons for 1 kg meat (Sakartvelos resp'ublik'a, 1993c, p. 5). The inflation indicator was three times higher than the average inflation rate in FSU countries. Even though the inflation rate decreased, there was still no stability for economic development. Price liberalization impacted the increase of trade deficits and the floating exchange regime influenced the increase of prices on imported goods. Furthermore, due to capital scarcity, capital investments also decreased (Tsikhelashvili et al., 2012, p. 11).

Gurgenidze et al. (1994, p. 268) argue that price liberalization (1992) played an important role in inflation. Prices increased dramatically after liberalization in 1992. For example, milk became 60 times more expensive and bread cost 100 times more (World Bank, 1993, p. 6). A survey from 1993 (conducted by the Committee for Social and Economic Information of Georgia) demonstrates that there was an expectation of price increases for raw materials and goods among enterprise managers. At that point, these enterprises had easy and cheap access to credits. Thus, prices were set above market levels in order to reduce demand and keep the goods for future sale at higher prices (Gurgenidze et al., 1994, p. 267). GDP declined in 1992 by 46% and the yearly average inflation was more than 900% (World Bank, 1993, p. 7). Thus, the expansionary monetary policy, price liberalization and the refusal of the IMF in the early 1990s to assist with the introduction of a national currency accelerated hyperinflation, as Russia started to play a geopolitical game with the ruble. However, this disastrous inflation cannot fully be blamed on the IMF and shock therapy or Russian tricks. The processes within Georgia and decisions made by the key actors significantly determined the fate of coupon and the national currency.

Even at the time of its issue, the Georgian prime minister stated that 'the coupon was doomed from the start' (Gurgenidze et al., 1994, p. 270). This had a certain influence on the trust of the society towards coupons. In order to understand this statement and hyperinflation, the fiscal and monetary situation of Georgia at that time shall be shortly reviewed. The Georgian government was running a high budget deficit of 35% of GDP (including extra-budgetary expansion) along with the fiscal crisis in 1992. The only way of financing this deficit was through bank credit. Even though in 1992 personal income and enterprise profit taxes were established, they did not influence budget revenues positively, as tax collection simply did not function. Furthermore, budgetary expenditure was significantly influenced by price liberalization and high inflation. Financing imports (of energy and grains), social benefits, wages, and supporting internally displaced people (IDPs)[1] became a burden for the state budget. Furthermore, because of the indexation of household deposits at the Saving Bank, the net claims on the government rose, as the state was the guarantor of the mentioned savings (Gurgenidze et al., 1994, pp. 269–270). Thus, the Georgian government was in desperate need of financial resources to deal with budget deficits and there was no legal or formal possibility of raising money other than borrowing it from the national bank.

However, not only was domestic credit to the government increasing, but so was credit for state enterprises as refinancing banks increased. The NBG was feeding banks with money. It raised the refinancing rate in 1992–1993 and by the end of 1993 it had reached 300%. Thus, Georgian banks had no interest in attracting deposits and even paid negative real interest rates on savings, influencing the rate of deposits in the national currency negatively, while hard currency (mostly the US dollar) deposits increased drastically. People preferred to make deposits in the ruble either in Russia or other ruble areas, as they offered better rates than Georgia did; thus, capital flight occurred. Furthermore, with negative interest rates, there was no possibility of financing the government budget deficit through government securities. Georgia was experiencing a ruble shortage in cash, whereas the economy was cash based (Gurgenidze et al., 1994, pp. 269–270). By 2003, the share of currency stock to broad money, which was outside the banks, still made up more than 40% (World Bank, 2003, p. 44).

The shortage of rubles created issues as the Georgian economy was cash based. The Georgian government announced that if the population put money in an account in the Savings Bank, then the level of savings would be doubled within one year. However, the government used this money to pay pensions and wages and the money supply did not decrease despite restrictions on the receipt of cash from Moscow. The liabilities of banks also increased and they could not return money to the population, which negatively influenced public trust. The former minister of finance, Khaduri called this plan a 'fraud [...] on national level' (Khaduri, 2005, p. 30). This action, as well as the reliance of the Georgian government on National Bank money and the financing of idle state enterprises through irresponsible banks, allow several observations to be made. The Georgian government had no plan about how to act and made ad hoc decisions. Such a situation was not caused only by the lack of knowledge of the government, but it was also triggered by rent-seeking gains – the National Bank was financing banks and state enterprises in a country in which the political and economic elites were inseparable. The central bank of Georgia was a newly established institution, which was expected to transform fundamentally along the rules of a market economy. Yet, there was no theoretical possibility to expect such a transformation in such a short time and therefore, the decisions of the National Bank of Georgia cannot be judged through the transition expectation prism only.

The NBG is often blamed for causing the hyperinflation through its irresponsible policies. Papava considers that the way credits were issued by the central bank was one of the main reasons for the inflation. Furthermore, the limits to cash circulation set by the Georgian central bank caused a gap between cash and non-cash monetary values that created barriers for the coupon to circulate. 'Also, state commercial banks tolerated excessive overdrafts, which promoted hidden credit emission' (Papava, 2005, p. 131) (see Sakartvelos resp'ublik'a, 1993b, p. 2, 1993f, p. 1). The expansionary monetary policy of the NBG was debated in public in the 1990s and it was explained through two main factors. One version pictured the NBG as naive in its decisions, wanting to encourage the development of business through increasing credit lines. The minister of finance even stated at that time: 'inflation is not always destructive, it can contribute to the rational development of the economy' (Gurgenidze et al., 1994, p. 272). The second narrative explained the NBG's actions as the greed of certain officials who made profit via liberalized lending and borrowing (Gurgenidze et al., 1994, pp. 272–273). The central bank president in 1993–1998, Nodar Javakhishvili, also argued that the lack of experience and wrong policies of the NBG caused hyperinflation. Another central bank president Gotsiridze (2005–2007) says that a significant share of Georgian foreign debt was due to speculative coupon transactions. The coupon did not have reserve back-up in the NBG, especially in foreign currency (Kitia & Akhobadze, 2015). Papava describes how privileged groups of people made fortunes in the beginning of the 1990s by having access to state credits; they had '"legally unlimited" opportunity to become rich through rapid currency or commodity transactions' owing to the 'devaluation of national currency and an increase in prices' (Papava, 2005, p. 58). Yet, the speech of the NBG president – Demur Dvalishvili – at the plenary session of the parliament (1993, May 27) reveals that expansionary monetary policy was also promoted by the needs of a country with a deteriorated economy to stimulate economic activities and avoid hunger (see Stenographic Report of the Parliament Meeting May 27, 1993, pp. 43–51). The central bank could not have avoided hyperinflation without a stable macroeconomic and political situation.

Moreover, the Georgian central bank was at that time too weak and lacked the necessary tools to influence the inflation process properly, even if the decision makers had been willing to do so. The National Bank of Georgia had very limited control on commercial or public banks and the president of the central bank at that time – Demur Dvailishvili – worryingly referred to this situation as a closed circle, from which he did not see a way out (see Stenographic Report of the Parliament Meeting May 11, 1993, pp. 102–103). The foreign exchange (FX) reserves of the NBG were far from extensive and it had no possibilities of increasing them – the only mechanism was an export tax on enterprises. With the issue of the coupon, the NBG and commercial banks established the Tbilisi Foreign Exchange Auction, but the volume of transactions, as well as the number of participants remained scarce. Thus, deficits in both areas – the FX reserve and the FX market – left very few options to the NBG regarding the exchange-rate regime and it was also not able to influence coupon depreciation as it could not intervene with FX reserves (Gurgenidze et al., 1994, p. 270).

Thus, the heated debate on hyperinflation positioned the government and the NBG on opposing poles and there was a blame game going on between them. It is not surprising that the National Bank and the political leadership no longer got along with each other. The government could not directly influence NBG policies, as the central bank president was appointed by the parliament. Dvalishvili, the president of the NBG at that time, was harshly criticized at a parliament hearing. After a month, the government resigned and 'the most pro-reform members of the cabinet were replaced by former *apparatchiki* and state enterprise sector managers' (Gurgenidze et al., 1994, pp. 271–272) (italics original). Shortly afterwards, the key governing figures of the central bank were also released from their positions as they were blamed for corruption and causing the hyperinflation (Gurgenidze et al., 1994, pp. 271–272).

However, shifting the blame to either the National Bank or the government contains a threat of seeing the problem in one dimension only. As already argued above, the government–central bank–state enterprises–commercial banks circle is inseparable from hyperinflation and there is not just one scapegoat. These practices might seem plausible if one views them through the lenses of path dependencies and Soviet legacies. The rent-seeking motives of the privileged people from political to civil societies, the dependency of state enterprises on state subsidies, and the dependence of the central bank on the government can easily be traced back to the Soviet Union. Soviet legacies can be identified in terms of lack of experience or milking the state and corruptive rent-seeking practices. Moreover, the mere helplessness of the central bank of a chaotic state to cope with poverty and economic catastrophes should not be underestimated.

Thus, the hyperinflation of the early 1990s resulted from a cocktail of various national, regional, and international factors, mistakes, lack of knowledge, rent-seeking motives, and wrong timing. It can even be considered as a historical momentum when three factors coincided – Soviet thinking in policymaking and the experience of twisted interests of the National Bank and state enterprises; transition pressure caused by the lack of knowledge in monetary affairs; and the burden of Russian geopolitical tricks. Yet, the experience of hyperinflation still influence the attitudes of the Georgian public towards national money and is often named by policymakers as a major driver of dollarization both in the government (Participant 11, personal communication, 8 June 2017; Participant 13, personal communication, 21 April 2017) and the central bank (Participant 2, personal communication, 6 May 2017; Participant 3, personal communication, 18 April 2017; Participant 4, personal communication, 3 May 2017).

The birth of the lari

The lari, the first national Georgian currency, emerged from the ruins of the coupon and the trauma of hyperinflation in an economy where the ruble and the dollar played important roles. The attitude of Georgian society towards a national currency was shaped by the negative experiences of hyperinflation. As a response to hyperinflation, Georgia started a stabilization and currency reform under the supervision of the IMF in 1994. According to this programme, the following steps should have been implemented – a drastic decrease of the NBG's financing of government budget; the termination of commercial banks' access to overdrafts at NBG anytime; the abolition of consumer subsidies; a decrease in the fiscal deficit by reducing government expenditure; and an increase in fiscal revenues through taxes; and the establishment of a floating exchange rate (Wang, 1999, p. 9). This programme was accompanied by price liberalization and a privatization processes (Papava & Chikovani, 1998, p. 7).

After the government and the NBG had implemented these steps, inflation decreased significantly but the demand for the coupon did not increase. Wang argues that this happened not only owing to people's lack of trust but also because they were not comfortable carrying substantial amounts of cash. The ruble was used for exchange and accounting, while the dollar and other currencies served the function of store of value (Wang, 1999, pp. 11–12). Thus, the Russian ruble still played an important role in Georgia and most remittances and export earnings were denominated in the ruble; even Russian military bases in Georgia received their salary in rubles (M. Kakulia, 2008, p. 181).

In 1995, the national currency the lari was introduced; one million coupons made one lari. Shortly after, the volume of domestic currency increased four times and the lari replaced the ruble as a means of exchange (Wang, 1999, pp. 11–12). The NBG pegged the lari to the dollar with the financial help of the IMF (credit) to increase trust in the new national currency. As a result, banks could no longer profit from currency trading, as the public did not need foreign currencies to the same extent as previously (Amaghlobeli et al., 2003, p. 51). After the introduction of the lari the level of dollarization fell from 66.7% to 40% in 1995 (De Nicoló et al., 2003, p. 33).

Even though inflation was tackled quite quickly and, shortly afterwards, a new national currency was issued, the impacts of inflation turned out to be long lasting. According to Wang, the success of stopping hyperinflation in only a couple of months was not due to the credibility of the Georgian government, but rather to the external IMF programme. The lack of credibility of the Georgian government explains, according to him, why currency substitution remained even after hyperinflation had ended (Wang, 1999, p. 17). Furthermore, inflation not only traumatized the attitudes of society towards a national currency and encouraged dollarization, but also marked the beginning of the IMF's official involvement in Georgia and the birth of the national currency.

Even though the lari was announced as the legal national currency on 2 October 1995, the idea and the name of the currency had been discussed as early as 1991. A special commission was set up to decide the questions around the name and design of the national currency banknotes (M. Kakulia, 2008, p. 178). There was an idea to call the currency the Georgian maneti, but the supporters of the word lari (which means treasure) managed to win. In 1992, it was officially decided that lari should be printed. The name of the Georgian currency comes from the Georgian classic poem '*Vephkhistkaosani*' ('The Knight in the Panther Skin' by Shota Rustaveli) from the twelfth century, and the banknotes portray important persons and facts from the history and culture of Georgia. As lari painter Bacha Malazonia says, money can be seen as a virus, as everyone who visits the country holds the currency. Therefore, it was important from the Georgian perspective to show on the banknotes that this country has a long history, rich literature, art, and architecture (Rekhviashvili, 2015). Here, the meaning of the money and national currency beyond its functions becomes very clear. The national currency for Georgia was not just about creating a means of exchange or store of value, but also was intended to be a symbol of sovereignty.

Discussions on the lari dated back to Zviad Gamsakhurdia's presidency. As the second president of the Georgian central bank, Nodar Javakhishvili recalls the first discussions on the currency, which were rather focused on the design of the banknotes, with no financiers or economists were attending these meetings. Yet, with the overthrow of Gamsakhurdia's government, the project of the national currency was postponed. Later, it was apparently an outcome of Shevardnadze's strong will to implement money reform in 1995 and issue the lari as a national currency. The lari was printed in France with the help of personal contacts, otherwise the Georgian government could not have afforded the costs (Kitia & Akhobadze, 2015).

These debates from the history of the lari demonstrate that the idea of national currency appeared in Georgia right after independence. Even though its implementation took several years, it was decided early on that Georgia did not want to use the Russian currency as a long-term measure. However, it is difficult to claim whether economic intentions were stronger or whether nationalist sentiments outweighed the economic goals in this decision. Yet, the discussions on the name of the currency demonstrate that an influential part of the political elite of independent Georgia were against the name 'manet'[2] for the Georgian currency, probably because they wanted to highlight the difference and separation from Russia, as well as from the Soviet Union. Furthermore, the political elite in Georgia considered the national currency as an important attribute of sovereignty despite the lack of economic knowledge on currency issues. Therefore, it is not surprising that so much attention was paid to the design of the banknotes. As Cooper argues 'If state leaders believed currency imagery did not matter, they would spend a lot less time designing and redesigning it' (Cooper, 2009, p. 13). Thus, the lari was not just the first national currency, but also a political statement of independence, national statehood, and a sign of distance from Russian influence.

Cooper remarks in his study on banknotes in post-Soviet currencies that all these states issued money which did not resemble the Soviet past (Cooper, 2009, p. 29). Yet, the patterns of national currencies differ from country to country and it is difficult to identify clearly dominant themes (Cooper, 2009, p. 1). The idea of a national currency is historically strongly connected with the emergence of the nation state and it played an important role in nation building. Governments have been using bank notes as a form of propaganda, which was even more powerful than a flag or anthem, because money was used on a daily basis by a large part of the population (Helleiner, 2011, p. 144). Trust, communication, and imaginaries of the state can be counted as the main functions of national currency (Cooper, 2009, p. 10).

A national currency played an important role for Georgia before the early 1990s, as well. Even within the Russian Empire, 'local silver and copper coins with markings in Georgian were minted in Tbilisi for over thirty years' (M. Kakulia, 2008, p. 176). The fate of Georgian money during the first Republic of Georgia was somewhat similar to the situation in the early 1990s. Georgia received an empty treasury from the Russian Empire and the emission of its own money was considered crucial by the social democratic government of that time (Kandelaki, 1960, p. 61). At the first stage, Georgia issued Transcaucasian bonds with other two Caucasian countries (Armenia and Azerbaijan) as a temporary arrangement, though there was a plan to issue a national currency, the marchili (the name of the money used in Georgia in the sixtenth century). The issue of the marchili was postponed, but the newly established state bank of Georgia was successful in increasing the credibility of and the trust in the Georgian bonds in its short time of existence (M.

Kakulia, 2008, p. 177). Among other factors, commercial banks in Georgia, which were mostly operating with foreign capital, opposed the Georgian currency. Therefore, the government preferred to postpone the issue of a national currency to avoid conflict with the banks (Kandelaki, 1960, pp. 63–66). Unfortunately, the issue of Georgian bonds (temporary currency) in 1919 was accompanied by severe inflation (Kandelaki, 1960, p. 69) due to geopolitical tensions, a capital deficit, and the lack of possibilities of raising money outside the country. Even though the marchili was never issued and the first state bank of Georgia could not exist for long due to the Soviet invasion in 1921, it managed to carry through a currency reform, to establish foreign currency reserves, and to initiate the process of creating a national currency (Gelashvili & Atanelishvili, 2016, p. 14). It is also remarkable that the Georgian government and the two other Caucasian republics agreed in 1918 on a number of measures to protect the value of the Transcaucasian bond. A set of rules was adopted to avoid capital flight or dollarization, as well as import dependency. It was forbidden to use Russian money, for example, and foreign currency trading was allowed only among state institutions (Kandelaki, 1960, p. 67). However, this historical knowledge was used neither throughout the 1990s nor later in Georgia.

The first test of the lari: the Russian economic crisis

The Russian financial crisis of 1998 had a significant influence on Georgia, which resulted in the depreciation of the lari, inflation, the decrease of GDP, and the further strengthening of the role of dollar. Thus, the role of geopolitics and trade relations can be quite significant in the historical development of dollarization. When neighbouring and trading partner countries have financial issues, there is a direct spillover of these problems into the local economy.

Russia was an important economic partner for Georgia. Almost 30% of Georgian exports went to Russia, and it received 20% of its imports from there. Furthermore, Russia was one of the most important destinations for Georgian emigrants. Thus, the 1998 financial crisis in Russia and the devaluation of the ruble (by 60%) had influence on Georgia as exports and remittances decreased sharply (M. Kakulia, 2008, pp. 183–184). Seventy per cent of the natural resource export was lost and Georgia started to increase its imports from Russia. In addition, prices increased and the state was incapable of paying pensions or salaries (Kochladze et al., 2002, p. 6). The GDP growth rate decreased twice compared to that at the beginning of 1998 (National Bank of Georgia, 1999, p. 5). The dollar deficit on Russian markets was soon transferred to CIS countries and Georgia as well. Papava describes how the illegal Tskhinvali corridor for smuggling was used for importing cheap Russian goods and 'for carrying huge amounts of US dollars out of the country to Russia' (Papava, 2005, p. 153). These developments influenced the value of the lari negatively.

Though no banking crisis occurred in Georgia, economic stagnation lasted long after this shock. On 23 February, the lari reached its historical minimum as one dollar equalled 2.4 lari (Tsikhelashvili et al., 2012, p. 12) with a depreciation rate of 40% (Amaghlobeli et al., 2003, p. 52). The Russian crisis caused a fiscal crisis in Georgia, which negatively affected trust in the national currency (M. Kakulia & Aslamazishvili, 2000, pp. 39–40). Thus, the 1998 crisis was the first serious test for the lari, highlighting the influence of economic partner countries on the national currency.

The NBG reacted by spending its dollar reserves, but this was a very limited policy tool. The IMF was advising the Georgian central bank to let the lari float and to stay away from currency interventions. Papava observed that such advice was harmful for Georgia at that time, as it could have caused panic or even bankruptcy of banks. However, the central bank did not listen to the IMF and continued spending its reserves until the value of the lari gradually stabilized (Papava, 2005, pp. 153–154). The 1998 NBG report also explains this decision: 'the NBG refused to quit FX interventions, since under existing monetary conditions it could have caused a large-scale banking crisis' (National Bank of Georgia, 1999, p. 27).

Thus, the central bank and the Ministry of Economy of Georgia decided that a gradual devaluation of the lari was better than a drastic devaluation. Despite more than the 30% devaluation of the lari against the dollar, prices increased by around 10% and banks did not go bankrupt. The NBG established a floating exchange regime in 1998. In 1999, the lari lost its value to the dollar again to the (then) historical minimum -2.45 lari. This was mainly triggered by the government's decision to use privatization revenues and WB loans for social programmes, which increased the supply of the lari and the demand for the dollar (M. Kakulia, 2008, pp. 183–184). Although the lari was depreciating against both the ruble and the dollar after the 1998 crisis, in 2003–2004, the lari started to appreciate against the dollar, while it was still depreciating against the ruble (International Monetary Fund, 2006, p. 52). The crisis did not turn into a banking crisis, as the population requested their deposits only in laris. However, most of these people wanted to change the national currency into the foreign one, which further sharpened the currency crisis (Gelaschwili & Nastansky, 2009, p. 6). Ironically, the high level of dollarization saved Georgia from a banking crisis and banks could even profit from the exchange-rate instability in 1999 through currency conversions (Amaghlobeli et al., 2003, p. 59).

The Russian crisis had a direct impact on dollarization. If the rate of deposit dollarization had decreased from 66.7% in 1994 to 40.1% in 1995 with the introduction of the lari, the share of foreign currency savings in total savings rose strikingly after the 1998 crisis and reached 79% in 1999 (De Nicoló et al., 2003, p. 33). One can observe the same trend of dollarization, measured as the share of foreign currency deposits to broad money (Havrylyshyn & Beddies, 2003, p. 339). Just in one year, from 1998 to 1999, deposit dollarization increased from 70% to 80% (M. Kakulia & Aslamazishvili,

2000, p. 23), while it almost doubled from 1995 to 1999 (De Nicoló et al., 2003, p. 33). If in 1998, there were 1.8 times more foreign currency loans issued by the Georgina banks, this number grew to 3.2 in 1999 (M. Kakulia & Aslamazishvili, 2000, p. 47). Yet, dollarization was mostly driven by deposit dollarization at this time, as the rate of loan dollarization was significantly lower than the one for deposits (see (Amaghlobeli et al., 2003, p. 56).

The absence of legal restrictions on domestic transactions in foreign currency also encouraged the process of dollarization (Amaghlobeli et al., 2003, pp. 54–55). By 2003, the level of financial dollarization had reached 86%. Thus, a two-currency zone functioned in Georgia. The national currency the lari was mostly used for current payments, consumption costs, small business contracts, whereas the dollar became the means of payment for big business arrangements and investments (Tsikhelashvili et al., 2012, p. 10).

Thus, the events of 1998 strongly contributed to the devaluation of the lari and the strengthening of the dollar. This was not just a temporary financial shock, but a significant blow against the new national currency, which was just about to gain confidence in the hearts of the Georgian population. The financial sector and banks, in particular, came out of the crisis unharmed and even made some profits out of exchange-rate volatilities. Dollarization saved the banks from a potential bank run. Furthermore, the lessons from 1998 show that the devaluation of a national currency and the enhancement of dollarization sometimes occurs due to external shocks. When a country like Georgia is not economically strong enough to deal with such shocks at the local level, the results might be damaging.

Conclusion

The geopolitical and economic developments of the early and mid-1990s had a significant influence on dollarization. It was already clear in the first years of the break-up of the Soviet Union that the Russian ruble did not have many chances against the dollar. Though a dual money system existed in Georgia in the beginning of the 1990s, where the ruble was used for transactions and exchange and the dollar for savings, the situation soon changed. After the hyperinflation of 1993–1994 and the introduction of the lari in 1995, the lari replaced the ruble in transactions and exchange, yet the dollar was still largely used for savings. However, the 1998 Russian crisis weakened the lari and led to a significant increase in the rate of dollarization.

The experience of hyperinflation shook the trust of the Georgian public in a national currency and in government institutions, as well as the central bank. These negative feelings proved to be long lasting and encouraged dollarization. Hyperinflation also marked the beginning of IMF's official entrance into Georgia and the birth of the national currency. Though the Georgian currency was successfully issued in 1995, it was predestined to be weak and vulnerable, emerging on the ruins of hyperinflation and facing the challenge of dollarization. The events around the period of hyperinflation also decided the fate of the Russian ruble in Georgia and the final victory of the dollar over the Russian currency. The 1998 Russian crisis caused the first important test for the lari and led to its depreciation. The role of the dollar was further strengthened in the aftermath of the crisis and this trend proved to be hardly reversible later.

The events of the 1990s, described in the chapter, highlight that wrong policies driven by a lack of knowledge and of alternatives, as well as the presence of rent-seeking aims, led to chaos in monetary affairs. Nor did the historical and geopolitical setting offer the best conditions for shaping a money-credit system in a newly independent state with a deteriorated production base and instable macroeconomic and political conditions.

Notes

1 IDPs in Georgia had to leave their homes due to wars in Abkhazia and South Ossetia in the beginning of the 1990s.
2 Manet used to be the name of the currency in Russia and in the Soviet Union.

References

Amaghlobeli, D., Farrell, J., & Nielsen, J. (2003). The evolution of commercial banking in Georgia, 1991–2001. *Post-Communist Economies*, 15(1), 47–74.

Aslund, A. (1995). *How Russia Became a Market Economy*. The Brookings Institution.

Aslund, A. (2007). *How Capitalism Was Built: The Transformations of Central and Eastern Europe, Russia and Central Asia*. Cambridge University Press.

Cooper, S. (2009). Currency, Identity, and Nation-Building: National Currency Choices in the Post-Soviet States. *American Political Science Association Annual Convention*, September.

De Nicoló, G., Patrick, H., & Ize, A. (2003). Dollarizing the Banking System: Good or Bad (No. 146; IMF Working Paper).

Fedorov, B. G., & Kazmin, A. I. (1994). 1993: The First Experiences of the Russian Financial and Monetary Stabilization Policy. In A. Aslund (Ed.), *Economic Transformation in Russia* (pp. 26–34). St. Martin's Press.

Fischer, S. (1994). Prospects for Russian Stabilization. In A. Aslund (Ed.), *Economic Transformation in Russia* (pp. 8–26). St. Martin's Press.

Gelaschwili, S., & Nastansky, A. (2009). Development of the Banking Sector in Georgia (No. 36; Statistische Diskussionsbeiträge, Issue 36).

Gelashvili, S., & Atanelishvili, T. (2016). Bank System Evolution in Georgia. *International Journal of Arts & Sciences*, 09(03), 13–20.

Gurgenidze, L., Lobzhanidze, M., & Onoprishvili, D. (1994). Georgia: From planning to hyperinflation. *Communist Economies and Economic Transformation*, 6(3), 259–281.

Gursoy, F., & Chitadze, N. (2012). Economic and Political Environment of Georgia After the Restoration of National Independence. *European Journal of Economic and Political Studies*, 5(2), 35–54.

Havrylyshyn, O., & Beddies, C. H. (2003). Dollarization in the Former Soviet Union: from hysteria to hysteresis. *Comparative Economic Studies*, 45(3), 329–357.

Helleiner, E. (2011). Denationalizing Money? Economic liberalism and the "national question" in currency affairs. In E. Gilbert & E. Helleiner (Eds.), *Nation-States and Money: The past, present and future of national currencies* (pp. 139–159). Routledge.

International Monetary Fund. (2006). Georgia: Selected Issues (Issue 06/170).

Jarocińsky, M., & Jirny, A. (1999). Monetary Policy and Inflation in Georgia 1996–98. *Russian & East European Finance and Trade*, 35(1), 68–100.

Kakulia, M. (2001). *savalut'o sist'emis ganvitarebis p'roblemebi sakartveloshi* [Challenges of Currency System Development in Georgia] (J. Meskhia (Ed.)). Research Institute for economic and social issues affiliated with the Ministry of economy, industry and trade of Georgia.

Kakulia, M. (2008). Before and After the Introduction of the Lari: Georgian National Currency in Retrospect. In E. M. Ismailov (Ed.), *Central Eurasia: National Currencies* (pp. 176–187). CA&CC Press.

Kakulia, M., & Aslamazishvili, N. (2000). *dolarizatsia sakartveloshi: massht'abebi, pakt'orebi, daz'levis gzebi* [Dollariztion in Georgia: Dimensions, Factors, Solutions*]* (J. Meskhia (Ed.)). Institute of Economy of the Georgian Science Academy.

Kakulia, R., & Khaburzania, L. (1993, June 10). k'up'oni mtavrobis mkhardach'eras moitkhovs [Coupon needs government support]. *Sakartvelos Resp'ublik'a N122*, 2.

Kandelaki, K. (1960). *sakartvelos erovnuli meurneoba* [Georgian national economy] (Book 2). Institute for the Study of the USSR.

Khaduri, N. (2005). Mistakes Made in Conducting Economic Reforms in Post-communist Georgia. *Problems of Economic Transition*, 48(4), 18–29.

Kitia, L., & Akhobadze, L. (2015). *Laris gza* [History of Lari]. Public Broadcaster of Georgia.

Kochladze, M., Gujaraidze, L., & Tavartkiladze, L. (2002). Decade of Independence Effects of Economic liberalization in Georgia: country report. https://greenalt.org/en/library/decade-of-independence-effects-of-economic-liberalization-in-georgia/.

National Bank of Georgia. (1999). Annual Report 1998. https://nbg.gov.ge/en/publications/annual-reports.

Papava, V. (2005). *Necroeconomics: The Political Economy of Post-Communist Capitalism (Lessons from Georgia)*. iUniverse Inc.

Papava, V., & Chikovani, E. (1998). *Georgia: Economic and Social Challenges of Transition* (V. Papava & E. Chikovani (Eds.)). M.E. Sharpe Inc.

Rekhviashvili, J. (2015). *Lari 20 Tslisaa* [Lari is 20 years old]. Radio Liberty.

Sachs, J. D. (1994). Prospects for monetary stabilization in Russia. In A. Aslund (Ed.), *Economic Transformation in Russia* (pp. 34–59). St. Martin's Press.

Sakartvelos resp'ublik'a. (1992a, May 12). resp'ublik'is saxelmts'ipo sabw'oshi edzeben k'rizisidan gamosvlis gzebs [The state council is looking for solutions for the crisis]. *Sakartvelos Resp'ublik'a N79*, 1.

Sakartvelos resp'ublik'a. (1992b, September 22). part'iebis ts'inasaarchevno p'rogramebi [Pre-election programs of political parties]. *Sakartvelos Resp'ublik'a N185–186*, 4.

Sakartvelos resp'ublik'a. (1993a, March 30). k'up'onebi autsilebeli et'ap'ia erovnul valut'aze gadasasvlelad [Coupon is an important step towards a national currency]. *Sakartvelos Resp'ublik'a N65*, 2.

Sakartvelos resp'ublik'a. (1993b, April 15). saertashoriso savalut'o pondis misiis dask'vniti gantskhadeba [A report of the International Monetary Fund]. *Sakartvelos Resp'ublik'a N77*, 2.

Sakartvelos resp'ublik'a. (1993c, July 31). bazari chveni mghelvarebisa [Market of our discontent]. *Sakartvelos Resp'ublik'a N166–167*, 5.

Sakartvelos resp'ublik'a. (1993d, November 11). k'up'onits, manetits da... ikneb gveshvelos [Coupon, Manet and... maybe everything will be fine]. *Sakartvelos Resp'ublik'a N244*, 2.

Sakartvelos resp'ublik'a. (1993e, November 13). k'up'onis pasi k'vlav etsema [Coupon is devaluating again]. *Sakartvelos Resp'ublik'a N245*, 3.

Sakartvelos resp'ublik'a. (1993f, December 2). pulad-sak'redit'o p'olit'ik'is gasaumjobeseblad [For improving money-credit policies]. *Sakartvelos Resp'ublik'a N255*, 1.

Stenographic Report of the Parliament Meeting June 10. (1993). Parliament of Georgia.

Stenographic Report of the Parliament Meeting May 11. (1993). Parliament of Georgia.

Stenographic Report of the Parliament Meeting May 27. (1993). Parliament of Georgia.

Tsikhelashvili, K., Shergilashvili, T., & Tokmazashvili, M. (2012). sakartvelos ek'onomik'uri t'ranspormatsia: damouk'ideblobis 20 ts'eli shualeduri angarishi [Economic transformation of Georgia: 20 years of independence A midterm report]. European Initiative Liberal Academy Tbilisi.

Wang, J.-Y. (1999). The Georgian Hyperinflation and stabilization (WP/99/65; IMF Working Paper).

Wheatley, J. (2005). *Georgia from National Awakening to Rose Revolution: Delayed Transition in the Former Soviet Union*. Ashgate.

White, S., Gill, G., & Slider, D. (1993). *The Politics of Transition shaping a post-Soviet future*. Cambridge University Press.

World Bank. (1993). Georgia Country Economic Memorandum from Crisis to Recovery: A Blueprint for Reforms (Issue May, No 11275).

World Bank. (2003). Georgia An Integrated Trade Development Strategy (Issue 27264).

6 A new financial system meets dollarization

The Soviet heritage as the foundation of the new financial system

The emergence of the financial system in Georgia and the roots of dollarization coincide in time. This kind of chronological parallelism allows an analysis of the intersections between these two processes. Soviet legacies played an important role in creating an unstable financial system in Georgia, which encouraged the advent and persistence of dollarization . This chapter focuses on the development of the financial system, especially commercial banking, in the 1990s, as banks represent the core of the financial sector in post-Soviet Georgia. A turbulent beginning was inevitable considering the lack of experience on the functioning of the financial system in a market economy and the absence of a financial culture. It is uncertain however to what extent this turbulence was manageable.

Banking activities and the existence of various credit organizations have a long history in Georgia, dating back to the first kingdoms on the Georgian territory in the sixth century BC. I the eighth century, credit-issuing institutions like banks already existed in Georgia and the first important currency reform can be traced back to the twelfth century, when it was forbidden to issue false coins. Since the beginning of the nineteenth century, with the start of the Russian colonization of Georgia, Georgian credit institutions were slowly replaced by Russian ones. In 1866, a branch of the Russian bank was opened in Tbilisi. In the mid-1870s, the first Georgian land banks were established in Tbilisi and Kutaisi by Chavchavadze and Ghoghoberidze, respectively (Mosiashvili et al., 2009, pp. 7–8). The Tergdaleuli generation (intellectuals of the 1860s, who were educated in Russia), known as the fathers of the Georgian nation, were determined about the need of banks, that would be built on Georgian capital for the Georgian purpose (Chavchavadze, 1889, 1893, 1894, 1897).

The historical context of establishing the banks in the nineteenth century is relevant for highlighting the difference with the 1990s. If the opening of the first Georgian banks was directly linked with nation building and were supposed to serve this aim, modern banks emerged beyond the state building realm in post-Soviet Georgia. The idea of banks in the nineteenth century emerged during the

DOI: 10.4324/9781003240174-8

national awakening of the Georgian people within the Russian empire. At this point, changes happened not only in nationalist feelings but also in the economic system. From the mid-1860s, feudalists had been losing their rights over serfs and had to adapt to capitalist thinking to survive. The wealth of the Georgian nobles was no longer protected by the Russian empire. For a significant number of these nobles it was too challenging to live without free labour that caused high indebtedness and the loss of estates in many cases. As Suny documents it, 'by the early twentieth century more than half of the privately held land in Tiflis province had been mortgaged' (Suny, 1994, p. 116) and the nobles could not keep up competing with the urban bourgeoisie (Suny, 1994, pp. 114–118). Lang quotes Sergei Meskhi, a liberal journalist at that time in Georgia, about the attitudes of nobles towards doing business: 'The landlord proudly declared: "What do I want with business, what do I want with money? My peasants' labour is my money!" Since the abolition of serfdom [...] Everyone has come to feel that the era when it was possible to live an insouciant, idle existence at the expense of other people's efforts has vanished completely' (Meskhi, 1874 cited in (Lang, 1962, p. 106).

The first ideas about a Georgian bank emerged among the new generation of Georgian writers and poets (Chavchavadze, Tsereteli, Nikoladze, Ersitavi, Orbeliani, etc.), who had started to agitate for the need of the Georgian language in literature from the 1860s and established several newspapers that later turned into the main platform of intellectual debates (Suny, 1994, pp. 127–130). Chavchavadze aspired to an agricultural society and considered it important to give lands in ownership to peasants, and to prevent the taking over of lands by Armenians (Suny, 1994, p. 133). In 1875, Ilia Chavchavadze became a chairman of the Land Bank of the Nobility in Tbilisi, "an institution designed to put the impoverished landed gentry on their feet by providing credit and capital" (Lang, 1962, p. 109). The Land Bank spent a large share of its profits for charity and public needs (Gelashvili & Atanelishvili, 2016, p. 14).

Thus, the idea of establishing the first Georgian banks emerged alongside the development of nationalistic feelings within the Russian empire and was oriented around the needs and challenges of Georgian society at that time. On the one hand, the banks should have helped nobles, who were left without serfs to develop business and regain control on their lands. On the other hand, they should have enabled peasants to buy land or develop agriculture. Furthermore, the core idea connected with banks was their role in funding education. These economic and social goals were supposed to serve the idea of nation formation. Yet, the role of banks and the understanding of their functions went through a dramatic shift in Georgia. The post-Soviet Georgian financial system emerged on the back of Soviet legacies and the new imperatives of transition and marketization; the Georgian banks had nothing to do with the socio-economic development of the country.

The financial system of the Soviet Union differed from that found in market economies. Money did not represent a universal means of payment in socialist economies, as there was no guarantee that firms or households could buy domestic goods at any time, even if they had money. Also, it was rather difficult to use money for international transactions. The function of money as a store of value was restricted, as the incentive to save was low due to low interest rates and the lack of liquidity of deposits (in terms of receiving cash at any time) (Buch, 1996, p. 10). Thus, the main function of money in a planned economy was limited to a unit of account. In the two-track financial system, cash transactions were used by households, but state and state enterprises did not use monetary payments. The main function of the central bank was bookkeeping. The state bank represented a mediator between savers and borrowers, as it provided directed credits to state enterprises. However, there was no credit risk assessment for such decisions (Bonin & Wachtel, 2003, p. 11). The fiscal and monetary sectors were not separated in the Soviet Union and monetary policy was not based on the market. Market prices or information on the value of assets and liabilities did not exist and the main aim of the accounting system was to check compliance with a production plan (Buch, 1996, pp. 11–13).

As one of the characters from Svetlana Alexievich's book *Second-Hand Time* says:

> Before [the breakdown of the Soviet Union I.E.], I had hated money, I didn't know what it was. My family never talked about it – it was considered shameful. We grew up in a country where money essentially did not exist. […] Money became synonymous with freedom [i.e. after the break down of the Soviet Union].
>
> (Alexievich & Translator Bela Shayevich, 2017, p. 55)

> Instead of the red flag, it's Christ is risen! And the cult of consumerism. […] That life is nothing but pyramid schemes and promissory notes. That freedom is money and money is freedom.
>
> (Alexievich & Translator Bela Shayevich, 2017, pp. 88–89)

The banking system went through a number of changes before and within the Soviet Union. In 1920, a decision was made to destroy the banking system in Russia. There were no credit institutions left in the country. In the frame of the new economic policy in the Soviet Union, the development of money-commodity relations was planned. Thus, in 1921, a branch of the Russian state bank was established in Georgia and which from 1924 was transformed into the central bank of Georgia. From 1922 to 1925 a number of specialized banks were founded with various industrial focuses. As the new economic policy was annulated in 1930, the banking system was also drastically transformed. Despite the existence of specialized state banks, banking practically did not exist, and the main function of banks was to save money (Mosiashvili et al., 2009, pp. 8–9) (see Garvy, 1977).

In the socialist banking system, the commercial and central bank functions were merged in the monobank system from the end of 1940s. The main function of a monobank was to provide money to enterprises in various sectors: agriculture, foreign trade, and investment projects. Household loans for consumption or housing were issued by saving banks. The excessive liquidity of saving banks was channelled by monobank to enterprises (Buch, 1996, pp. 7–8; Rona-Tas & Guseva, 2014, p. 33). The main function of the monobank was to develop a financial plan in reference with the planned production. Money did not play a decisive role, as 'money demand determined money supply, and [...] financial flows merely served to accommodate the financing needs of the production plan' (Buch, 1996, p. 8).

Thus, the state bank was not independent from the political establishment, it was under the direct control of the government. It was also not able to implement money and credit policy independently. Its main function was to provide cheap credits for state enterprises. These entities were quite privileged and received subsidies and other types of financial privileges, so they could resist the competition on the real market. However, in post-socialist countries, central banks acquired completely distinct functions such as the development of the money-credit policy and the banking system, the support of price stability, economic growth and employment (Bakhtadze et al., 2012, pp. 159–160) (see Andreassen, 1963; Garvy, 1977; Lane, 2001 on state bank policies in the Soviet Union).

After the dissolution of the Soviet Union, similar developments occurred in the banking systems of most of the former Soviet Union (FSU) countries. State banks were commercialized and they turned into key financial actors with their simple institutional structures and no specialization; hardly any development banks were established. Furthermore, the share of foreign capital and ownership increased in the region (Safarov, 2015, p. 59). A two-tier banking system with a central bank and commercial banks is typical of FSU countries. The retail part of the Soviet monobank was transformed into saving banks in some FSU countries (Rona-Tas & Guseva, 2014, p. 35). A relatively high number of banks appeared on the market, as the rules were loose for setting up a bank (Rona-Tas & Guseva, 2014, pp. 40–41). As commercial banks became the key players of the financial system, stock exchanges were not important in FSU countries (Kolodko, 2000, p. 190).

Except for the monobank, specialized banks (Promstroibank, Agroprombank, Zhilsotsbank) were also abolished and destroyed throughout the transition process. On the ruins of these big networks, several commercial banks emerged, 'which operate as ordinary commercial entities and do not wish to participate in solving socio-economic problems at national scale' (Safarov, 2015, p. 57). As Winkler argued: 'These banks are not agents of change. Instead, they defend the status quo ante by granting bad loans to prop up ailing, former state-owned enterprises or by financing other companies belonging to the banks' owners' (Winkler, 2003, p. 10). Because of such practices numerous banks went bankrupt and many countries suffered from economic and currency crises.

Thus, the heritage of the Soviet Union was the inseparable government–central bank–commercial bank–state enterprise nexus. Though a new system with new institutions emerged during this transition process, Soviet legacies remained decisive not only in terms of institutional functioning, but also in shaping relations among new commercial banks, central banks, and governments. The analysis of the newly emerged financial system in Georgia shows that the nexus remained unbroken in the 1990s. More importantly, the financial system had little to do with the interests and needs of society and was predominantly oriented towards rent seeking.

The new financial system takes off

There were two major ideas about the development of the banking system in Georgia in the beginning of the 1990s. On the one hand, there were supporters of the new banks and, on the other hand, there were those who wanted to encourage a slower rehabilitation process of state-owned banks from the Soviet Union. The first group managed to enforce their ideas (Amaghlobeli et al., 2003, p. 49). The debate on new entry or rehabilitation approach was taking place in other post-Soviet and Central and East European (CEE) countries as well. In 1996, Georgia recorded the second-worst indicators after Albania in the ranking of the best and worst quality of banks among transition states (Claessens, 1996, pp. 21–22).

A two-tier banking system emerged in Georgia, as was typical for the post-Soviet space, although the world bank (WB) referred to it in 1993 as a one-tier system due to close linkages between the central bank, government, and commercial banks. In 1992, five specialized state banks[1] and 71 commercial banks were present in the market along with the National Bank of Georgia (NBG); state banks played more a important role than commercial banks at that point, with an 85% share of the total credits (World Bank, 1993, p. 45). By 1992, the share of commercial banks was only 20% in enterprise deposits and 12% in short-term credits. The assets of the major state banks were made up by enterprise savings and NBG refinancing. The loan policies were mostly determined by government instructions and orders (World Bank, 1993, pp. 47–48). The privatization of state banks started soon and as the WB noted in its 1993 report, 'Banks are enthusiastic about this prospect [privatization] and believe they will be able to raise additional resources [...] and make greater profits' (World Bank, 1993, p. 48).

By 1995 the transformation of state commercial banks had begun which suffered from high levels of non-performing loans, inherited from the Soviet Union. Three of these specialized banks (they were the third tier of the banking system), SberBank, EximBank, and Promstroi Bank, turned into a united Georgian bank, while Binsotsbank became the Bank of Georgia. The Gosbank (Soviet state bank) was transformed into the central bank of Georgia. The other five state banks were privatized and in 1991–1993, 179 new commercial banks emerged. It was easy to establish a bank, as there were no regulations. After the hyperinflation of 1993, the amount of starting capital needed for a bank was reduced further. Thus, by 1994, the number of banks reached 226 in Georgia (Bakhtadze et al., 2012, pp. 139–143). The commercial banks that emerged in Georgia shortly after independence had little in common with their predecessors in the nineteenth century. The development of the banking system in Georgia throughout the 1990s and early 2000s is a story of incompetence, greed, private gains, Ponzi schemes, and failures.

As with commercial banks, Georgia had a historical experience of a central bank before Sovietization as well. This knowledge was also disregarded after the break-up of the Soviet Union. Nevertheless, the model of the state bank, opened in 1920 in the first Republic of Georgia and the debates around it could have provided fruitful grounds for the discussion on the new central bank (see Eradze, 2022). The establishment of the State Bank of Georgia in the twentieth century was not seen as a technical or institutional measure only, but was supposed to take over the function of saving the country, just like the army (Sakartvelos resp'ublik'a, 1920, p. 2). Thus, the central bank was perceived as a crucial pillar of statehood, not only in economic but also in political terms. Most importantly, the functions of the state bank were debated in search for an appropriate model for the Georgian context at that time, as the government did not want to copy any model. The main concept of the Georgian state bank was based on the Swedish model, as it was important for Finance Minister Konstantine Kandelaki to ensure that the central bank should not work under the subordination of the finance ministry or private shareholders, as happened in Russia or England. Thus, a supervisory council, as well as a governing board were set up to govern the central bank (Kandelaki, 1960, pp. 130–131). The state bank was responsible for supervising and controlling the financial system to avoid speculations; encourage the development of trade, industry, and agriculture through specialized credits; and guarantee the stability of the currency (Kandelaki, 1960, p. 122). Thus, the functioning of the central bank was directly linked with the aims of economic development and financial stability. Nevertheless, this historical experience was forgotten at the beginning of the 1990s and the National Bank of Georgia was established on an empty paper. The Soviet past and the powerful propaganda machine against the first Georgian Republic were successful in covering up this period in Georgian history and Georgians have not started to rethink these experiences until now.

The 1995 Organic Law of Georgia announced the National Bank as 'the central bank of Georgia, the bank of banks, the banker or fiscal agent of the Government of Georgia' (Sakartvelos Organuli k'anoni Sakartvelos Erovnuli Bank'is Shesakheb [Organic Law of Georgia on the National Bank of Georgia], 2009), Article 1.1; author's translation). The main tasks of the National Bank were to ensure price stability, financial stability and encourage economic growth (Sakartvelos Organuli k'anoni Sakartvelos Erovnuli Bank'is Shesakheb [Organic Law of Georgia on the National Bank of Georgia], 2009), Articles 3.1, 3.2; author's translation). Though there was a special department for banking supervision, it was difficult for the NBG to do so due to the weak information systems in the beginning of the 1990s (World Bank, 1993, p. 50). Thus, the functions of the new central bank of Georgia were not directly embedded in the overall economic development aims of the country, and it did not have the power to supervise all financial institutions.

The Georgian central bank was declared as independent from the influence of legislative, executive, or other authorities (Sakartvelos Organuli k'anoni Sakartvelos Erovnuli Bank'is Shesakheb [Organic Law of Georgia on the National Bank of Georgia], 2009, Article 4), but this independence was fragile in two regards. First, the independence of the National Bank throughout the 1990s was relative in the context of the strong government–central bank–commercial bank–state enterprise nexus inherited from the Soviet Union. (These linkages were particularly evident in the analysis of the hyperinflation of 1993–1994.) Furthermore, the dependence of the Georgian government on the National Bank in terms of dealing with fiscal deficits presupposed political influences on the bank. In the beginning of the 1990s 'the NBG was obliged to automatically finance government deficits and administer direct credits' (Amaghlobeli et al., 2003, p. 49). For example, in 1996, the Georgian central bank was financing more than 70% of budget deficit (Cukrowski, 2000, p. 6), and in 1998 more than 97% of central bank credit was issued to the government (Cukrowski, 2000, p. 17). Thus, the National Bank of Georgia was not really independent from the government and executive power was also directly involved in matters of regulation (Gelashvili & Atanelishvili, 2016, p. 15). The independence of the Georgian central bank was ambiguous if one considers its dependence on the international monetary fund (IMF). The role of the IMF was crucial in monetary policy. The main monetary policy instrument for the NBG – the foreign exchange – was basically provided by the Fund. As the credit market was not developed in Georgia, a discount rate policy played an insignificant role for the NBG (Wellisz, 1996, p. 15).

Thus, though the Georgian central bank was set up at the beginning of the 1990s as an independent institution, its role and power were rather limited, and its mandate was narrow, focusing on currency and price stability. The instruments of monetary policy were very limited and its impact on financial and monetary stability had very little scope in terms of a very high dollarization rate and the underdevelopment of local financial market. The capability of the central bank was under a double constraint in terms of its dependencies on the IMF and its embeddedness in the Soviet-influenced state structure. Yet, the problem here shall not be reduced to the question of independence of the central bank, as this cannot be a guarantee of the societal well-being-oriented functioning of this institution. What matters instead are the aims of the central bank and their relationship with the needs of the society, as well as the policy space to realize these aims. The Georgian national bank seems to have lacked both throughout the 1990s.

New banks – new rules?

During the first years of transition (until 1994) banks in Georgia started out quite idly as they had access to cheap money from NBG, which they lent to state enterprises at high interest rates (Amaghlobeli et al., 2003, p. 59). This encouraged many, including state enterprises, to open banks to have access to cheap credit (Gurgenidze et al., 1994, p. 274). By 1992, banks relied almost completely on central bank money and the money was spent for projects that were favoured by the government and the central bank (World Bank, 1993, p. vii). However, the performance of banks could not have been measured according to the fulfilment of their real functions, as they pretty much did not have to worry about deposit or external funds; the banks could still survive with the credit rate differentials, as mentioned above (Amaghlobeli et al., 2003, p. 59). Thus, Georgian banks neither attracted savings from society nor provided money to businesses in the early 1990s.

Commercial banks had serious issues with non-performing loans, which were assessed by the WB as a potential cause for financial instability in 1993, especially because of the direct linkage between banks and enterprises that were often under the same ownership (World Bank, 1993, pp. vii–viii). In addition, 'banking activities continue to be directed by the state, either directly through government dictate, or indirectly by the refinancing policies of the NBG' (World Bank, 1993, p. 45). The loss of assets after the dissolution of the Soviet Union and lending money to risky borrowers, under government directions, caused the increase of non-performing loans (World Bank, 1993, p. 49).

This situation soon proved to be unsustainable, causing financial instability and harming the overall economic development of the country, also indirectly encouraging dollarization. Issues in the banking sphere became dramatic in a few years as the level of bad loans rose, deposits drastically decreased, and enterprises did not function properly. At this point, the NBG started to interfere with tightened regulations – the minimum capital requirements and capital adequacy ratios were raised, lending limits were lowered for individuals in relation to the total loan portfolio, and banks were requested to prepare business plans in the framework of bank certification programme. After one year, one-half of the banks no longer existed as they could not keep up with the new rules (Amaghlobeli et al., 2003, p. 50). However, it was difficult to get an insight into the balance sheets of banks at that time, as the process of classification of non-performing loans and the rescheduling of these loans was rather non-transparent and corrupt, based on informal arrangements. Bank managers profited from such deals without letting the shareholders know about the real situation (Gurgenidze et al., 1994, p. 276).

In 1996, NBG gained more legal power to regulate banks (Amaghlobeli et al., 2003, p. 51), though it had started prudential regulations already in 1994 (International Monetary Fund, 1998, p. 24). In 1996, a law on commercial banks and an anti-monopoly law and in 1997, a law on bankruptcy were adopted (International Monetary Fund, 1998, p. 35). In 1997, further reforms started in the banking system. The NBG raised the capital requirements for banks again. A further change in the capital requirement happened in 2003 (Bakhtadze et al., 2012, pp. 142–143). By 2001, the number of banks equalled 26 (Amaghlobeli et al., 2003, p. 51). In 2000, the ratio of assets of commercial banks to gross domestic product (GDP) was 13%. By this time, almost 80% of all assets were under the control of ten banks, whereas one-half of these assets were divided among three banks. The share of the former state banks was shrinking in the market throughout the 1990s (International Monetary Fund, 2001, p. 62).

The early banking trends in Georgia are directly linked with dollarization. The banks not only caused financial instability through irresponsible lending, but also discouraged saving in the national currency, while making deposits in dollar attractive through high interest rates. Here, the role of the national bank was also crucial. The NBG had lower refinancing rates than the Russian Central Bank until 1993; this discouraged commercial banks from attracting deposits and they even offered negative interest rates on savings. However, deposits in the US dollar had positive rates. Thus, 'hard currency deposits grew from virtually zero at the end of 1991 to over 6.5 billion ruble by end November 1992, and continued to grow thereafter' (Gurgenidze et al., 1994, p. 269). The World Bank explained that the low level of savings was because of the dependence of banks on the NBG's money and government instructions in their functioning (World Bank, 1993, p. 45). Most household savings were accumulated at the savings bank in early 1990s, which in turn experienced liquidity problems. Georgians were known as the second biggest savers (on a deposit per capita rate) in the Soviet Union after Lithuania (World Bank, 1993, p. 48).

The policy of discouraging savings in the national currency continued throughout the 1990s. As Amaghlobeli et al. explain, towards the end of the 1990s, it was not even possible to make long-term deposits in lari in many banks. On the one hand, society had little trust towards the national currency and, on the other hand, it was not in the interest of banks to attract long-term money resources in the lari (Amaghlobeli et al., 2003, p. 61). Georgian banks offered high interest rates on dollar deposits (Jarociński & Jirny, 1999, pp. 72–73) and this encouraged deposit dollarization. The IMF also explains the increase in the dollarization rate in 1997 through the differential between the interest rates in foreign and domestic currency deposits (International Monetary Fund, 1998, p. 52). Such a trend in deposits did not only occur because of interest rates; it is important to observe the policies of the central bank and commercial banks to understand their roles in the process.

Commercial banks could have influenced the development of the economy through their selection of loan provision to different economic sectors. Development of local production and the support of local firms were crucial in terms of dollarization, as currency stability can be backed up by a strong economy. Yet, Georgian banks did not encourage this process. Most of the income of banks originated from fees, commissions and FX conversion. Interest rate spreads were quite high. Risk assessment was not developed and banks faced problems in mobilizing capital; collateral lending was also undeveloped (International Monetary Fund, 2001, p. 65). Loan policies were largely influenced and shaped by patronage schemes throughout the 1990s. As the IMF documented in its 1998 report 'it is not unusual for government departments to operate businesses in areas which they regulate' (International Monetary Fund, 1998, p. 36).

Despite some fundamental changes in the banking sector, commercial banks did not play a significant role through their loans in the development of the economy. In 1997, the share of commercial bank loans to the private sector was little more than 2% of GDP (International Monetary Fund, 1998, p. 34). Even export-oriented firms had difficulties in accessing money through banks. Interest rates, at almost 20%, were too high to borrow and the requirements for collateral was also unaffordable. Another issue was connected to the fact that banks only provided short-term, one-year loans that made it more difficult for businesses to finance themselves. Small and new firms encountered special problems in this regard (World Bank, 2003, p. xix). Most loans (70%) were issued to trade, due to the geopolitical location of Georgia and the international trade routes through its territory. As international trade mainly operates in foreign currency, demand on foreign currency loans was increasing. Manufacturing and construction followed trade in terms of receiving most loans. However, heavy industry suffered from the lack of access to loans (Amaghlobeli et al., 2003, pp. 55–56) and agriculture received only 4% of the total loans, even though this sector of economy made up 20% of the GDP (World Bank, 2003, p. 45).

Thus, the credit and savings policies of Georgian banks were neither directed at strengthening the lari, nor at the development of the economy. Furthermore, irresponsible banking practices triggered financial instability and a decrease in trust towards the system. In the first years, banking was associated with criminal activities, as some of these banks attempted to access money through speculative methods by offering unrealistically high interest rates. There was a boom of dubious firms under that offered the Georgian population unrealistic interest rates on their savings and promised them enrichment (see Sakartvelos resp'ublik'a 1993a, 1993b, 1993c, 1993e). Moreover, these banks and financial firms were directly encouraging deposit dollarization, trying to attract dollar savings by offering high financial gains in a very short period of time (Sakartvelos resp'ublik'a, 1992, p. 2, 1993d, p. 4).

In 1995, many of these firms went bankrupt (Gelaschwili & Nastansky, 2009, p. 2). A significant part of the population lost their savings and their trust towards banks decreased (Jarocińsky & Jirny, 1999, p. 72). According to the survey of the statistical department, conducted in Georgia in 1998–1999, people's preference to keep savings at home rather than in banks had increased ten-fold (Kakulia & Aslamazishvili, 2000, pp. 28–29). Thus, there were no incentives for the public to keep savings in banks and thus create long-term money resources in the national currency. Even after hyperinflation and economic stabilization, the integration of banks into the economic system did not occur in the context of little trust and a large informal economy in the country. The 2000 NBG poll documented that only a little more than one-third of the population regarded banks as trustworthy and more than one-half of those surveyed showed absolute distrust towards banks (Amaghlobeli et al., 2003, p. 57).

Thus, the ill-functioning banking system in Georgia supported and strengthened the role of the dollar in the economy. This was done through the following channels – the discouragement of savings in the lari and making dollar deposits attractive; not encouraging the development of the real economy through loans; losing the trust of the society upon speculative deals; and encouraging financial instability. All these factors had a direct influence on creating more demand for dollars in the country.

Conclusion

The continuation of Soviet practices in the relations between the government, the central bank, commercial banks, and state-owned enterprises encouraged the evolution of an unstable financial system in Georgia, and one which disregarded societal needs. This kind of an 'isolation' from public interests caused public distrust in financial institutions (which was later strengthened by speculative banks). Furthermore, the lack of knowledge and experience of market-based banking, the presence of barriers to accessing capital, and the context of a deteriorated economy made it even more difficult for the banks to cope with multiple challenges. They turned out to be incapable of taking responsibility for contributing to state building. Quite the opposite, banks further destabilized the system and supported the process of dollarization.

Thus, Georgian commercial banks encouraged foreign currency domination directly and indirectly. First, as saving in the national currency was discouraged, the creation of money resources in the lari for the banking system beyond the NBG money was affected negatively. Also, households were more motivated to make deposits in other currencies than the lari, and the level of deposit dollarization was increasing. Second, the sectoral loan policy of commercial banks demonstrated that access to credit was hardly guaranteed to the production sectors. Third, the commercial banks of the 1990s managed to shake public trust in the financial system and the national currency through their speculative and irresponsible practices.

Note

1 There were the following state banks: Agropromobank for agriculture, Promstoibank for heavy industry and construction, Gilsostbank (Social Development

Bank) for light industry and trade, Vneshekonombank (its Georgian successor was Eximbank) for foreign transactions, Sberbank, a major saving bank (World Bank, 1993, pp. 47–48).

References

Alexievich, S., & Translator Bela Shayevich. (2017). *Second-Hand Time: The Last of the Soviets* (6th ed.). Fitzcarraldo Editions.

Amaghlobeli, D., Farrell, J., & Nielsen, J. (2003). The evolution of commercial banking in Georgia, 1991–2001. *Post-Communist Economies*, 15(1), 47–74.

Andreassen, K. (1963). Features of Banking Organization, Monetary and Credit Policy in the Soviet Union. *Economics of Planning*, 3(1), 41–52.

Bakhtadze, L., Barbakadze, K., & Khandashvili, T. (2012). *Pinansuri inst'it'ut'ebi da bazrebi* [Financial Institutions and Markets]. Ivane Javakhishvili State University, Faculty of Economics and Business.

Bonin, J., & Wachtel, P. (2003). Financial Sector Development in Transition Economies: Lessons from the First Decade. *Financial Markets, Institutions and Instruments*, 12(1), 1–66.

Buch, C. M. (1996). *Creating Efficient Banking Systems Theory and Evidence from Eastern Europe*. J.C.B. Mohr Tübingen.

Chavchavadze, I. (1889). saglekho bank'is sak'itkhistvis [On the peasants' bank]. Georgian Democracy Initiative. https://gdi.ge/ge/publication/ilia-chavchavadze1.page.

Chavchavadze, I. (1893). tbilisis saurtierto sameurneo k'redit'is sazogadoeba [A mutual economic society of Tbilisi]. Georgian Democracy Initiative. https://gdi.ge/ge/publication/ilia-chavchavadze1.page.

Chavchavadze, I. (1894). *k'redit'i sakartvelos mevenakhetatvis* [Credit for Georgian vinedressers]. Georgian Democracy Initiative. https://gdi.ge/ge/publication/ilia-chavchavadze1.page.

Chavchavadze, I. (1897). *dzveli da akhali chveni ek'onomik'uri tskhovrebisa* [*Our old and new economic life*]. Georgian Democracy Initiative. https://gdi.ge/ge/publication/ilia-chavchavadze1.page.

Claessens, S. (1996). Banking Reform in Transition Countries (No. 1642; World Bank Policy Research Working Papers).

Cukrowski, J. (2000). *Financing the Deficit of the State Budget by National Bank of Georgia (1996–1999)*. Center for Social and Economic Research (CASE).

Eradze, I. (2022). sakartvelos sakhelmts'ipo bank'is p'olit'ik'uri ek'onomia [Political Economy of the Georgian State Bank]. In L. Nakhutsrishvili (Ed.), *sakartvelos demok'rat'iuli resp'ublik'a (1918–1921): pormisa da shinaarsis dziebashi* [The Democratic Republic of Georgia (1918–1921): in quest of form and meaning]. Ilia State University.

Garvy, G. (1977). The Origins and Evolution of the Soviet Banking System: An Historical Perspective. In G. Garvy (Ed.), *Money, Financial Flows, and Credit in the Soviet Union* (pp. 13–35). National Bureau of Economic Research.

Gelaschwili, S., & Nastansky, A. (2009). Development of the Banking Sector in Georgia (No. 36; Statistische Diskussionsbeiträge, Issue 36).

Gelashvili, S., & Atanelishvili, T. (2016). Bank System Evolution in Georgia. *International Journal of Arts & Sciences*, 09(03), 13–20.

Gurgenidze, L., Lobzhanidze, M., & Onoprishvili, D. (1994). Georgia: From planning to hyperinflation. *Communist Economies and Economic Transformation*, 6(3), 259–281.

International Monetary Fund. (1998). Georgia: Recent Economic Developments and Selected Issues. https://www.elibrary.imf.org/view/journals/002/1998/099/002.1998.issue-099-en.xml.

International Monetary Fund. (2001). Georgia: Recent Economic Developments and Selected Issues. https://www.elibrary.imf.org/view/journals/002/2001/211/002.2001.issue-211-en.xml.

Jarociński, M., & Jirny, A. (1999). Monetary Policy and Inflation in Georgia 1996–98. *Russian & East European Finance and Trade*, 35(1), 68–100.

Kakulia, M., & Aslamazishvili, N. (2000). *dolarizatsia sakartveloshi: massht'abebi, pakt'orebi, daz'levis gzebi* [Dollarization in Georgia: Dimensions, Factors, Solutions] (J. Meskhia (Ed.)). Institute of Economy of the Georgian Science Academy.

Kandelaki, K. (1960). *sakartvelos erovnuli meurneoba* [Georgian national economy] (Book 2). Institute for the Study of the USSR.

Kolodko, G. W. (2000). *From Shock to Therapy: The Political economy of Post-socialist Transformation*. Oxford University Press.

Lane, D. (2001). Russian Banks and the Soviet Legacy (No. 9; Research Papers in Management Studies).

Lang, D. (1962). *A Modern History of Soviet Georgia*. Grove Press.

Mosiashvili, V., Lomidze, P., & Qoqosadze, P. (2009). *sabank'o sakme (lektsiebis k'ursi)* [Banking (lecture course)] (M. Vanishvili (Ed.)). Tbilisi David Aghmashenebeli University.

Rona-Tas, A., & Guseva, A. (2014). *Plastic Money: Constructing Markets for Credit Cards in Eight Postcommunist Countries*. Stanford University Press.

Safarov, A. M. (2015). On the Significance of Development Banks in the Economies of post-Soviet Countries. *Review of European Studies*, 7(10), 53–67.

sakartvelos organuli k'anoni sakartvelos erovnuli bank'is shesakheb [Organic Law of Georgia on the National Bank of Georgia] (2009).

Sakartvelos resp'ublik'a. (1920, July 28). Sakartvelos Sakhelmts'ipo Bank'is Gakhsna [The Opening of the Georgian State Bank], 1–4.

Sakartvelos resp'ublik'a. (1992, September 22). part'eibis ts'inasaarchevno p'rogramebi [Pre-election programs of political parties]. N185–186, p. 4.

Sakartvelos resp'ublik'a. (1993a, May 19). Advertisement Section, N102, p. 4.

Sakartvelos resp'ublik'a. (1993b, June 15). Advertisement Section, N125, p. 4.

Sakartvelos resp'ublik'a. (1993c, August 5). Advertisement Section, N170.

Sakartvelos resp'ublik'a. (1993d, August 6). Advertisement Section. N171, p. 4.

Sakartvelos resp'ublik'a. (1993e, November 17). Advertisement Section. N247, pp. 2–4.

Suny, R. G. (1994). *The Making of the Georgian Nation* (2nd ed.). Indiana University Press.

Wellisz, S. (1996). *Georgia: A brief survey of macroeconomic problems and policies*. CASE Foundation.

Winkler, A. (2003). The CEE and NIS Regional Context for Microfinance. In S. Forster, S. Greene, & J. Pytkowska (Eds.), *The State of Microfinance in Central and Eastern Europe and the New Independent States* (pp. 7–15). Consultative Group to Assist the Poor (CGAP).

World Bank. (1993). Georgia Country Economic Memorandum from Crisis to Recovery: A Blueprint for Reforms (Issue May, No 11275).

World Bank. (2003). Georgia An Integrated Trade Development Strategy (Issue 27264).

Part III

The persistence of dollarization

> A modern nation-state is not only a political concept, but also an economic organism, embedded within the production relations and the local market. [...] Therefore, the state is primarily concerned with territorial security, education and health of its population, revival of economic activities which are appropriate for the time being, support of national production etc. [...] Only the development of local economy can help nation-states survive global economic pressures.
>
> (Kandelaki, 1935, p. 38)

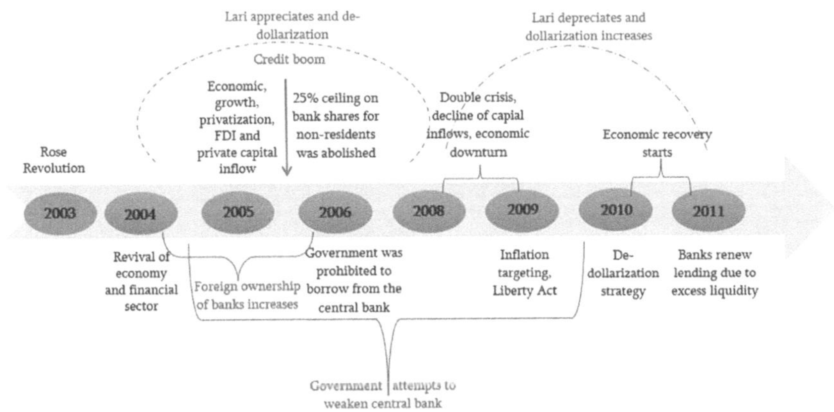

Figure T2 Timeline 2: The persistence of dollarization
Source: Author's illustration.

DOI: 10.4324/9781003240174-9

7 The birth of the new Georgian state

Roses in action: revolution on TV screens[1]

November 2003 was an exciting month in Georgia. Thousands of demonstrators in front of the Georgian parliament and many more in front of their televisions had hope for the first time after 1991 – a hope for a new, better life. The only vivid picture in my memory from that November is of our family in front of the television, trying to make sense of a fuzzy screen – showing a mass of people in the street. I somehow cannot recall joy and celebration of the revolution results, but there was hope afterwards.

The ill-functioning state, frozen (unpaid) pensions and salaries, gas and electricity shortages, corruption, unemployment, poverty, and political instability had become unsustainable. By 2003, Georgia was the seventh most corrupt country of those assessed globally by Transparency International, according to their Corruption Perception Index (Timm, 2013, p. 5). A budget crisis[2] expressed in the issues over tax collection, budgetary wars with the Adjara region, and the decrease in foreign aid, triggered the revolution (Papava, 2005, pp. 160–162). The Georgian state could have probably kept functioning if it had received further funding from abroad, but it had become clear to international organizations (IOs) (such as the international monetary fund) that the situation in Georgia was not going in the right direction.[3] Thus, the Fund withdrew funding shortly before the 2003 elections (Broers, 2005, p. 335). However, from 1999, international donors did not want to issue money to the Georgian government and there was no longer a possibility of debt restructuring through the Paris Club (Papava, 2006, p. 660).

It was exactly within the context of pressure from IOs that Shevardnadze decided to allow young and active politicians such as Saakashvili (president after the revolution) or Machavariani to take over important positions in the early 2000s, respectively as a minister of justice and a minister of taxes. Furthermore, Zurab Jhvania (prime minister after the revolution) was unofficially named as Shevardnadze's successor (Christophe, 2004, pp. 15–16). These people later turned into a core revolutionary team (Jobelius, 2011, p. 78). Saakashvili had already made his name during Shevardnadze's

DOI: 10.4324/9781003240174-10

presidency through his aggressive reform initiatives in the sphere of justice (Gegeshidze, 2011, pp. 31–32).

The political economy of the Rose Revolution remains as fuzzy as our tiny TV screen 15 years ago. Although a significant quantity of academic texts have been produced on the revolution, surprisingly the literature remains silent about its political economy. Most of the texts explain the revolution through socio-economic problems in the country and Shevardnadze's inability to cope with them, the activism of Georgian non-governmental organizations (NGOs) and of the so called young reformers, the special role of the media, as well as the support of western organizations and donors (see Angley, 2013; Broers, 2005; Cheterian, 2008; Jones, 2006; Wheatley, 2005; Zurabishvili et al., 2012). Nevertheless, it is unclear what kind of capital fractions within or outside the country supported or opposed the revolution; the economic base of the revolution requires further research.[4]

The revolution was planned and implemented as a top-down process. According to Mitchell (2004, p. 345), most of the population were observers of the revolution in front of their TVs. The old intelligentsia was split between the supporters of Shevardnadze and supporters of the revolution (Kakachia & Lebanidze, 2016, p. 141). Though a significant role of IOs and the United States of America (USA) in this process is undeniable, one should be careful not to attribute too much importance to it. Shevardnadze was already considered as an enemy by the public. According to a 2003 poll, only 5% of the respondents considered that developments in Georgia were right (Angley, 2013, p. 46; Cheterian, 2008, p. 694). Georgian society had lost faith in the government and Shevardnadze had also lost the support of the army and police. This was one of the reasons that the protests went on peacefully in November 2003 (Mitchell, 2009, p. 173). Shevardnadze had been keeping the army underfinanced during his presidency as he wanted to prevent the military from becoming powerful (Aprasidze, 2016, p. 111). Thus, he succeeded neither in winning the hearts of the Georgian people (see Christophe, 2004, p. 24), nor had he the support of the military.

The prominence of NGOs as a revolutionary force was visible already in 2001 in anti-government protests against a government raid of the opposition TV channel Rustavi 2 (Angley, 2013, p. 46). The parliamentary elections of November 2003 were a crucial point for sharpening the critique and NGOs did not miss this chance. One strategy that was used by two big NGOs, the International Society for Fair Elections and Democracy (ISFED) and the Georgian Young Lawyers Association (GYLA), was that of election observation. These organizations managed to mobilize several thousands of observers all over Georgia, with the financial help of the USA and other international donors (Broers, 2005, p. 341). Furthermore, NGOs started to publish on human rights violations (such as torture in prisons), as well as about obscure payments allowing prisoners to buy their freedom from detainment and the 'planting [of] drugs and arms on suspects' (Broers, 2005, p. 346). A few months before the elections, an activist student group 'Kmara'

(Enough!) was founded by the Liberty Institute, which was also closely linked with Saakashvili's and Jhvania's political parties. Thus, from the beginning, cooperation emerged between the opposition parties and civic activists (Broers, 2005, p. 340). This protest movement, inspired by the Serbian experience, played a significant role in making the Rose Revolution happen. A trip to Serbia was initiated and financed by the Open Society Georgia Foundation (OSGF) in the beginning of 2003 with the participation of future leaders of the Rose Revolution (Saakashvili and Zhvania among them). A further trip for activists was organized later for activists from the Liberty Institute, Young Lawyers Association, and the OSGF (Giga Bokeria,[5] Tinatin Khidasheli,[6] and Alexander Lomaia[7] participated in this trip). Yet, 'Kmara' members, as well as the OSGF, denied that the group received significant funding from the foundation (Angley, 2013, pp. 46–48).

Thus, the Rose Revolution was an outcome of more than two decades of public frustration, at the inability and unwillingness of the government to tackle socio-economic issues; the emergence of western-educated political opposition and NGOs; the loss of trust of international organizations towards Shevardnadze's government; the right timing of protests before and after the parliamentary elections of 2003; and the support of the Western governments to the new political elite. However, the revolution started and was implemented from above by the political and civil society elites, without tight cooperation with the broader society and the involvement of economic forces or capital fractions.

A new political elite with new values? Consolidation of state power and the premises of authoritarian neoliberalism

The post-revolution political elite had experience of working for the previous government and for the two key opposition parties (Saakashvili's National Movement from 2001 and Zhvania's United Democrats from 2002) that had roots in Shevardnadze's party, incorporating its former members. Yet, both opposition parties claimed to be western and democratic (Broers, 2005, p. 336). The post-revolution political elite is an example of a mixture of the Soviet past and western values.

The desire of the new elite to eradicate everything old was quite strong, which was clearly demonstrated in the radical change of personnel at public institutions. Staff in ministries were completely changed, and mostly young people with western education were hired (Papava, 2006, p. 663). For example, the traffic police were completely changed in Tbilisi (Mitchell, 2009, p. 177). In one day, 15,000 policemen were fired, and a few thousand public registry employees lost their jobs within a single day. In sum, almost one-half of all public officials were made unemployed (Gugushvili, 2016, p. 3). Nevertheless, the removal of the old Soviet nomenklatura from the government provided no guarantee for the disappearance of old practices and methods of governance.

In contrast with Shevardnadze's government, Saakashvili managed to capture central state power including the region of Adjara (in 2004). If Shevardnadze had to keep a balance among various formal and informal power groups in order to exercise political power, Saakashvili had it all. His police and military reforms reshaped these institutions and the president gained their full support (see Cheterian, 2008, pp. 701–702). The authoritarian aspirations of the post-revolution government were clearly visible from the very beginning. Saakashvili consolidated his power by strengthening the executive body and turning Georgia into a one-party state. He won the presidential elections of 2004 with more than 96% of the votes. The early spring parliamentary elections, in the same year, highlighted the dominance of the revolutionary National Movement-Democrats coalition with more than 67% of votes. Other than the coalition, only one other party (the New Right) managed to enter the parliament (the threshold was 7%) (Broers, 2005, p. 344). Saakashvili changed the constitution to gain more power (Jones, 2006, p. 45; Khidasheli, 2004; Muskhelishvili & Jorjoliani, 2009, p. 693). Though a semi-presidential system was introduced, the power of the president increased by enabling him/her to form a government without parliament's agreement. These changes were enforced without any public participation, within one day (Broers, 2005, pp. 345–346; Jobelius, 2011, p. 80). Consequently, the role of the parliament was significantly weakened, and it was often referred to as the 'Government's Notary' (Papava, 2009, p. 202). Thus, it became clear from the beginning that Georgia was turning into a party state. The flag of Saakashvili's party (National Movement) was declared as the national flag of Georgia (Cheterian, 2008, p. 696). The Soviet tradition of strengthening the executive government's power over the legislative body (Wheatley, 2005, p. 95) was continued by the post-revolution government.

A further aspect of power consolidation was Saakashvili's success in literally removing thieves in law from national life within a few years. Slade (2012, p. 627) describes the 2005 campaign against this power group that had three main pillars: the criminalization of thieves in law and permitting the confiscation of their illegal properties; the removal of the patronage of thieves in law in the police system; the introduction of education programs to raise awareness about organized crime. The cool, attractive icon of a thief in law was rapidly replaced by a trustworthy, professional image of the patrol police with their brand-new cars, new uniforms, and good salaries. Police reforms were accompanied with a mass renewal of staff, as well as the reform of the Ministry of Interior Affairs. European countries, United Nations Development Program (UNDP), and Open Society Institute (OSI) supported these reforms financially. Georgian media played an important role in popularizing the changes as well. If in 2006, 80% of the surveyed population considered the police as corrupt, by 2012 only 25% thought so. The police reforms had played a significant role in state building – increasing security and trust, combating corruption, and providing legitimacy for the government (Lehmbruch & Sanikidze, 2014, pp. 93–94). Thus, Saakashvili's power was strongly backed up by coercion, if needed. Furthermore, it was important for the government to provide a secure environment in which society would trust the state. This was well symbolized in the new glass buildings for police (Saakashvili & Bendukidze, 2014, p. 152).

The post-revolution government not only centralized and strengthened the power of the executive branch, but were also very self-centred in planning and implementing new reforms. They did not communicate their goals and policies with the wider public. The government was not willing to hear criticisms (Aprasidze, 2009b, p. 68), even though in his inaugural speech Saakashvili (2004) highlighted that the time had come for the government to listen to the people. As Mitchell argues, government officials were very confident in what they were doing and thought they 'did not need to "waste" time on deliberation or debate' (Mitchell, 2009, p. 180). Freedom House reports reveal that NGOs did not have any significant influence over Saakashvili's policymaking – the uncontested power of the ruling party; the United National Movement (UNM) in parliament enabled the government to disregard the opinions of these organizations (Kakachia & Lebanidze, 2016, p. 149). The government was thus abolishing a system of checks and balances at the domestic level (De Waal, 2011, p. 3; Gegeshidze, 2011, p. 33).

Thus, Saakashvili's government managed to gain central power, defeat informal power groups and old elites, and ensure the strength and loyalty of the army, as well as start gaining the heart of society by reforming the police into a trustworthy institution. However, too much power was accumulated in the hands of the governing party, as well as by the president, turning Georgia into a party state. Such a setting not only paved the way towards radical reforms, but also signalled the early signs of authoritarianism. Even though the post-revolution government was equipped with all necessary tools and sources of power for tackling foreign currency domination, they did not do so. A strong currency was neither perceived as an important medium for state building nor for the increasing trust of the society towards the government.

Dollarization through the prism of state-building

The Rose Revolution not only brought a regime change, but it also marked the beginning of the new Georgian state. Saakashvili claimed that Georgia started to be a state only after the revolution (Jones, 2006, p. 34), making a shift from a failed to a proper state (European Stability Initiative, 2010b, p. 17). Saakashvili and his team picked up pretty much the same themes and foci as had Tergdaleuli[8] in the nineteenth century – of building a democratic European state with a strong and modern economy, achieving national unity, and settling relations with Russia and Europe (Cheterian, 2008, p. 696; Jones, 2006, p. 37). In his inaugural speech in 2004, president Saakashvili (2004) highlighted that Georgia was an ancient European country and a part of European civilization, which had to regain its place in Europe, thus declaring its integration with Europe as the key aim. At the same time, the state-building rhetoric of the government was quite nationalistic and the constant focus on territorial integrity was backed up by increased spending on defence (Mitchell, 2009, p. 180).

The new Georgian state had to break links with the Soviet past. This aim went hand-in-hand with the goals of modernization (Cheterian, 2008, p. 694). Yet, these goals served as a façade as well as a power base of the government. Saakashvili was hoping to be seen as a modernizer of the Georgian state. Aprasidze (2009a, p. 10) refers to the process started by Saakashvili's government – 'state-managed nation building' – where the main aim of the government was to increase the trust of society in formal state institutions, and where new reforms were based on the increasing power of the state security system. The war against corruption was also part of the de-Sovietization process (Di Puppo, 2012, p. 162; Jones, 2006, p. 38). Although the trust of society was important for the government, trust in the national currency was not seen as part of the state-building process.

Thus, Saakashvili pictured modernity, functionality, and the western state as the key pillars of the Georgian state, which had to leave its Soviet past behind. The modernization agenda as a foundation for the new state building can be traced in three interlinked narratives – of democratization, the minimal state, and economic growth. The democratization paradigm enjoyed top priority not only within the political elite, but also within civil society. However, democracy was mostly understood in terms of fair elections, freedom of speech, and human rights. Creation of a minimal state served a crucial purpose of legitimizing the radical libertarian reforms of the government. Economic growth was a driver of all economic reforms. Though these three pillars created the context of the 'new' state, they were not to be taken for granted. These narratives provided a nice cover up for the façade of the Georgian state. An analysis of each of the three pillars demonstrates why and how dollarization was completely compatible with the new state-building narrative and why it was not problematized in the post-revolution rush to reform. The sections below shed more light on each of these three aspects.

Dollarization beyond the discourse of democratization

The dominance of the democratization paradigm was nothing new to Georgia. Throughout the 1990s, Georgian civil society was occupied with this aim. However, a major difference between Shevardnadze's and Saakashvili's governments can be found in the expansion of this paradigm towards the state apparatus level. It became a declared goal of the post-revolution state to become democratic (see Saakashvili, 2004). Yet, the understanding of democracy was rather 'political', focusing on freedom of speech, free elections, civil liberties, and political pluralism. Such a perception of democracy, shared by the government and most actors of civil society, did not offer any space for questioning socio-economic developments and problematizing dollarization. The knowledge and spirit to democratize was strengthened in the post-revolution government, as many civil society activists and NGO practitioners occupied government positions after the revolution. The new political elite heavily relied on these people (Angley, 2013, p. 53). Former civil society actors held such important positions as minister of education, culture, and sport, minister of justice, as well as mayor of Tbilisi, and they were represented in parliament (Broers, 2005, p. 345).

Democratization discourse was dominant within civil society. The old intelligentsia who were nostalgic about the Soviet Union and sympathized with Russia (as their career and work was well appreciated in Russia), did not problematize socio-economic issues either. They did not have any specific ideas about alternative ways of development and mostly opposed Saakashvili's autocracy (Kakachia & Lebanidze, 2016, pp. 141–143). Even the opposition parties in Georgia did not think in terms of development (Muskhelishvili & Jorjoliani, 2009, p. 697). The opposition was weak and had little access to resources. Their access to media was limited and they had financial difficulties; most businesses were afraid to support them (De Waal, 2011, pp. 8–9). More general weaknesses of Georgian political parties applied to the post-revolution party landscape as well; there was an absence of programmes and fuzzy ideologies which were hard to allocate to the left or to the right (Kakachia & Lebanidze, 2016, pp. 146–147).

Therefore, socio-economic issues and currency related problems were not problematized even during the first legitimacy crisis of Saakashvili's government in 2007. The protests were triggered by the ethical misdeeds of the government and its violation of human rights. The main requirement towards the government in the course of the 2007–2008[9] demonstrations was the improvement of the political system and of democracy (International Crisis Group, 2007, p. 3; Muskhelishvili & Jorjoliani, 2009, p. 697). Within the dominant democratization discourse, the critique of the government also remained focused on political pluralism, fair elections, and human rights. Though these issues are indeed crucial for the functioning of the state, the overlooking of socio-economic developments explains why dollarization remained beyond the scope of the government and the civil society. Furthermore, democratization was rather used as a cover-up for the authoritarian governance of Saakashvili's party, as described in the following section. Such a setting further shrank the space for raising a critique of government policies. Thus, democratization, both in official rhetoric and its violation in practice, enabled the dollar hegemony to persist in Georgia after the revolution.

Wilted roses and thrones of the revolution: authoritarianism uncovered

George Bush referred to post-revolution Georgia as a 'beacon of liberty' in 2005 (CNN.com, 2005), but Saakashvili's state-building project has been criticized for its neglect of democracy. The motto of the government was 'modernization before democracy' (Aprasidze, 2016, pp. 92–93); the government thought state building was superior to democracy and that the latter would follow naturally (Mitchell, 2009, p. 179). Even though neoliberalism is associated with depoliticization mostly, it shall be analysed in terms of governmentality, as it would allow one to explain state interventions or the usage of other non-market tools for governance (Madra & Adaman, 2018, p. 113).

Weak democracy during Saakashvili's governance had several dimensions. One of the most obvious signs was the immediate weakening of civil society through the brain drain from NGOs to the government. The function of civil society as a watchdog was significantly weakened. Organizations that did not directly support the revolution dealt with a number of problems in terms of accessing the government for their work (Broers, 2005, p. 345). Georgian NGOs were further weakened through reduced international funding (Cheterian, 2008, p. 699). These actors believed that the Georgian government could democratize the country from the top down (Muskhelishvili & Jorjoliani, 2009, p. 595). American and European donors shifted their money from civil society towards government programmes, focusing on good governance rather than democracy (Lazarus, 2013, p. 16). This shift to governance had happened already at the end of the 1990s at the international level, when the international financial institutions (IFIs) realized that Washington Consensus policies did not work (see Babb & Kentikelenis, 2018, p. 20). Good governance was supposed to make up for the failures of Washington Consensus by 'getting politics right'. 'The word "governance" allowed the Bank [World Bank] (and IMF) to discursively enter the realm of state politics without transgressing its explicitly 'non-political' original Articles of Agreement' (Lazarus, 2013, p. 6). It was thus no coincidence that the assessments of Freedom House and the World Bank on democracy and good governance, respectively, in Georgia were contrasting. While Georgia was demonstrating success in terms of good governance, it was failing in democracy (Lazarus, 2013, p. 3; Rekhviashvili & Polese, 2017, p. 8). Especially in the years right after the revolution, from 2005 till 2008, scores for political rights and civil liberties were at a lower level than before the revolution (apart from civil liberties score in 2005 which remained unchanged) (Aprasidze, 2016, p. 96). Thus, not only had the Georgian government subordinated its democratization plans to modernization, it was also part of an international trend to shift the focus from democratization towards good governance, raising the questions – in whose interest exactly the governance should serve. Although Saakashvili's government strengthened the executive power and weakened civil society, the West continued supporting his state-building project (Mitchell, 2009, p. 172), because the government was considered reliable in terms of implementing economic and administrative reforms (Kakachia & Lebanidze, 2016, pp. 139–140).

Saakashvili's government weakened civil society not only by transferring its most active leaders to the government, but also by attacking the media.

Several important talk shows were shut down to limit the possibilities of political critique, thereby increasing the pressure on print media. Rustavi 2 turned into a pro-government channel and (Mitchell, 2009, p. 180) two TV channels (Iberia and the Ninth Channel) has already been closed down in the first year of governance, as 'a new mood of self-censorship seemed to have settled in' (Broers, 2005, p. 345). Such repressive practices against media continued throughout Saakashvili's presidency (Papava, 2009, p. 202). A prominent example of this policy was the attack on the TV channel *Imedi* (Georgian word for hope), which was founded in 2003 by a Georgian businessman, Badri Patarkatsishvili, and had been one of the main voices for the opposition. In culmination of the November 2007 demonstrations against the government, *Imedi* was raided, its equipment was destroyed, and the TV channel was shut down. A smaller TV channel Kaukasia was also closed and a state of emergency was announced (International Crisis Group, 2007, p. 4; Wheatley & Zürcher, 2008, p. 10). In response to international pressure, Imedi TV was reopened in December (International Crisis Group, 2007, p. 5). Imedi gradually turned into one of the main supporters of the government, along with Rustavi 2 and Georgian public broadcaster. The phrase 'it came down from above' was one of the most common sentences used by journalists (De Waal, 2011, p. 22). In 2011, press freedom was assessed as being worse in Georgia than it had been in 2004 (Jobelius, 2011, p. 81).

Thus, while building an authoritarian neoliberal state, Saakashvili was doing his best to marginalize and discipline various opposition forces and social groups through a strong executive power, instead of trying to gain their consent. These kinds of practices were often legitimized through economic necessity and legal or constitutional tools were given priority over democratic discussions (see Bruff & Tansel, 2019) on authoritarian neoliberalism). Massive changes started at universities, as well. In the spirit of education reforms, elderly academicians were fired. Saakashvili's party maintained its control over student self-governance organizations (Muskhelishvili & Jorjoliani, 2009, p. 696), which were directly supporting government policies (International Crisis Group, 2007, p. 19). Government relations with artists, academics, and intelligentsia were disregarding and disrespectful. The government was not open to their critique and tried to discredit them by contextualizing the intelligentsia as 'charetskhili' – a Georgian word for flushed down (International Crisis Group, 2007, p. 24). A prominent Georgian political scientist, Alexander Rondeli (2008) describes how various social groups in Georgia felt humiliated at this time. Saakashvili confronted the old Soviet intelligentsia openly and radically. This part of society not only lost their status after the revolution, but also the sources of income and privileges that they had enjoyed under Shevardnadze (Kakachia & Lebanidze, 2016, pp. 141–142). Thus, Saakashvili's party had a significant influence on various social groups. As the international crisis group 2007 report claimed: 'the threat of losing employment makes civil servants compliant. State universities are an example' (International Crisis Group, 2007, p. 19).

Authoritarian practices were noticeable to some civil society actors from the very beginning. Tina Khidasheli (head of an NGO, Georgian Young Lawyers Association, that actively supported the revolution) published a letter in 2004, just a year after the revolution, pointing at the authoritarian governance of the Rose Revolution government (Khidasheli, 2004). Furthermore, civil society organizations addressed Saakashvili in 2004 with an open letter, where they warned the president that authoritarian means of governance would not do the country any good. They highlighted the appearance of enemy discourse to marginalize the opposition (Civil.ge, 2004). Furthermore, in 2004, the Ombudsman and human rights activists had already published information on the torture and ill treatment of more than 1,000 people. Such practices constituted an integral part of post-revolutionary rush on tax collection, alongside the arrest of old officials or businessmen on tax evasion charges (Cheterian, 2008, p. 704).

The International Crisis Group (2007) published a report on Georgia under the title: 'Georgia: Sliding toward Authoritarianism?' Also, in the same year (November) the *New York Times* published an article with a title 'Georgia's Future Looks Like More of the Past' (Levy, 2007). Yet, these practices remained beyond an explicit critique of western actors (USA, EU, NATO). They missed the chance of putting pressure on Saakashvili's government to respect democratic rules (International Crisis Group, 2007, p. ii).

Though the situation improved significantly in terms of corruption (Georgia demonstrated one of the best results in the post-Soviet space; Rekhviashvili & Polese, 2017, p. 7), a new type of corruption started to flourish (Papava, 2006, p. 663). Authors and practitioners highlight the shift of corruptive practices from daily life towards higher governmental levels. Privatization deals, the seizure of buildings without warning or disregard of property rights provide good examples of the so-called elite corruption (Cheterian, 2008, pp. 702–703; De Waal, 2011, pp. 25–26).

Papava describes the government's scheme of raising money on the basis of allegations of corruption. Extra-budgetary accounts were created where money was transferred from those who were found guilty on corruption charges to buy their freedom. These accounts were also filled by money from the voluntary contributions of businesses (Papava, 2006, p. 663). Dubious funds were set up to develop military and law-enforcement agencies, which were not under state budget control and which received money from businesses, but not always on a voluntary basis (Anjaparidze, 2006). Fighting corruption and criminality was used as an excuse for violent, illegal practices and mass imprisonments. The number of people in prisons was continuously increasing and the police often abused the use of force (Muskhelishvili & Jorjoliani, 2009, p. 694). The number of prisoners increased four times between 2004 and 2010, due to Saakashvili's 'zero-tolerance policies'. Any kind of corruption or theft was punished by long-term imprisonments and the age of criminal responsibility was reduced from 14 to 12 years (Lazarus, 2013, p. 11).

The events of 2007, when protests broke out against Saakashvili's government, also clearly demonstrate authoritarian governance. The demonstration was violently attacked by the police, followed by an attack on the opposition TV channel Imedi (De Waal, 2011, pp. 6–7; Muskhelishvili & Jorjoliani, 2009, pp. 696–698). Saakashvili tried to marginalize the 2007 protest by linking it with Russian influence and blaming some opposition leaders of conspiracy against the government (International Crisis Group, 2007, p. i). The factor of Russia as an enemy was used to cover up other problems. As Gegeshidze (2011, p. 39) argues, as soon as a threat came from Russia, people forgot about freedom and democracy. Furthermore, a state of emergency was announced, opposition TV channels were closed, and some activists were put in prison (Wheatley, 2008). Saakashvili appointed preponed presidential elections to January 2008, which he won by 53% of the votes (Muskhelishvili & Jorjoliani, 2009, p. 698).

Thus, the Georgian state did not manage to fully break with the Soviet past. The renewal of civil servants and erasing the institutional memory did not establish a new political culture. Promises of a democratic state remained hollow words. Georgia was becoming an authoritarian state. Nevertheless, this is not to argue that the post-revolution government did not care about democracy. But the importance of democracy for the government shall be seen in relation with and in terms of the political aspirations of the West. Though Georgia turned into an institutionalized, formalized state, it never really adopted democratic values. Democracy was once again used as a façade and the hybrid character of the Georgian state did not change in this sense. The authoritarian practices of Saakashvili's government were eradicating spaces for critical debate at schools, universities, public workplaces, or in the media. These practices were not always critically assessed by international actors. Thus, even if a critical assessment of overall socio-economic developments and dollarization persistence appeared within civil society, spaces for debate and reflection were becoming more and more limited.

The minimal state and libertarian monetary policy[10]

> To ask the government for help is like trusting a drunk to do surgery on your brain.
>
> (Minister of Economy; Bendukidze cited in (Jobelius, 2011, p. 84)

The second pillar of the state-building rhetoric was the aspiration to a minimal state. The concept of the minimal state was used as a justification for radical reforms as well as for deregulation. Saakashvili and Bendukidze (minister of economy and later of reform coordination after the revolution) explain the logic behind their reforms in a 2014 article: that Georgia as a failed state needed radical reforms, under which the role of the government should remain as limited as possible. Therefore, they had to free businesses from illegal and legal influences, integrate Georgia into the world market, and fight against corruption (Saakashvili & Bendukidze, 2014, p. 150). The Georgian government was not alone in these ideas – libertarian and conservative think-tanks such as the Cato Institute, the Frazer Institute, and the Heritage Foundation actively supported them (Jobelius, 2011, p. 85). Yet, Bendukidze, the father of major economic reforms after the revolution, claimed in one interview that he had discovered these ideas himself, without reading Hayek, Mises, or any other thinkers. Moreover, he was not interested in the academic roots of libertarianism (European Stability Initiative, 2010a, p. 10). Bendukize named two of his Russian friends as his main inspirations – Andrei Illarionov, a libertarian economic advisor to Putin till 2005, and Vitaly Naishu, a mathematician and economic thinker (European Stability Initiative, 2010a, p. 11).

The post-revolution government started a mass closure of state agencies and public institutions to demolish the bureaucratic state and eradicate corruption. According to the former energy minister, Nika Gilauri, 'More regulation creates more opportunity for corruption and more obstacles for growth' (Gilauri, 2017, p. 25). The logic of abolishing regulation agencies because of corruption is rather puzzling. The post-revolution government did not try to improve these agencies by eradicating corruption; the solution was found in closing them down. Negative historical experience of the 'mother state', since the Soviet Union, was on their side. The Georgian public perceived no good from their governments, so this logic was not challenged and it provided a nice legitimation for the new reforms. Thus, if corruption was used as the main technology of governance by Shevardnadze (which later became the main reason for its collapse), Saakashvili used it as the key excuse and legitimation for reducing the regulatory role of the state. It was believed that small government would affect economic growth positively. Thus, 'Georgia's regulatory framework was reduced to the immediate essentials: fighting corruption, protecting public safety, and collecting taxes' (Gilauri, 2017, p. 27). This quote of the former minister of energy (2004–2007) and of finance (2007–2009) summarizes very well how the government understood the main functions of the state, resembling a liberal understanding of the state as a watchdog for markets and the mediator of societal conflicts.

A WB report describes meetings headed by the Minister of Economy, Bendukidze (described as a 'liberal radical') to decide the need of public agencies as being '"guillotine"-style meetings' (World Bank, 2012, p. 96). Out of 28 ministries only 13 were left (Gugushvili, 2016, p. 2). For example, food safety and motor vehicle inspection agencies were abolished; the anti-monopoly agency was also closed in 2005. There was even an idea to get rid of the NBG in order to avoid a state monetary policy (Timm, 2013, p. 9). The idea of replacing the central bank by a currency board was also debated, which would mean that the rate of Georgian lari would be fixed to a foreign currency or currency basket; no loan could be issued to the government and commercial banks would be given a right to refuse involvement in the fiscal deficit projects (Papava, 2007, p. 7). Bendukidze wanted to abolish the ministry of economy, as well (Jones, 2015). It is also puzzling that the Georgian central bank did not have an official de-dollarization strategy until 2010 (National Bank of Georgia, 2011b, pp. 9–10), as one would expect a central bank of a highly dollarized country to care about currency stability (see (Eradze, n.d.).

These perceptions of the roles of the state, central bank, and national currency were in line with Hayekian views. Hayek questioned the need of a government monopoly on issuing money and suggested the use of private money suppliers instead (Hayek, 1990, pp. 26–27). He picked up the idea of universal money in the 1970s, because he was disappointed by how governments had been managing their national currencies since the gold standard (Helleiner, 2011, pp. 143–146). Hayek believed that governments did not have enough information to manage money supply and if they did, he doubted their intention of serving public interests (Hayek, 1990, pp. 100–103). Therefore, he advocated for denationalization of money and supported free banking and the free flow of currencies. With the absence of a monetary policy, central banks would also disappear (Hayek, 1990, pp. 92–93). Hayek also suggested dissolving 'the unholy marriage between monetary and fiscal policy' (Hayek, 1990, p. 117).

The National Bank of Georgia was not abolished, but shifted to the regime of inflation targeting in 2009, where price stability turned into the central bank's highest priority and the independence of the National Bank was strengthened. Inflation targeting not only redefines the main functions and aims of a central bank, but also calls for more independence of this institution (McNamara, 2002, p. 48). Inflation targeting should be seen as part of a broader ideological debate on states and markets. This monetary regime reflects the understanding of the state in terms of providing proper conditions for the market to function (Gabor, 2010, pp. 808–809). Therefore, inflation targeting fits well within the rhetoric of mainstream economics and the aim of establishing neo-liberal central banking in a minimal state. This regime is widely supported by monetary economists (for example, Mishkin, Laubach, Posen) and institutions like the IMF (Epstein, 2001, pp. 3–4). The shift to inflation targeting had political and strategic motives, as it should have signalized guarantees to foreign investors and attracted foreign capital. Peripheral countries are often being pursued by international actors that inflation targeting will help them to access international capital (Epstein, 2001, pp. 4–5). Thus, the Georgian government had to make a trade-off between abolishing the central bank or instrumentalizing it for achieving economic aims.

The radical deregulation policies of the Georgian government were not always supported by international actors. There were tensions between the EU and the Georgian government on a number of regulatory issues, also with regard to certain licenses for export products or domestic markets

(European Stability Initiative, 2010b, p. 23). For Bendukidze, those Georgians who advocated regulations as a part of harmonization with the EU, were 'betrayers' (De Waal, 2011, p. 3). Saakashvili and Bendukidze (2014, pp. 159–161) recall in their joint article that the IMF was initially also sceptical about the government plans on the deregulation of government agencies in 2004. The Fund was afraid of negative budgetary results of such changes.

The Liberty Act is also a nice demonstration of such relations and the determination of the Georgian government to enforce minimal state aims. The Law on Economic Freedom, Opportunity and Dignity (Liberty Act) (2009) aimed to canonize the ideology of the minimal state in the Georgian constitution. The law was supposed to forbid the establishment of new regulatory bodies and make a referendum obligatory for increasing taxes. The goal was to maintain the liberal trend in the economy and make Georgia "a flagship of worldwide economic liberalism" (Saakashvili, 2009 cited in Jobelius, 2011, p. 85). The Liberty Act introduced some of the Maastricht rules in terms of government expenditure, budget deficit, or debt to GDP ratios. This law also granted absolute freedom for currency exchange and conversion operations. Saakashvili and Bendukidze describe the Act as one being contested within the government, as many could not understand the necessity of the small state. The ministry of finance was not happy either.

The Liberty Act not only reflects the notion of a minimal state, but also echoes the aspiration of the government to get Georgia integrated into the global market and more importantly to attract foreign capital. Here, the timing of the Act was decisive. Already in 2008 there was a plan to create a financial hub and tax haven in Georgia, so the government had to create favourable conditions for capital flows. Yet, the exchange rate of the lari could have suffered from such flows (Lashkhi et al., 2008, pp. 24–28). Moreover, after the 2008–2009 double crisis[11] Georgia needed to turn on the green light for international investors, therefore, constitutionalizing certain freedoms and guarantees for the capital was important. As Saakashvili and Bendukidze themselves argue, they wanted to 'design a straitjacket for the irreversibility of reforms [...] to create the basis for the inviolability of the principles of economic freedom. It was vital for the economy to remain attractive for investors' (Saakashvili & Bendukidze, 2014, p. 159). This is why any limitations of currency conversion or bank accounts in foreign currencies were forbidden and the law also constitutionalized freedom of capital movement so that the Georgian central bank would not have a possibility to change it. The Liberty Act was criticized by the European Parliament and the IMF. Due to pressure from IOs, especially from the EU, the Georgian government made some compromises such as enabling it to raise taxes temporarily (for 3 years) without a referendum or allowing the government to introduce new regulatory bodies. The Liberty Act was adopted in 2011 (Saakashvili & Bendukidze, 2014, pp. 159–161).[12]

Thus, the minimal state as a dominant state-building narrative explains why dollarization was not perceived as a problem during Saakashvili's presidency. The government did not see it as its job to interfere into the market and even considered the closure of the ministry of economy or the central bank. The ideas on a currency board or a free currency zone fitted perfectly within the libertarian understanding of the monetary system and did not challenge the dollar hegemony in the country. Therefore, the role of the national currency was rather insignificant in the state building rhetoric.

The Georgian minimal state

Despite all the reforms described above and the official rhetoric on free markets, the Georgian state under Saakashvili's presidency was never a minimal one. Publicly declared libertarian ideology coexisted with interventionist practices of the post-revolution government. Georgia was praised continuously for its achievements in institution building and the creation of a business-friendly environment, labour freedom, and trade freedom on the international political arena. The WB even attributed it the status of a top reformer (in 2005–2010) (Timm, 2013, p. 1). Yet, these reforms often remained a facade, as deregulation in Georgia turned into a different kind of regulation (Jones, 2013, p. 184). The government forcefully gained control over land and capital from private owners, but used these resources for financing state projects as well. Saakashvili's government was enforcing informal authoritarian governance (Rimple, 2012; Timm, 2013). The post-revolution government did not care much about property rights or freedom of businesses. The state was supreme over the economy (Timm, 2013, p. 1). This was, for example, demonstrated in the new division of property in favour of the new political elite after the revolution (Timm, 2014, p. 10). Papava calls this process of property redistribution deprivatization, as is characteristic of authoritarian countries (Papava, 2006, pp. 666–667). Some businessmen from Shevardnadze's times were forced to give up their property, part of which was later sold by the state to newly established companies (Timm, 2013, pp. 11–12). Transparency International (TI) Georgia has explored the expropriation of different types of property in post-revolution Georgia – real estate, land, restaurants, businesses, cars, office equipment, small shops etc. These goods were usually registered as gifts to the state in an officially signed document by the ministry of economy. The public defender's investigations reveal cases of the government threatening its 'victims' through planting drugs. According to the TI Georgia, these practices had no legal basis (Transparency International Georgia, 2013). Practices such as 'parallel tax collection' or as TI calls it, 'tax terrorism' (Transparency International Georgia, 2010, p. 9), were very common during Saakashvili's presidency. A journalist, Paul Rimple (2012), identifies the key businesses where government control was significant; it included firms in the telecommunications, media, advertising, gasoline, pharmaceutical market, and mining sectors. He describes common tactics and strategies of the government by which it acquired businesses through tenders, corruption or violent means. Many of such companies were later registered in offshore zones (for example, in the British Virgin Islands).

Even though neoliberalism does not deny the role of governments and even more, calls for state-led markets, the modes of economic governance in Georgia acquired a different pattern than that of governments protecting markets based on an agenda 'which is attuned to the dependence of economic liberalism on competition laws, property rights, a culture of enterprise, a strong police force, strict monetary policies, and so on' (Davies, 2018, p. 273). Neoliberal motives were merged with historical legacies from the Soviet Union of directly taking over control of markets. For example, direct interventions of the government into the market were expressed in influencing prices before elections or forcing certain businesses to employ people (Timm, 2013, pp. 17–18). For example, in 2006, Saakashvili initiated an employment programme under which businessmen had to provide jobs for 50,000 people for three months and the government would pay these people $85 a month. This programme brought nothing; people were not really employed, nothing was produced, but $12.7 million was spent from the national budget. A similar programme was repeated in 2007 again for 10,00,000 people (Papava, 2009, p. 202).

The post-revolution government tried to manipulate statistics about the economic development of the country as well. The statistics department constituted an integral tool of the governance process.[13] This department came under governmental control after the revolution, as it became integrated into the ministry of economy. Papava draws a parallel with the Soviet Union, when statistics were produced for government rhetoric and political aims (Papava, 2009, p. 203). Jones also argues that financial data had a strong political dimension during Saakashvili's presidency, as in the Soviet Union. '[N]either GDP nor GNP measured the cash economy, nor the unregistered remittances on which most Georgians depended. [...] Aggregate unemployment and poverty rates told us nothing about their depth' (Jones, 2015).

The authoritarian interventionist character of the Georgian state became even more evident after 2008. Rekhviashvili and Polese argue that in the second term of his presidency (from 2008), Saakashvili's government realized it had destroyed its mechanisms of legal intervention while creating a minimal state. Thus, in order to handle post-war (2008) and financial crisis problems, it turned to informal practices of governance. The government wanted to deal with the social costs of marketization in this manner. This is also the period when the state became 'the biggest investor' (Rekhviashvili & Polese, 2017, p. 1). Yet, as argued above, informal intervention into the market (often illegal) had been a major governance strategy for Saakashvili's government from the beginning. After 2008, the government started to dominate the economy even more openly, for example, financing certain sectors (wine, tourism, agriculture) or promoting state-owned enterprises (Timm, 2014, p. 12).

Just as democracy never became a skin for Georgia, it also never turned into a minimal state. Quite the opposite, the government had control over businesses and the market. Georgia was shaped rather as a neoliberal state, where the state's power did not decrease, but was further expanded. Saakashvili's neoliberal governance applied authoritarian rule and discipline not only to the opposition groups, but also to the market. In theory, this could have created the perfect preconditions for imposing restrictions on market actors and limiting the usage of foreign currency. However, the libertarian understanding of currency on the one hand and global pressures on the other hand eliminated the possibility of strict de-dollarization politics. Moreover, de-dollarization would have required a long-term strategy and would not have brought such quick gains as fake employment programmes or infrastructure projects financed forcefully by businesses. Furthermore, the dollar hegemony fitted well in the interests of the local financial elite or international investors, as explained in the following sections. Thus, neoliberalism does not necessarily cause the retreat of the state, but social and political life is rather restructured around markets by the state elites. Here, informality is one of the key themes in peripheral states (Connell & Dados, 2014).

Economic growth as a new religion: foreign currency domination in an FDI-driven economy

Shevardnadze's legacy provided no easy starting point for the post-revolution government. Georgia was a poor, corrupted country, where the state budget comprised only 15% of GDP, salaries and pensions had not been paid for years and the basic infrastructure did not function (Gugushvili, 2016, p. 2). The level of external debt had reached 50% of GDP (Dadalauri, 2009, p. 180) and the government had to deal with energy and budget crises (Papava, 2009, p. 200).

Kakha Bendukidze, who was invited from Russia as the minister of economy in 2004, became the father of major economic reforms. Admitting in one of his interviews that he did not know much about Georgian economy, Bendukidze was sure that this was not needed as he knew the universal principles of economy (European Stability Initiative, 2010b, p. 19). Bendukidze's aim was for the Georgian economy to grow rapidly through radical deregulation. To quote him:

> Any economic policy should have maximum deregulation of the economy as its priority. In Georgia, this should take the form of ultraliberalism, since if Georgia wants to build a normal country, its economy has to grow at very high rates.
>
> (Bendukidze cited in European Stability Initiative, 2010b, p. 20)

It was exactly this pressure of economic growth through deregulation that made the strength of the national currency secondary in comparison to the openness to foreign capital and ease of transactions in foreign currency.

The new minister wanted to create a new team with young people, who had nothing in common with communism. He believed that these people did not need to have specific knowledge, but rather to be creative and enthusiastic (European Stability Initiative, 2010b, p. 22). Bendukidze's attitudes towards the economy and economic development reveal the neglect of country-specific knowledge or the need of policies derived from the local context. They also demonstrate the understanding of the economy as a field in which skills and intuition matter more than specific knowledge. These principles became the guiding vectors of the economic policies in Georgia after the revolution. These ideas on the economy were not challenged by local economists. Neoclassical economics had haunted Georgian universities. Kahka Bendukidze even founded his university, the Free University of Georgia, in 2007 (Free University, n.d.). Furthermore, the International School of Economics at the Tbilisi State University was founded in 2005, upon an appeal of the Georgian Prime Minister Zurab Jhvania to the WB President Wolfensohn to provide support 'to train young economists in modern economics as it is taught all over the world and to conduct economics research here in Georgia' (ISET, n.d.). These universities (also state universities) played an important role in institutionalizing the ideas of the post-revolution government on the economic development, providing academic back-up for their arguments, preparing the staff for ministries, central bank, and other decision-making institutions. These ideas remain uncontested within Georgian policymaking or academic context to this day.

Saakashvili's government did not have a broad development plan beyond the narrow aim of economic growth. This was well reflected in the eclectic and contradictory role models that Saakashvili named from time to time – from Singaporization to creating another Switzerland in Georgia (see De Waal, 2011, p. 3), imitating New Zealand or the United Arab Emirates (Gogolashvili, 2011, pp. 187–188). The holy aim of economic growth rested on the main pillar of attracting foreign direct investments (FDI).[14] Accelerated privatization was one of the major ways of inviting international capital to Georgia. The government was ready to sell everything, including energy distribution lines, water utilities, ports, airports, land, long-term rights for fisheries, mineral deposits, and so on. Russia was not excluded from the privatization process[15] either (Saakashvili & Bendukidze, 2014, p. 153). Saakashvili and Bendukidze did not want to set any barriers to foreign capital, even if it came from Russia: 'in an open and competitive new Georgia it did not matter where the money originated' (Saakashvili & Bendukidze, 2014, p. 154).

A tax reform encouraged the process of privatization and the entry of international investors as tax competitiveness was crucial for the government to increase FDI (Dadalauri, 2009, p. 182). This reform cut the number of taxes drastically, freed employers from social tax, decreased VAT and corporate income tax, and introduced a flat income tax (20%). The number of taxes was reduced from 21 to six and custom duties were abolished (Timm,

2013, p. 7). In 2009, Georgia was one the least taxed countries (Gugushvili, 2016, p. 3). The core aim of this reform was to make life easier for corporations, while labour had to pay its costs (Dadalauri, 2009, p. 184). Saakashvili's government offered foreign investors tax exemptions and assets for symbolic prices, freeing them from visa or work permit obligations (Gugushvili, 2016, p. 3). In addition, the labour code was changed in 2006 – making the Georgian labour market attractive for investors (Gugushvili, 2016, p. 3; Lazarus, 2013, p. 9). Moreover, workplace inspections were abolished, bargaining rights were taken away from trade unions and strikes were criminalized (punishable by two years' imprisonment) (Jobelius, 2011, p. 84). A minimum wage, overtime payments, and health and safety rules at work were considered to be unnecessary and working hours (though defined as 41 hours a week by law) were made negotiable in terms of increasing them (Gugushvili, 2016, p. 3). Georgia was ranked as the sixth country in the Ease of Doing Business in 2007 for its deregulated labour market and employer freedoms. Georgia's prime minister, Lado Gurgenidze, even referred to the new labour code in 2008 as an 'entrepreneurial revolution' (European Stability Initiative, 2010b, p. 27). The International Labour Organization was dissatisfied with such changes, as they violated basic social rights; the European Commission also highlighted mismatches between the Georgian Labour Code and the European Social Charter (Lazarus, 2013, p. 9).

Further reforms and legal changes were enforced to improve international rankings of Georgia (for example, Ease of Doing Business), to attract foreign capital (European Stability Initiative, 2010b, p. 26). Marketing work was financed in the international media (CNN, *Financial Times, The Economist*, etc.) to create a brand for Georgia and assure investors that it was worth investing in the country (European Stability Initiative, 2010b, p. 30). As Saakashvili and Bendukidze argue, their aim was to open up the Georgian economy to international trade through signing free trade agreements with neighbouring countries, abolishing import tariffs, and opening markets, even unilaterally in some cases. After implementing all these changes, Georgia was praised for ease of international trade, as its rate of customs duties was one of the lowest in the world (Saakashvili & Bendukidze, 2014, p. 153).

Georgia was making progress in the WB's Ease of Doing Business rankings, moving from 137th in 2004 to the 15th place by 2009 (Mitchell, 2009, p. 176), and earning a 'Global top reformer status' from the WB in 2010 (Timm, 2013, p. 1). Georgia was also leading in the region with its results in the WB's state capacity and governance scores (Rekhviashvili & Polese, 2017, p. 7). Yet, who profited from these titles and how sustainable was such a development path for the country?

The large-scale privatization programme, implemented between 2004 and 2010, brought $1.4 billion and had a significant influence on fiscal politics. High levels of FDI (due to privatization) positively contributed to GDP and budget growth (Rekhviashvili & Polese, 2017, p. 9). Budget revenues increased by 700% in the first five years due to improved tax collection, as well (Mitchell, 2009, p. 175). By 2006, the shadow economy had reduced by 10%, though in certain sectors there was a rebound of underground activities (International Monetary Fund, 2006, pp. 33–37). However, Georgia was facing danger of the 'Dutch Disease', which caused a decline in exports and rise in inflation in 2004–2008 (Anguridze et al., 2015, p. 14). The main driver of the Dutch disease was the inflow of foreign capital due to privatization, as well as the increase in tax payments and remittances that strengthened the value of the national currency but negatively influenced the current account (Papava, 2007, p. 8). According to Aslamazishvili, the first signs of the Dutch Disease were already visible in 2003 as foreign investments increased due to the Baku-Tbilisi- Ceyhan pipeline project (Aslamazashvili, 2006, pp. 62–63).

Positive macroeconomic developments in the first years after the revolution encouraged de-dollarization, though only for a short period (Figure 7.1). The level of deposit dollarization decreased from 86% to 74% within a year (2004) (National Bank of Georgia, 2006a, p. 58). The legalization of the economy and the reduction of the share of shadow economy (in which the dollar had been the key currency) played an important role in this dynamic (National Bank of Georgia, 2004, p. 33). Deposits in the national currency increased by 79% and those in the foreign currency by 31% (National Bank of Georgia, 2004, p. 40). Loan dollarization remained above 70%, until it started to decrease towards the end of 2007 until the beginning of 2009. The trend of de-dollarization was reversed after the crisis of 2008–2009. The persistence of high levels of dollarization was especially remarkable within long term loans and term deposits (National Bank of Georgia, 2010b, p. 31).

The transparency of the privatization process as well as its long-term results were highly questionable. Most of the factories were sold like real estate buildings and the new owners could easily send workers home, due to flexible labour law of Georgia (Lazarus, 2013, p. 19). Furthermore, Papava

Figure 7.1 Deposit dollarization
Source: National Bank of Georgia (2011a, p. 39).

points at such violations as indicating lower sums of money in official contracts, after selling certain properties or privatizing state property to some dubious companies (Papava, 2010, p. 48). European diplomats were critical about the mass privatization project as well, especially because of the selling off of sea ports (Saakashvili & Bendukidze, 2014, pp. 159–161). Apart from the issues in transparency of the privatization process, the allocation of foreign capital in terms of economic development was also questionable. The investment boom touched only few economic sectors – construction, real estate, commercial banks, infrastructure, and energy projects (Livny, 2016, p. 176; Nadaraia et al., 2013, p. 16). Such trends encouraged the development of a consumer economy in the country, which was highly dependent on capital inflow from abroad (Anguridze et al., 2015, p. 10). Thus, a further impact of FDI growth on the Georgian economy was the increase in imports; GDP and imports were in positive correlation in 2003–2009 (National Bank of Georgia, 2009, p. 18). The annual report of the National Bank of Georgia (NBG) in 2004, highlighted the danger of the Dutch disease in terms of a disbalance between investment and export sectors, which had a negative influence on price stability and competitiveness of Georgian products on the world market (National Bank of Georgia, 2004, p. 26). Nevertheless, FDI played an important role in the development of the export sector, as well. By 2013, more than one-half of the firms in exports had Georgian-foreign equity. Without the re-exporting segment, the share of the mentioned companies made up two-thirds of real exports. Furthermore, these organizations contributed 30% of VAT and employed 20% of total employees in Georgia (Anguridze et al., 2015, p. 28). Yet the export structure in terms of exported products did not change significantly after the revolution (see Eradze, 2021; International Monetary Fund, 2006, p. 56; National Bank of Georgia, 2010a, p. 27).

The increase of the FDI influenced economic growth positively but this was not reflected in the social welfare of the broader society (Figure 7.2). Socially vulnerable groups, unemployed people, and the poor did not enjoy the fruits of economic growth (De Waal, 2011, p. 2; Gegeshidze, 2011, p. 34). As the Rose Revolution resulted in mass reorganizations especially in the public sphere, a lot of people remained unemployed. Owing to the amount of people employed in construction, transportation, and communications, financial intermediation was increasing, employment in agriculture, industry, public sector, and trade was decreasing (National Bank of Georgia, 2006b, p. 25). Overall unemployment[16] did not decrease and urban unemployment even increased after the Rose Revolution (Gugushvili, 2016, p. 5). According to the United Nations Children's Fund (UNICEF), the number of employed people decreased by 213,000 from 2003 to 2008; 64% of the employed were self-employed and most of them worked in small farms; 22% of the Georgian population lived in poverty, whereas almost 10% belonged to the extremely poor category (UNICEF, 2010, pp. 7–8). The rate of undernourishment also increased after the revolution. In addition to rising poverty rates, the

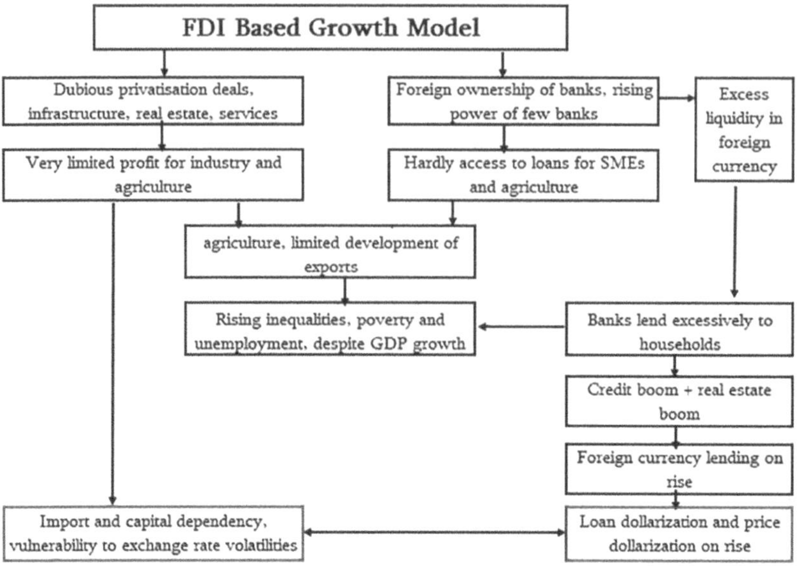

Figure 7.2 FDI-led accumulation regime
Source: Author's illustration.

inequality gap was also widening. Georgia's Gini coefficient (42% in 2010) was one of the worst in the region (Rekhviashvili & Polese, 2017, pp. 13–15).

Thus, the distributional effects of economic growth were very limited in Georgia. This can be explained through a closer examination of the drivers of this growth. Economic growth did not occur due to fundamental changes in the economic structure and most importantly, the productive sphere was not developed. The drivers of economic growth was the service sector, especially infrastructure, energy, real estate, finance and trade, as well as construction (see National Bank of Georgia, 2010c, p. 18, 2011b, pp. 18–19). This can be explained by the focus on finance, energy, and security areas. As Tatum claims, the aim of the government was to show the international community (IMF, WB, European Bank for Reconstruction and Development, North Atlantic Treaty Organization, etc.) its commitments and socio-economic issues on the ground were ignored. To quote him: 'The international focus has blurred the lens pointed towards the domestic scene, and this approach has alienated much of Georgia's population, which still suffers from widespread poverty, unemployment, and income inequality' (Tatum, 2009, p. 168). For example, agriculture decreased by 20% in 2011 in comparison with 2005, whereas this sector employed one-half of the population but could not produce enough food for the Georgian market (Gogolashvili, 2011, p. 191). In 2010, the government spent less than 1% of GDP on agriculture (De Waal, 2011, p. 17). Although in 2007 Saakashvili realized the social costs of his economic policies and announced the combat of poverty as his main aim (Civil.ge, 2007), not much changed in the general line of policies, despite some unsuccessful attempts at poverty reduction (Gogolashvili, 2011, p. 185; Rekhviashvili & Polese, 2017, p. 17). Thus, it was clear that the strategy of prioritizing economic growth before addressing poverty did not work.

It is widely acknowledged that although capital inflows can be beneficial for the recipient country, they can cause problems. If a country cannot absorb capital in a productive way, it can encourage risky and increased lending in these countries that might cause harm to the financial system and economy. In addition, capital inflows can lead to an appreciation of the real exchange rate which negatively affects the international competitiveness of exports (Priewe & Herr, 2005, p. 121). This applies to the developments in Georgia after the 2003 revolution. The overall impact of mass privatization and the increase of FDI was ambivalent in post-revolution Georgia. The economic policies of the post-revolution government were effective for promoting short-term growth, but they did little for developing the Georgian economy in the longer term. These reforms did not improve the social welfare of the population and significantly weakened the power of labour in favour of employers. Economic growth did not happen in Georgia not only due to the development of productive sphere, but rather owing to the development of services and privatization revenues. Though economic growth had a positive influence on the value of the lari and on de-dollarization, this process did not have a solid economic basis. De-dollarization was not a result of a fundamental change in the composition of GDP or of the development of the export sector, but was driven by short-term capital inflows. The mentioned policies did not transform or revive the Georgian economy to create a solid economic back-up for the Georgian currency. They also did not improve the trade balance to decrease the country's vulnerability to exchange-rate fluctuations. The FDI-financed imported consumption boom further strengthened dollarization and increased the import dependency of the country. The trade balance was influenced negatively and money supply in foreign currency also increased. The increased dependency of the Georgian economy on foreign capital was making the country vulnerable to capital flight and crisis.

Conclusion

The Rose Revolution of 2003 marked a beginning for a new Georgian state. Even though the state building reforms of Saakashvili's government were successful in terms of institution building, the elimination of corruption (at least on a micro level) and GDP growth, dollarization persisted at high levels. Not only was the role of the dollar still significant for the functioning of the accumulation regime, but foreign currency domination also remained unquestioned and unproblematized. A strong national currency and sovereign monetary policy did not appear on the agenda of state building, even in the context of trust in the government, which was in fact important for Saakashvili's administration.

The analysis of the state-building narratives of Saakashvili's government sheds more light on dollarization hysteresis. Saakashvili's declared aim was to create a modernized, democratic, minimal state, where economic growth was the main driver of all socio-economic developments. Yet, the practices differed from the announced goals. Georgia emerged as an authoritarian neoliberal state which turned out to be compatible with foreign currency domination. A strong national currency did not play an important role in this agenda of state-building. The global neoliberal pressure of competitiveness to attract foreign capital, as well as the catching-up aims of modernization paradigm required the free circulation of foreign currencies in the peripheral state of Georgia. The radical deregulation policies of the post-Rose Revolution government created a suitable environment for foreign capital inflow and encouraged the persistence of dollarization.

Moreover, it is not surprising that dollarization was not perceived as a problem within a minimal state narrative, where even the abolishment of the ministry of economy and the central bank was debated. The Hayekian line of questioning the need for a central bank and national currency well corresponded with Bendukidze's ideas on an 'ultra-liberal' economy. If in the 1990s, the development of the Georgian state disregarded currency issues (other than a symbolic level) due to its ignorance of the economic sphere, the post-revolution government did not ignore the economy, but wanted to subordinate everything to a market logic, under which foreign currencies and the free float of monies were welcomed. FDI-driven economic growth further strengthened the role of dollar by granting freedom to foreign capital. Economic growth was not driven by economic development; import and foreign capital dependency made the Georgian economy more vulnerable to capital flows and exchange-rate fluctuations. Yet, the democratization-oriented civil society and political elites did not pay much attention to issues other than fair elections, political pluralism, or human rights. However, even if a critique had emerged from the civil society, Saakashvili's government would have supressed and discredited any opposite views on its socio-economic development pathways or political governance. Thus, dollar hegemony remained unshaken and uncontested in Georgia, as foreign currency and foreign capital again played a key role in the functioning of the accumulation regime.

Notes

1 Reference to (Mitchell, 2004, p. 345) regarding TV screens.

2 In 2003, the budget deficit was \$90 million – 15% of the planned revenue, internal debt was \$120 million, and half of the population was under poverty level (Papava, 2006, pp. 660–661).

3 The IMF had called on anti-corruption measures in the country which Shevardnadze's government did not deliver (Broers, 2005, p. 335).

4 Even a text called 'Political Economy of Rose Revolution' does not analyse the role of such capital fractions (see (Papava, 2006).
5 Deputy minister of foreign affairs and secretary of interior affairs' council after the revolution.
6 Young Lawyers Association.
7 Minister of education after the Rose Revolution.
8 Political activists and writers, who were educated in Russia and encouraged the awakening of the Georgian national spirit in the 1860s.
9 A tipping point of the protest was a public allegation of the former defence minister Okruashvili against Saakashvili on crime. Okruashvili was arrested but a number of people (around 100,000) went on to the street in Tbilisi and demanded a parliamentarian republic instead of a presidential one (Muskhelishvili & Jorjoliani, 2009, pp. 696–698) see (De Waal, 2011, pp. 6–7)
10 This section is based on the author's journal article 'Dollarization Persistence in Georgia in the Prism of State Building', which is currently under review (Eradze, n.d.).
11 The double crisis was caused by the war against Russia in 2008 and the world financial crisis.
12 Yet, the final version of the law allowed tax increase without referendum upon a specific organic law (Civil.ge, 2011). The law on taxes and referendum is part of the Georgian constitution, Article 94 (1).
13 For example, in 2006, according to the Statistics Department, the inflation rate in Georgia was 14.5%, which was assessed critically by the IMF. The Georgian government replaced the head of the department, who managed to 'decrease' the inflation rate to 9.2% within four months (Papava, 2009, p. 203).
14 In 2004, The United Centre for Serving the Investors was established (Dadalauri, 2009, p. 195).
15 For example the united Georgian Bank was sold to Russian Vneshtorgbank (Papava, 2009, p. 204).
16 Measuring unemployment in Georgia is a contested issue. The data from the statistics department differs from independent research results. Mismatches in the data are related to different definitions of unemployment and the status of self-employed people, especially in agriculture.

References

Angley, R. E. (2013). Escaping the Kmara box: Reframing the role of civil society in Georgia's Rose Revolution. *Studies of Transition States and Societies*, 5(1), 42–57.

Anguridze, O., Charaia, V., & Doghonadze, I. (2015). *Security Problems and Modern Challenges of the Georgian National Currency.* Ivane Javakhishvili Tbilisi State University TSU Center for Analysis and Forecast, Tbilisi.

Anjaparidze, Z. (2006). Georgian Government Questioned about Secret Funds. *Eurasia Daily Monitor*, 3(71), 10–12.

Aprasidze, D. (2009a). Lost in Democratization and Modernization: What Next in Georgia? *Caucasus Analytical Digest*, 02, 9–11.

Aprasidze, D. (2009b). State-Building and Democratization in Georgia: Have the Limits Been Reached? *OSCE Yearbook 2008*, August, 63–74.

Aprasidze, D. (2016). 25 Years of Georgia's Democratization: Still Work in Progress. In G. Nodia (Ed.), *25 Years of Independent Georgia: achievements and unfinished projects* (pp. 91–130). Konrad Adenauer Stiftung, Ilia State University.

Aslamazashvili, N. (2006). "holandiuri daavadeba" sakartvelos ek'onomik'ashi: arsebuli realoba da shesaz'lo saprtkheebi ["Dutch disease" in Georgian economy:

existing situation and possible threats]. In L. Bakhtadze, G. Tutberidze, & V. Schneider (Eds.), *sakartvelos ek'onomik'uri t'endentsiebi* [Economic trends in Georgia] *Quarterly Review* (pp. 60–67). GEPLAC.

Babb, S., & Kentikelenis, A. (2018). International Financial Institutions as Agents of Neoliberalism. In D. Cahill, M. Cooper, M. Konings, & D. Primrose (Eds.), *The SAGE Handbook of Neoliberalism* (pp. 16–28). SAGE.

Broers, L. (2005). After the 'revolution': Civil society and the challenges of consolidating democracy in Georgia. *Central Asian Survey*, 24(3), 333–350.

Bruff, I., & Tansel, C. B. (2019). Authoritarian neoliberalism: trajectories of knowledge production and praxis. *Globalizations*, 16(3), 233–244. doi:10.1080/14747731.2018.1502497.

Cheterian, V. (2008). Georgia's rose revolution: Change or repetition? Tension between state-building and modernization projects. *Nationalities Papers: The Journal of Nationalism and Ethnicity*, 36(4), 689–712.

Christophe, B. (2004). Understanding Politics in Georgia (No. 22; DEMSTAR Research Report).

Civil.ge. (2004, October 18). An Open Letter of Civil Society Representatives to President Saakashvili. https://civil.ge/archives/106354.

Civil.ge. (2007, December 16). Saakashvili Lays Out Priorities. https://civil.ge/archives/113785.

Civil.ge. (2011, July 1). Revised 'Economic Liberty Act' Passed with Final Reading. https://civil.ge/archives/185962.

CNN.com. (2005, May 11). Bush: Georgia 'beacon of liberty'.

Connell, R., & Dados, N. (2014). Where in the world does neoliberalism come from? The market agenda in southern perspective. *Theory and Society*, 43(2), 117–138.

Dadalauri, N. (2009). Transnationalization and the Georgian State: Myth or Reality? In L. Bruszt & R. Holzhacker (Eds.), *The Transnationalization of Economies, States, and Civil Societies New Challenges for Governance in Europe* (pp. 179–219). Springer.

Davies, W. (2018). The Neoliberal State: Power against Politics. In D. Cahill, M. Cooper, M. Konings, & D. Primrose (Eds.), *The SAGE Handbook of Neoliberalism* (pp. 271–284). SAGE reference.

De Waal, T. (2011). *Georgia's Choices: Charting a Future in Uncertain Times.* Carnegie Endowment for International Peace.

Di Puppo, L. (2012). Anti-Corruption Policies in Georgia. The Construction of Images of Success. In L. Kosals & H. Pleines (Eds.), *Governance Failure and Reform Attempts after the Global Economic Crisis of 2008/2009 Case Studies from Central and Eastern Europe. Changing Europe (Volume 9)* (pp. 161–171). ibidem-Verlag.

Epstein, G. A. (2001). *Financialization, Rentier Interests, and Central Bank Policy* (pp. 1–43). Political Economy Research Institute.

Eradze, I. (n.d.). Dollarization Persistence in Georgia in the Prism of State Building. *Globalizations.*

Eradze, I. (2021). Imbalanced foreign trade, debt, and investment in developing countries: The case of Georgia (Issue June). https://eu.boell.org/en/2021/06/16/imbalanced-foreign-trade-debt-and-investment-developing-countries-case-georgia.

European Stability Initiative. (2010a). Georgia's Libertarian Revolution Part one: Georgia as a model (Issue April).

European Stability Initiative. (2010b). Georgia's Libertarian Revolution Part Three: Jacobins in Tbilisi (Issue April).

Free University. (n.d.). Kakha Bendukidze. Freeuni.edu.ge.

Gabor, D. (2010). The International Monetary Fund and its New Economics. *Development and Change*, 41(5), 805–830.
Gegeshidze, A. (2011). Georgia's Political Transformation: Democracy in Zigzag. In *South Caucasus 20 Years of Independence* (pp. 25–41). Friedrich Ebert Stiftung South Caucasus.
Gilauri, N. (2017). *Practical Economics: Economic Transformation and Government Reform in Georgia 2004–2013* (1st ed.). Palgrave Macmillan.
Gogolashvili, K. (2011). In search of Georgia's economic model. In *South Caucasus 20 Years of Independence* (pp. 173–192). Friedrich Ebert Stiftung South Caucasus.
Gugushvili, D. (2016). Lessons from Georgia's neoliberal experiment: A rising tide does not necessarily lift all boats. *Communist and Post-Communist Studies*, 50(1), 1–14.
Hayek, F. A. (1990). *Denationalisation of Money: The Argument Refined* (3rd ed.). The Institute of Economic Affairs.
Helleiner, E. (2011). Denationalizing Money? Economic liberalism and the "national question" in currency affairs. In E. Gilbert & E. Helleiner (Eds.), *Nation-States and Money: The Past, Present and Future of National Currencies* (pp. 139–159). Routledge.
International Crisis Group. (2007). Georgia: Sliding towards authoritarianism? (Issue December, N 189).
International Monetary Fund. (2006). Georgia: Selected Issues (Issue 06/170).
ISET. (n.d.). About us. Iset.tsu.ge.
Jobelius, M. (2011). Georgia's authoritarian liberalism. In *South Caucasus 20 Years of Independence* (pp. 77–92). Friedrich Ebert Stiftung South Caucasus.
Jones, S. (2006). The Rose Revolution: A Revolution without Revolutionaries? *Cambridge Review of International Affairs*, 19(1), 33–48.
Jones, S. (2013). *sakartvelo: polit'ik'uri ist'oria damouk'ideblobis gamotskhadebis shemdeg* [Georgia: A Political history since independence] (M. Chitashvili (Ed.)). Center for Social Sciences.
Jones, S. (2015). Kakha Bendukidze and Georgia's failed experiment. opendemocracy.net.
Kakachia, K., & Lebanidze, B. (2016). Georgia's Protracted Transition: Civil Society, Party Politics and challenges to Democratic Transformation. In G. Nodia (Ed.), *25 Years of Independent Georgia: Achievements and Unfinished Projects* (pp. 130–161). Konrad Adenauer Stiftung e. V, Ilia State University.
Kandelaki, K. (1935). *sakartvelos erovnuli meurneoba: t'erit'oria da mosakhleoba* [National Economy of Georgia: territory and population], Book I. D. Kheladze Publishing.
Khidasheli, T. (2004, December 8). Georgia: The Rose Revolution has wilted. *The New York Times*.
Lashkhi, I., Evgenidze, N., Narmania, D., & Gabedava, M. (2008). *sakartvelos mtavrobis '50 dghiani p'rograma' – analizi da shepasebebi* ['50 Day Programm' of the Georgian government – analysis and assessments]. Open Society Foundation Georgia, Tbilisi.
Lazarus, J. (2013). Democracy or Good Governance? Globalization, Transnational Capital, and Georgia's Neo-liberal Revolution. *Journal of Intervention and Statebuilding*, August, 1–28.
Lehmbruch, B., & Sanikidze, L. (2014). Soviet Legacies, New Public Management and Bureaucratic Entrepreneurship in the Georgian Protection Police. Agencifying the Police? *Europe-Asia Studies*, 66(1), 88–107.

Levy, C. J. (2007, November 15). Georgia's Future Looks Like More of the Past. *The New York Times.*

Livny, E. (2016). Georgia's Revolutions and Economic Development. In Gia Nodia (Ed.), *25 Years of Independent Georgia: Achievements and unfinished Projects* (pp. 162–208). Konrad Adenauer Stiftung e. V, Ilia State University.

Madra, M. Y., & Adaman, F. (2018). Neoliberal Turn in the Discipline of Economics: Depoliticization Through Economization. In D. Cahill, M. Cooper, M. Konings, & D. Primrose (Eds.), *The SAGE Handbook of Neoliberalism* (pp. 113–129). SAGE reference.

McNamara, K. R. (2002). Rational Fictions: Central Bank Independence and the Social Logic of Delegation. *The Politics of Delegation*, 25(1), 47–76.

Mitchell, L. A. (2004). Georgia's Rose Revolution. *Current History*, 103(675), 342–348.

Mitchell, L. A. (2009). Compromising democracy: State building in Saakashvili's Georgia. *Central Asian Survey*, 28(2), 171–183.

Muskhelishvili, M., & Jorjoliani, G. (2009). Georgia's ongoing struggle for a better future continued: democracy promotion through civil society development. *Democratization*, 16(4), 682–708.

Nadaraia, O., Gorgodze, O., Utiashvili, D., & Sharumashvili, N. (2013). ek'onomik'uri zrda da st'rukt'uruli t'ranspormatsia [Economic growth and structural transformation]. *Ek'onomik'a Da Sabank'o Sakme*, 1(2), 7–21.

National Bank of Georgia. (2004). Ts'liuri angarishi [Annual Report]. https://nbg.gov.ge/publications/annual-reports.

National Bank of Georgia. (2006a). Ts'liuri angarishi [Annual report]. https://nbg.gov.ge/publications/annual-reports.

National Bank of Georgia. (2006b). Ts'liuri anagarishi [Annual Report]. https://nbg.gov.ge/publications/annual-reports.

National Bank of Georgia. (2009). Ts'liuri angarishi [Annual report]. https://nbg.gov.ge/publications/annual-reports.

National Bank of Georgia. (2010a). Annual Report. https://nbg.gov.ge/publications/annual-reports.

National Bank of Georgia. (2010b). Financial Stability Report. https://nbg.gov.ge/publications/annual-reports.

National Bank of Georgia. (2010c). Ts'liuri angarishi [Annual report]. https://nbg.gov.ge/publications/annual-reports.

National Bank of Georgia. (2011a). Ts'liuri angarishi [Annual report]. https://nbg.gov.ge/publications/annual-reports.

National Bank of Georgia. (2011b). Ts'liuri angarishi [Annual report]. https://nbg.gov.ge/publications/annual-reports.

Papava, V. (2005). *Necroeconomics: The Political Economy of Post-Communist Capitalism (Lessons from Georgia)*. iUniverse Inc.

Papava, V. (2006). The Political Economy of Georgia's Rose Revolution. *East European Democratization*, Fall, 657–667.

Papava, V. (2007). Currency Board against the Background of Dutch Disease. *Georgian Economic Trends Quarterly Review*, October, 7–8.

Papava, V. (2009). Georgia's economy: Post-revolutionary development and post-war difficulties. *Central Asian Survey*, 28(2), 199–213.

Papava, V. (2010). The "Rosy" Mistakes of the IMF and World Bank in Georgia. *Problems of Economic Transition*, 52(7), 44–55.

Priewe, J., & Herr, H. (2005). *The Macroeconomics of Development and Poverty Reduction: Strategies beyond Washington Consensus*. Nomos.

Rekhviashvili, L., & Polese, A. (2017). Liberalism and shadow interventionism in Liberalism and shadow interventionism in post-revolutionary Georgia (2003–2012). *Caucasus Survey*, 1–24.

Rimple, P. (2012). *Who owned Georgia 2003–2012*. Transparency International Georgia.

Rondeli, A. (2008). Georgia's search for itself *Opendemocracy.net*. (pp. 1–3). opendem ocracy.net.

Saakashvili, M. (2004). *Mikheil saakashvilis sitkh'va ts'armotkmuli pitsis dadebis tser-emoniaze* [Inaugaural Speech of Mikheil Saakashvili]. National Library of the Georgian Parliament.

Saakashvili, M., & Bendukidze, K. (2014). Georgia: The most radical Catch-up Reforms. In A. Aslund & S. Djankov (Eds.), *The Great Rebirth: Lessons from the Victory of Capitalism over Communism* (pp. 149–165). Peterson Institute for International Economics.

Slade, G. (2012). No Country for Made Men: The Decline of the Mafia in Post-Soviet Georgia. *Law & Society Review*, 46(3), 623–649.

Tatum, J. D. (2009). Democratic Transition in Georgia: Post-Rose Revolution Internal Pressures on Leadership. *Caucasian Review of International Affairs*, 3(2), 156–171.

Timm, C. (2013). Economic Regulation and State Interventions: Georgia's Move from Neoliberalilsm to State Managed Capitalism (2013/03; PFH Research Papers).

Timm, C. (2014). A liberal developmental state in Georgia? State dominance and Washington Consensus in the post-communist region (2014/02; PFH Research Papers).

Transparency International Georgia. (2010). The Georgian Taxation System – An Overview. https://transparency.ge/en/post/report/georgian-taxation-system-overview.

Transparency International Georgia. (2013). Voluntary Gifts or State Robbery. transp raency.ge.

UNICEF. (2010). rogor umk'lavdebian sakartveloshi bavshvebi da mati ojakhebi pinansuri k'rizisis zegavlenas? k'etildgheobis k'vleva [How do Georgian children and their families cope with the results of the financial crisis? Research on social welfare]. https://www.unicef.org/georgia/media/3676/file/WMS_2009_ge.pdf.

Wheatley, J. (2005). *Georgia from National Awakening to Rose Revolution: Delayed Transition in the Former Soviet Union*. Ashgate.

Wheatley, J. (2008). Georgia's democratic stalemate. https://www.opendemocracy.net/en/georgia_democratic_stalemate/.

Wheatley, J., & Zürcher, C. (2008). On the Origin and Consolidation of Hybrid Regimes: The State of Democracy in the Caucasus. *Taiwan Journal of Democracy*, 4(1), 1–31.

World Bank. (2012). *Fighting Corruption in Public Services: Chronicling Georgia's Reforms*. World Bank.

Zurabishvili, D., Meladze, G., Nachkhebia, M., Chkhartishvili, L., & Gvakharia, G. (2012). *'vardebis revolutsiis' memk'vidreoba: ret'rosp'ek't'uli analizi da khedva momavali ganvitarebisatvis* [Rose revolution heritage: retrospective analysis and future development visions]. Heinrich Böll Foundation South Caucasus.

8 Peripheral financialization and the persistence of dollarization

The rise of finance: the role of foreign capital and foreign currency

The post-Rose Revolution (2003) accumulation process in Georgia can be characterized by the increasing power of the financial sector (especially banks) and the shift of profit making towards finance. The increasing power of banks was expressed not only in rising profits, but also in the expansion of commercial bank activities beyond the financial sector. Lending policies of banks also changed after the revolution, providing loans to big corporations and households, whereas small and medium size enterprises (SMEs) and start-ups could barely access credit. Commercial banks can be regarded as the key actors of financialization in Georgia, while the driving force of this process is foreign capital. In the banking sector foreign capital had a special importance (referring to the foreign ownership of banks) not only in reviving finance, but also in strengthening the dependence of the Georgian financial sector and economy on foreign money and encouraging the persistence of dollarization.

Reforms in the financial sector are a priority in transition countries as a part of structural adjustment (Barisitz, 2005, p. 58). Development of the financial sector is considered crucial for economic growth by international organizations (IOs). In the 1990s, the world bank (WB) announced finance as a very important area of development (Priewe & Herr, 2005, p. 123). Liberalizing the financial sector through deregulation was one of the essential pillars of transition. A general assumption was that money would flow from developed to developing countries and that this would solve the problems of capital scarcity in these states. Therefore, any restrictions on capital flows or convertibility of currencies was prohibited. Furthermore, the liberalization of foreign exchange (FX) markets was directly linked with non-discriminatory polices to enable free trade. By now, it has been proved that this set of policies did not bring about the presupposed results. Quite the opposite, in a number of countries, capital inflows rather led to current account deficits and currency crises, even as early as the late 1990s (Painceira, 2009, pp. 6–7).

Though fundamental changes in the financial sector had started in the mid-1990s in Georgia, a significant institutional change of the financial

DOI: 10.4324/9781003240174-11

system took off after the Rose Revolution. The Georgian government wanted to create a global financial centre in Georgia by attracting large financial companies (Papava, 2009, p. 205). According to the former advisor of the ex-president of Georgia, Giorgi Margvelashvili, Saakashvili hoped that if Georgia turned into a financially safe haven in the region, political security would be guaranteed as well (Participant 11, personal communication, 8 June 2017).

The financial sector turned into the fastest growing sector of the Georgian economy after the Rose Revolution (2003). The amount of assets, deposits, and loans had been increasing since the late 1990s, and this trend continued until the 2008 crisis (Gelaschwili & Nastansky, 2009, p. 8). In 2004, the share of banking assets to GDP reached 17% (it was 15.7% in the previous year) (National Bank of Georgia, 2004, p. 57). In 2005, the total assets of Georgian banks increased by 50%. Furthermore, loans increased in the same year by 85%; the ratio of loans to GDP was 14%, whereas in the previous year it was 9% (National Bank of Georgia, 2006c, p. 8). In 2006, the assets of Georgian banks increased by almost 66% (National Bank of Georgia, 2006e, p. 62). Furthermore, the share of long-term credits (longer than one year) was rising (National Bank of Georgia, 2004, pp. 57–58). If in 2000 the share of long-term credits was 27%, by the end of 2005, it reached 64.2% (National Bank of Georgia, 2006c, p. 10). Due to increasing trust towards banks, deposits in both the national and in foreign currencies were also increasing. One-half of deposits belonged to individuals (National Bank of Georgia, 2004, pp. 57–58).

Commercial banks emerged as the key players of the financial sector in Georgia and power was becoming consolidated in the hands of a few players. If in 2004 six big banks controlled more than 80% of all assets and deposits (National Bank of Georgia, 2004, p. 59), two banks possessed more than 70% of the market share in 2013. The TBC Bank owned around 29% of the banking sector shares, whereas the Bank of Georgia held almost 43% shares (European Investment Bank, 2013, pp. 7–8). The formation of banks as powerful actors was further supported by the decentralized banking system, as each commercial bank enjoyed the freedom to manage its financial risks, to restructure, or to manage non-performing loans (Gelaschwili & Nastansky, 2009, pp. 3–4).

Microfinance organizations and credit unions were also represented. Microfinance institutions in Georgia were allowed to lend money, provide insurance services, make transfers, and be involved in FX. Yet, they could not take deposits, obtaining funding through international markets. Therefore, microfinance organizations could not compete against commercial banks, creating an even more favourable environment for the banks. Other financial actors had even less significant power. Although there were 18 credit unions in Georgia in 2013, they had a very insignificant share (only 0.1%) of assets. Credit Unions have been under central bank regulation since 2003 and almost all their funding is dependent on deposits (European

Investment Bank, 2013, pp. 11–14). Thus, by 2012, commercial banks owned 91% of all assets in the financial sector, while the insurance sector held 5% and microfinance organizations less than 4%. The share of assets owned by credit unions and the stock market was close to zero (Bluashvili, 2013, p. 60). Furthermore, the capital market was not developed in Georgia. According to Khishtovani, the underdevelopment of the capital market was also related to the monopoly of banks as well (Khishtovani, 2012, pp. 4–6). Thus, the commercial banks became uncontested powerful actors in the financial sector of Georgia after the Rose Revolution.

The power of banks was not only expressed in their monopoly status or rates of profit, but also in terms of their expansion towards the non-financial sectors of the economy. Commercial banks were allowed to own firms (until 2014); they mostly engaged in insurance and stock companies. Banks could be both creditors and shareholders. Such rights were a result of the deregulation process of the financial sphere (Gelaschwili & Nastansky, 2009, p. 5). A 2006 strategy document of the National Bank of Georgia (NBG) highlighted the need to encourage the development of banks' investment politics in other companies (National Bank of Georgia, 2006c, p. 29). However, this document did not reflect on the negative sides of such practices.

In 2009 (after the 2008–2009 crisis), banks in Georgia were forbidden from involvement in non-profile activities, but they started to establish holding companies and continued their business this way. Commercial banks were not allowed to make investments directly, but only through their companies (Sharumashvili & Agladze, 2013, pp. 26–27). Commercial banks mostly invested in the financial sector (70% of all investments), from which 15% was allocated to insurance companies. As for investments in the non-financial sector, (with a 30% share of total investments), the most important sector was real estate. Georgian banks owned and rented out real estate. Most of the real estate owned by the banks was generated through taking over collaterals in case of loan default (Sharumashvili & Agladze, 2013, p. 25). In 2014, the NBG restricted commercial banks' non-profile activities, including investments through holding companies (National Bank of Georgia, 2014). However, according to interviewees from the Georgian central bank, owners and founders of banks were still represented in other sectors (Participant 4, personal communication, 3 May 2017; Participant 13, personal communication, 21 April 2017).

A major factor in the revival of the financial sector in Georgia, and one that especially shaped the role of banks as key actors was the presence of foreign capital. Foreign ownership of banks is common not only in post-Soviet countries, but also among Central and East European (CEE) countries. Most of the commercial banks are either directly or indirectly in foreign ownership in the post-Soviet, as well as in the CEE countries. The transition process paved the way for the liberalization of financial markets and made the banking sector dependent on foreign capital. It was not only this dependency that has been relevant here, but also the easy access of banks to dollar resources that influenced the supply of dollar loans (see Beckmann et al., 2015; Dübel & Walley, 2010; Mihaljek, 2007). Though usually the roots of dollarization are searched for in deposit dollarization, the relationship between foreign-owned banks and an increased supply of foreign currency loans demonstrates that it is not always deposits in dollars that come first.

The presence of foreign banks and their share in local banks increased since the 1980s in poor countries (World Bank, 2002, p. 64). IOs such as the WB were actively promoting the entry of foreign investors in the financial sector of transition countries. From the end of the 1990s, in particular, when the WB realized that transition reforms had not been successful, it started to advocate for the role of foreign ownership as a means of improving the performance and stability of the financial sector (Stein, 2010, p. 270). The transfer of good governance and banking practices were one of the main reasons for selling banks to foreign investors in the CEE during the period of transition. By 2013, more than 50% of banking assets were in foreign ownership in CEE countries, whereas in some states almost the complete domestic markets were taken over by foreign investors (Škarica, 2014, p. 46). The opening up of the financial system went hand in hand with integration 'into multinational financial groups with headquarters located outside their jurisdiction' (Pistor, 2012, pp. 143–144). In most of these countries, banks under foreign ownership established dominant positions on the market. Austrian, Italian, Belgian, French, and German banks are most present in the region (Beckmann et al., 2015, p. 25). The increasing share of foreign ownership in the region brought changes in the governance structure of financial institutions that were no longer completely under national jurisdiction (Pistor, 2012, p. 145) (see Eradze, 2022b).

A 2002 World Bank report provides a list of benefits of foreign-owned banks: efficiency in banking, better credit provision for the private sector through lower intermediation costs, knowledge transfer to the local staff, better access to loans for SMEs, and higher chances for these countries to receive loans from international banks (World Bank, 2002, pp. 66–67). Foreign ownership has brought positive changes in terms of increased competitiveness and efficiency, the transfer of know-how and technologies, and positively influencing confidence in the financial sector. Furthermore, in certain cases, parent banks have even taken over the role of the lender of last resort (Barisitz, 2005, p. 78). Nevertheless, empirical evidence has shown that foreign ownership can negatively influence capital flight, create challenges for SMEs in accessing credit, as well as encouraging lending in foreign currency (Steinmo, 2008, p. 258) or causing instability for the financial system in the case that parent banks face difficulties (World Bank, 2002, p. 69).

Different studies demonstrate that foreign ownership has been an important driver for increasing foreign currency loans, as banks are willing to have currency-matched portfolios (Beckmann et al., 2015, p. 25). In the event that banks have the possibility of borrowing abroad, carry trade[1] might take place, as banks are able to finance themselves in foreign currency under favourable conditions (see Eradze, 2022b). This will lead to an increase of short-term debt and banks might start issuing foreign currency loans on the domestic market (Priewe & Herr, 2005, p. 172). Furthermore, foreign or foreign-owned banks might also issue more and more loans during periods of economic problems or stop lending because of problems in the home countries of the parent banks even when the host economy was doing well (Modebadze, 2011, p. 11). This is why, because of high global liquidity and an increase in funding by parent banks, lending in foreign currency led to a credit boom in CEE countries (Škarica, 2014, p. 46).

Developments in the Georgian banking sector went hand in hand with global and regional changes.[2] In the late 1990s, Georgia also experienced an inflow of foreign capital. The number of state-owned banks was decreasing continuously and by the late 1990s the share of former state banks had declined to 30% of banking assets. If in 1997 the share of foreign capital in Georgian banks was almost zero (only two foreign banks, one Russian and one Turkish, were functioning in 1997 in Georgia) (International Monetary Fund, 1998, p. 23), by 2001, 11% of the total banking assets were held by foreign investors in seven banks of Georgia (International Monetary Fund, 2001, p. 63). By 2004, ten out of 19 banks had shares of foreign owners in Georgia and two were foreign banks (National Bank of Georgia, 2004, p. 57).

The IMF actively promoted foreign bank ownership in Georgia and perceived the entry of foreign capital into the financial sector as a means of combatting dollarization (International Monetary Fund, 2001, p. 81). The Fund found it essential for Georgia to attract foreign investments to the financial sphere to promote the development of skills and technology: 'Such investment could be in the form of either establishing new banks or buying shares of existing banks' (International Monetary Fund, 2001, p. 71). One can find a similar line of argumentation in favour of foreign ownership in the 2006 report of the Fund, as well:

> foreign bank ownership could also increase the overall level of confidence in the banking sector, and reduce the risk of a government bailout in case of a crisis, contributing to improved stability of the banking system and prospects of market integration with the West.
>
> (International Monetary Fund, 2006, p. 16)

In 2006, 10 banks with foreign ownership (that is, those with more than 50% of shares owned by non-residents) controlled almost 87% of total banking assets in Georgia (National Bank of Georgia, 2006e, p. 62). An important legal change in 2006 enabled a further increase of foreign capital in the banking sector. Before 2006, non-bank investors were allowed to own only 25% in a Georgian bank (International Monetary Fund, 2006, p. 8). The IMF considered this kind of limitation as one of the barriers to attracting foreign investors (International Monetary Fund, 2006, p. 14). The Georgian central bank initiated a legal change to remove this restriction, so that any individual or legal entity could own up to 100% of a Georgian bank (International Monetary Fund, 2006, p. 15). A strategy document of the National Bank for the development of the financial sector in 2006–2009 positively assessed the influence of foreign capital in the banking sector, as it would encourage higher levels of investments from abroad and better international ratings for Georgian banks. Good ratings would help banks to gain access to cheap capital and investments. Therefore, the central bank was determined to enforce the liberal currency regime (National Bank of Georgia, 2006d, p. 18).

The share of foreign capital was increasing continuously. By 2013, there were 20 banks on the market which were liquid. Nineteen out of the 20 banks were in foreign ownership (including three branches of foreign banks). State-owned banks did not exist, and only one bank, Progress Bank, was under Georgian ownership. Foreign institutions such as the European Bank for Reconstruction and Development (EBRD), the International Financial Corporation (IFC), the FMO (Dutch Entrepreneurial Development Bank), and the Deutsche Investitions und Entwicklungsgesellschaft (DEG) were among the major shareholders in Georgian banks. Despite the importance of foreign shareholders, Georgian owners of banks also had significant power (European Investment Bank, 2013, pp. 7–8) (see Modebadze, 2011, p. 34 for detailed information on foreign shareholders for the key Georgian banks).

Even though foreign capital became the driving force for the development of the Georgian financial sector, it also strengthened the role of dollar and triggered a credit boom in 2005–2006, driving households into over-indebtedness (as discussed in more detail in Chapter 9). With the increase of foreign capital ownership, Georgian banks started to borrow in foreign currency and 'lending in foreign currency has increased faster than foreign currency deposits' (Amaghlobeli et al., 2003, p. 56). Hardly any long-term credits were issued in the national currency (Gelaschwili & Nastansky, 2009, p. 11). Among the main lenders of Georgian banks were the IFC, the EBRD, the KfW, the DEG, and others (National Bank of Georgia, 2004, p. 58). International institutions play an important role in terms of providing credit guarantees for Georgian financial institutions, as the state does not make such provision. For example, the United States Agency for International Development (USAID) Development Credit Authority provided a guarantee for almost one-half of the loans of local institutions that were borrowed either locally or internationally. In 2007–2008, the KfW also provided such a guarantee (10 million Euros) for the Bank of Georgia, TBC Bank, and Bank Republic to borrow from Commerzbank (European Investment Bank, 2013, p. 11). However, increased foreign ownership made the Georgian financial system dependent on foreign capital. Being in its early development phase, the Georgian stock market has not advanced and the national money supply has remained limited, and economic growth has been strongly dependent on foreign capital (Sattler, 2014, p. 6).

The dominance of foreign capital shaped the loan policies of commercial banks and influenced the development trajectory of the Georgian economy.

Banks have been focusing on big corporations (mostly in the services sector) and households, while small and medium businesses had hardly any access to credit. Commercial banks did not finance innovation as they tried to avoid financing risky projects (Sharumashvili & Agladze, 2013, pp. 26–27). In 2011, more than 70% SMEs named accessing credit as the main barrier. A 2013 WB research also found out that only 14% SMEs were using bank loans for investments. Loan conditions were rather unfavourable – 96% of such loans required a collateral of 220% of the loan volume. Therefore, SMEs often took credit as individuals (Soldatuk & Zoninashvili, 2015). Furthermore, while big companies had access to foreign capital, SMEs have remained rather dependent on local financial markets (Bluashvili, 2013, p. 61), highlighting the importance of bank lending policies in developing these businesses. In interviews with representatives of the central bank (Participant 2, personal communication, 6 May 2017), the IMF (Participant 7, personal communication, 25 May 2017), and the KfW (Participant 9, personal communication, 10 May 2017) in Georgia, higher risks and the underdevelopment of risk-assessing procedures for SMEs have been identified as the explanation for these lending policies.

Apart from the trend of focusing on big corporations and households, the sectoral loan division of banks is also relevant. Among corporate loans, trade and infrastructure received most loans, while mortgages and consumer loans were on the rise in retail lending (National Bank of Georgia, 2006e, p. 66). For example, in 2007 (during the credit boom), banks issued 35% of their loans to individuals, 30% to trade and services, whereas only 8% went to industry, and less than 1% to agriculture (Lashkhi et al., 2008, pp. 30–31). Thus, Georgian commercial banks neither contributed to the development of the real economy nor supported SMEs or innovative start-ups. With the absence of development banks, this gap in the provision of capital to the mentioned sectors remains a major issue.

Thus, post-revolution reforms supported the revival of the financial sector in Georgia. Finance grew faster than other sectors of the economy. The increasing power of the financial actors, especially banks, has been demonstrated along the following major lines – the growth of commercial banks, the development of banks as the most powerful actors with the absence of a capital market, an increase in loan portfolios, as well as the involvement of banks in the non-financial sectors of the economy. However, the success story of finance did not have a clear-cut positive influence on the development of the Georgian industry or export sectors. Georgian commercial banks tended to concentrate on big corporations and retail lending. The sectoral division of loans demonstrate that bank credits usually ended up in infrastructure, trade, or energy projects. Moreover, the increased share of foreign ownership in banking and easy access to foreign money triggered lending in foreign currency, and also to households. Household credits (mostly consumption and mortgages) hardly supported the development of the economy, as consumption loans increased imports and worsened the trade balance, while mortgages further strengthened price dollarization on the real estate market.

The financialization of monetary policy[3]

A closer look at developments in the Georgian economy enables us to identify two periods – from 2004 until the double crisis of 2008–2009; and 2009 to the 2012 presidential elections. This division is plausible not only in terms of observing different development trajectories in the economy but also regarding dollarization and a shift in central bank's monetary policy. The year 2009 marked a new monetary regime for the NBG – inflation targeting, which further limited the functions and policy tools of the central bank. Before the crisis, due to economic growth, the legalization of the economy, and foreign capital inflow, the lari was appreciating and the level of dollarization was declining, however the 2008–2009 crisis reversed the situation and, among other factors, a sharp decline in foreign capital negatively influenced both the stability of the lari and dollarization. Therefore, the following analysis of monetary policy is also divided into the aforementioned periods in order to trace the major linkages between monetary policy aims, economic developments, and dollarization.

The political economy of central banking

Central banks have been contested terrain throughout history. Perceptions about the form or functions of these institutions have been debated within major discussions on the interaction of politics and economics. Daniela Gabor identifies and explains three main historical debates on central banking – Keynesianism from the 1930s to the 1970s; monetarism from the 1970s; and neoliberal inflation targeting since the 1990s (Gabor, 2011, pp. 15–16). The major points of disagreement in these discussions have focused on the key functions of a central bank and the relations of this institution with the government. Monetarist theory was dominant throughout the 1980s and 1990s as a focus on employment (as had existed under Keynesianism) was not compatible with the orthodox views on markets (Gabor, 2010, pp. 809–810).

The Georgian central bank was following monetarism until 2009 and its main functions were defined by the Organic Law (Article 2) in the following way: the bank was responsible for maintaining the value of the national currency, price stability, functional money-credit system, and a liquid financial sector (National Bank of Georgia, 2006e, p. 39). Apart from inflation, issues such as currency stability were among the main aims of the central bank. This is important for a highly dollarized country like Georgia. Under monetarism, the NBG used the exchange rate as an instrument and intervened in the foreign currency market in case of volatilities, as money supply was used as the main tool for influencing inflation. Thus, in contrast to inflation targeting, it was important to keep a stable linkage between money supply and inflation (National Bank of Georgia, n.d.). In 2009 the National Bank of Georgia switched to a policy of inflation targeting. For monetarism and inflation targeting, low inflation is the main aim of monetary policy, where inflation is defined through increasing aggregate demand. Both approaches rely on the assumption of market efficiency and that banks simply respond to the changes implemented by the central bank. Both monetary regimes try to tackle inflation through addressing excessive aggregate demand, but in different ways. If for monetarism, open market operations are the key, inflation targeting focuses on short-term interest rate as its main instrument (Gabor, 2010, pp. 813–814). Yet, under inflation targeting, 'monetary policy is operated by adjusting the *price* of money, not by controlling the *quantity* of money' (International Monetary Fund, 2017, p. 14; italics original), as it is in monetarism. Moreover, one of the major differences between monetarism and inflation targeting is that monetarism allows the management of flexible exchange rates, while inflation targeting does not consider such interventions and disregards the exchange rate as an instrument (Gabor, 2010, p. 815). Understanding the mission of central banks in terms of managing increasing money supply and maintaining a stable money multiplier has been criticized by post-Keynesian endogenous money theorists, because of the disregard for the institutional characteristics of the banking sector (Gabor, 2010, pp. 809–810).

Central bank–government relations have been widely discussed as well. Central bank independence is the key issue in this debate, which is usually discussed along the following dimensions – independence from political influence on the staff and policies, as well as its financial separation from the government (McNamara, 2002, p. 52). If the laissez faire ideology prohibited any kind of involvement of the government in monetary matters under the gold standard, after World War I, this idea was questioned, especially with regard to the Great Depression and appraisal of Keynesian ideas. Many central banks lost their independence after the Great Depression as they were blamed for the economic catastrophe. Thus, before the 1970s, the interference of governments into monetary politics increased (see Capie et al., 1994, pp. 22–33). During these times, Keynes called for the subordination of monetary policy to fiscal policy to achieve full employment (Gabor, 2011, pp. 30–31). Yet, central bank independence gained popularity again from the 1970s. Among the active supporters of this idea were the IMF and the Organisation for Economic Cooperation and Development (OECD). Independence of central banks was advocated in the context of good governance to 'protect' this institution from political influence, especially before elections (McNamara, 2002, p. 47). Despite such attempts to depoliticize central banking, central bank policies cannot become apolitical, as they are directly linked with distribution politics and are therefore linked with certain values (McNamara, 2002, pp. 53–54). In addition, the idea of central bank independence is questionable in terms of democratic legitimacy, as well as accountability (McNamara, 2002, p. 49). Epstein raises a plausible question:

'If a central bank becomes independent, then it would seem that it would be accountable to nobody but itself. How can advocates then claim that along with independence comes accountability?' (Epstein, 2001, p. 7). He argues that in such a case central banks might indeed become independent from government influences, but then become accountable to financial markets (Epstein, 2001, pp. 7–8). Furthermore, there is no clear-cut evidence that central bank independence is directly linked with the improvement of macroeconomic outcomes in developing or developed countries (McNamara, 2002, p. 58) (see Balls et al., 2018; Crowe & Meade, 2008; Posen, 1995).

The question of central bank independence is rather complex in the Georgian case. The NBG and its relations with the Georgian government went through a complex trajectory of development from the 1990s. If in the first half of the 1990s, Soviet style practices of central banking continued in terms of lending to state enterprises and commercial banks owned by politicians, the reforms of the late 1990s triggered substantive changes in the banking sphere (although the central bank remained a fiscal agent of the government). After the Rose Revolution (2003), even the need for a central bank was questioned (Timm, 2013, p. 9). Yet, in 2006, the Georgian government was forbidden to borrow from the central bank (National Bank of Georgia, 2006e, p. 50) and it was planned to remove the liabilities and assets from the balance of the NBG that were not directly linked with the bank (for example, the KfW loan to the energy sector should have been transferred to the government) (National Bank of Georgia, 2006d, p. 45). Furthermore, the central bank should not have provided direct credits to the government (National Bank of Georgia, 2006d, p. 44). The Georgian government attempted to weaken the power of the central bank several times after the revolution. In 2006, the plan of removing the banking supervision function from the central bank was not successful, as NBG directors and the parliamentary committee for budget and finance were against it. Yet, in spring 2008, 'the government [...] deprived the NBG of the power to exercise banking oversight, leaving it the sole function of regulating inflation' (Papava, 2010, p. 51). Until 2007, three different actors supervised the financial system: the NBG supervised commercial banks, microfinance organizations, credit unions, and currency exchange shops. Due to changes in 2007–2008, one supervisory agency was formed as an independent entity, not subordinated to any other institutions, but which received money from the NBG (National Bank of Georgia, 2008a, p. 27). The reform of the central bank was part of the 50-day action plan of 2008, which aimed to create a financial hub in Georgia. This is when it was decided to limit the central bank functions to inflation targeting (Lashkhi et al., 2008, pp. 27–28). Yet, in 2008, the NBG claimed economic independence from the government, removing responsibilities for government spending or liabilities; the Georgian government would not have any responsibility towards the bank either (National Bank of Georgia, 2008a, p. 15). In 2009, the central bank regained its supervisory functions (Gelaschwili & Nastansky, 2009, p. 5) and with the shift to inflation targeting in 2009, was declared institutionally independent in organic law (National Bank of Georgia, 2009, p. 8) (on government central bank relations see Eradze, n.d.).

Thus, despite government attempts to reduce the power of the central bank, the NBG was trying to become independent from government influence after the revolution. A higher degree of independence was supposed to increase the trust of financial actors in the central bank and its policies. Even though central bank independence is discussed in terms of depoliticizing finance and neoliberal central banking, as independent central banks are considered to be best serving financial markets and their interests (Epstein, 1992, pp. 1–3), this issue is rather controversial for countries like Georgia. On the one hand, one can legitimately be critical of the separation of the central bank from politics and question its accountability towards the public; on the other hand, it is challenging to advocate a model of central banking in which the bank would be in close cooperation with the government. The recent history of post-Soviet Georgia does not provide evidence of any benefit to be obtained from such cooperation between the government and financial institutions. Thus, in a country in which the public does not trust the state apparatus and its institutions and where political and financial elites are inseparable, the idea of a central bank which works together with the government faces historical, psychological, and legitimate obstacles.

Monetary policy 2004–2009: coping with the challenges of a strong lari

The legalization of the economy after the Rose revolution, as well as increased budgetary transactions, raised the demand for the lari and the volume of money in circulation increased. The NBG was able to encourage the process of the monetization of the economy (National Bank of Georgia, 2004, pp. 32, 39–40). The monetization of the economy refers to 'the ration of a money aggregate to annualized GDP in current prices' (Jarociński & Jirny, 1999, p. 74). The level of monetization not only gives an idea of the amount of money in economy, but also on supply-demand relations, financial market depth and intermediation, as well as overall stability (Jarociński & Jirny, 1999, p. 74). Monetization can also be understood as 'the degree to which money is accepted and used as a medium of exchange, a unit of account, and a store of value' (Mcloughlin & Kinoshita, 2012, p. 3). In the 1990s, the Georgian economy suffered from low monetization, especially after hyperinflation. A specific feature of post-Soviet economies is that the decrease in inflation does not necessarily lead to an increase in the level of monetization, as would be expected by economists; households stick to old habits of avoiding holding money despite changes in the macroeconomic situation (Jarociński & Jirny, 1999, pp. 74–75). Yet, remonetization started after the Rose Revolution and M3 (money supply) increased to 16.5% in 2006 (National Bank of Georgia, 2006e, p. 48); in 2002, this indicator was 11% (International Monetary Fund, 2006, p. 7).

As a result of rising demand for the lari, as well as of increased foreign capital inflows, the lari was appreciating in the first years after the Rose Revolution and de-dollarization was taking place (Figure 8.1). Since 1998, there was a managed floating exchange rate in Georgia, which was determined by its supply and demand on the internal market (National Bank of Georgia, 2008a, p. 29). The Georgian central bank had to terminate interventions in the FX market in 1998 due to the low level of reserves. However, in 2004, trust of investors increased and a three-year contract with the IMF ensured reserve inflows. As a result, international reserves doubled and the Georgian central bank renewed interventions at the FX market. Yet, if until 1998 the aim of the central bank was to achieve a fixed exchange rate, in 2004, it only intervened to avoid significant fluctuations (National Bank of Georgia, 2004, pp. 36–38).

According to the IMF the Georgian lari was underappreciated before the revolution, so it was getting close to equilibrium. The Fund was suggesting that the central bank should let the exchange rate float freely, while keeping a watch over inflation. Fiscal policy measures should have also addressed lari appreciation (International Monetary Fund, 2006, pp. 51–52). Nevertheless, there was fear that lari appreciation would negatively influence export competitiveness and increase the current account deficit (International Monetary Fund, 2006, p. 51; National Bank of Georgia, 2004, p. 34). The central bank of Georgia was sterilizing the effects of foreign capital inflow, as it was purchasing more USD than it was selling in 2004–2007 (National Bank of Georgia, 2006a, p. 37, 2007a, p. 32) (see Eradze, 2022a). Yet, according to the National Bank, the appreciation of the lari did not affect the export sector negatively, as (among other factors) the major export product of Georgia was raw materials, the prices of which were not dependent on the exchange rate. Furthermore, the low cost of Georgian labour contributed to the competitiveness of export goods. Thus, while allowing the lari to appreciate to a certain extent, the Georgian central bank could avoid inflation and the competitiveness of the country was not damaged (National Bank of Georgia, 2004, pp. 37–39).

The fear of national currency appreciation in Georgia resembles a broader debate on exchange rates in transition countries – whether the exchange rate should be undervalued for the sake of exports or not (Brabant, 1998, p. 198). Though the National Bank of Georgia was allowing the lari to appreciate to a certain degree, it was also intervening into the FX market against and buying foreign currency. This was leading to an increase in the volume of money (National Bank of Georgia, 2004, p. 34) and creating a dilemma for the central bank because of price stability aims. It is remarkable that the central bank was the main actor on the local currency market after the revolution. Its interventions accounted for 86.6% of the total turnover of this market in 2007 (National Bank of Georgia, 2008b, pp. 23–24).

In the opinion of the IMF, currency appreciation does not always influence export competitiveness in transition countries. The lari had been so

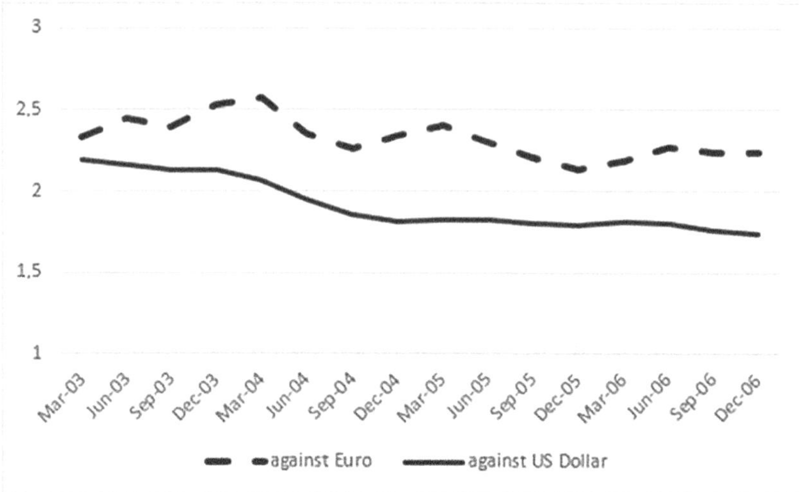

Figure 8.1 The exchange rate of the Lari against different currencies, 2003–2006
Source: National Bank of Georgia (2022).

undervalued in the past that through appreciation it was moving closer to the equilibrium rate (International Monetary Fund, 2006, p. 51). According to an interviewee from the central bank, the lari's depreciation against the dollar did not have such positive effects for Georgian exports as textbooks teach; Georgia's trading partner is not the United States. However, if the lari were to depreciate against the Turkish lira, then it could have a positive effect on the balance of trade. In addition, in a dollarized economy currency depreciation has negative impacts for consumers and businesses (Participant 4, personal communication, 3 May 2017) (Figure 8.2). Thus, the currency appreciation – decreasing export competitiveness dilemma – was not quite applicable for Georgia. Yet, the central bank was still intervening in the FX market and facing another dilemma of price stability and dollarization. Although the depreciation of the national currency might lead to positive results for the balance of trade, for dollarized countries 'the degree of pass-through from depreciation to inflation becomes direct and much higher.[…] The important channel between dollarization and inflation is the exchange rate, which drives a depreciation-inflation spiral' (Priewe & Herr, 2005, p. 176). For a highly dollarized country like Georgia, where the volatility of inflation is high in relation to changes in the exchange rate, it is rather costly to devaluate the national currency in terms of increasing inflation and financial instability (Mkhatvrishvili et al., 2016, p. 72). On the other hand, the fear of depreciation might lead to too much appreciation and cause a currency crisis over time or low growth and unemployment that harms development (Priewe & Herr, 2005, pp. 175–176). The appreciation of the lari

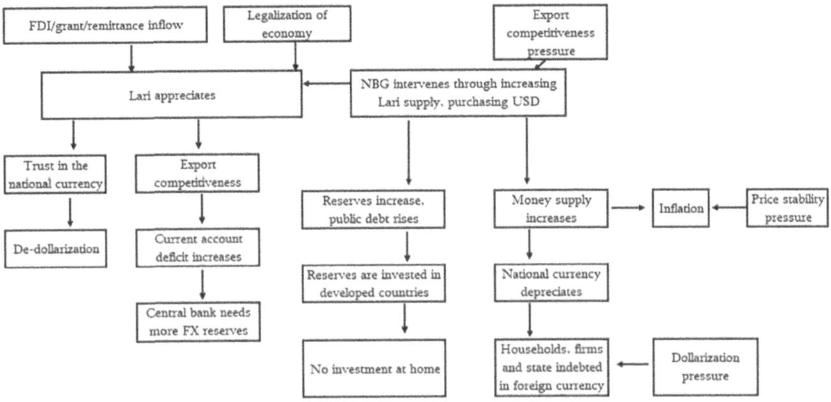

Figure 8.2 The dilemmas of the Georgian Central Bank, 2004-2007
Source: Author's illustration.

had positive implications for dollarization as trust in the national currency was increasing and the de-dollarization of deposits and loans was taking place. Yet, the central bank had to decide whether to enjoy the perils of currency appreciation or to counteract it due to the fears of its negative impacts on the trade balance (see Eradze, 2022a).

Thus, shortly after the revolution, positive economic and political developments, legalization of the economy and an inflow of foreign capital led to lari appreciation and to de-dollarization. Yet, the main dilemma of the Georgian central bank during the first years after the revolution was to decide whether to allow the lari to appreciate, despite its possible negative impact on the current account deficit or to intervene against currency evaluation, facing the danger of inflation. Therefore, fear of losing export competitiveness was the major obstacle for the trend of de-dollarization in 2004–2008. Yet, this trend was completely reversed after the crisis of 2008.

Double crisis: the inflation–export competitiveness–dollarization triangle

The trend of lari appreciation and de-dollarization changed after the August war (2008), as the inflow of foreign currency decreased significantly, and overall economic development regressed. Georgian GDP decreased by 3.9% in 2009 (National Bank of Georgia, 2009, p. 10). The Georgian central bank was challenged by satisfying the demand for foreign currency. The National Bank fixed the exchange rate of the lari to the dollar, but it was soon forced to allow the lari to depreciate (National Bank of Georgia, 2008b, pp. 23–24). In 2008–2010, the lari nominal exchange rate depreciated by 11.2% to the USD (real effective depreciation to the USD was 8.7%). Loan dollarization increased in 2008–2009; this trend was reversed towards the end of 2009, yet dollarization remained at a higher level than before the crisis. The same trend could be observed with deposit dollarization. The persistence of high levels of dollarization is especially remarkable within long-term loans and term deposits (National Bank of Georgia, 2010b, pp. 55–56).

Due to the critical situation in 2008, the Georgian central bank lowered reserve requirements for banks from 13% to 5% and shifted from a strict to an expansionary monetary policy (National Bank of Georgia, 2008b, p. 27). During the war, the NBG was managing a floating exchange rate through FX interventions to avoid significant changes in the exchange rate (National Bank of Georgia, 2008b, p. 30). The rate of monetization decreased, and the rate of deposit dollarization reached 75.8% by the end of 2008, having been 60% at the end of July 2008 (National Bank of Georgia, 2008b, p. 29). However, from 2009, the trend of de-dollarization and an increase in monetization continued again, but at a rather slower speed than before 2008 (National Bank of Georgia, 2009, pp. 39–40). The lari depreciated by 20% by mid-2009 in relation to its peak in October 2008. The main driving force behind the lari depreciation was the decrease of capital inflows (International Monetary Fund, 2011, p. 5).

The devaluation of lari during the crisis provided a good test for the currency depreciation-export competitiveness transmission channel, which was the major central bank dilemma in the pre-crisis period. Even though Georgian exports decreased by 24% in 2009 (National Bank of Georgia, 2009, p. 10), it is difficult to argue that the transmission through exchange rate to exports was strong. Other factors besides exchange rates were important in influencing Georgian exports: the loss of export markets due to conflict, limitations in domestic financing, and the decrease of foreign direct investment (FDI). The IMF considered the last factor as the most relevant for the Georgian case, as FDI had played an important role for the Georgian export sector (especially mining, metal industries, and tourism). Around 20% of FDI was directed to export industries and if tourism is also considered then the share of FDI was 30% (International Monetary Fund, 2011, pp. 9–12). Thus, the decline of FDI made it even more difficult to encourage the export competitiveness of the country (International Monetary Fund, 2011, p. 14). Therefore, FDI inflow appears to have major importance for the Georgian export sector. Yet, it also leads to the appreciation of the national currency as experienced in the pre-crisis period. This controversy highlights once again the limited nature of policy choices for countries like Georgia that are dependent on foreign capital and have a high level of dollarization. In this case, de-dollarization goals are squeezed between the aims of low inflation, foreign capital inflow and export competitiveness, which makes it difficult for the central bank to prioritize what to tackle first (National Bank of Georgia, 2008a, p. 18).

Thus, the downward economic trend after the crisis made it obvious how fragile and vulnerable the Georgian economic success story was. The crisis highlighted that this success depended on capital inflows; as did the de-dollarization trend. Thus, it took the next crisis (2008 war with Russia) for the house of cards to collapse and the dollarization trend to progress again.

The Georgian central bank on guard against inflation

In 2009 an inflation targeting regime was introduced in Georgia. Article 3 of the Organic Law announced price stability as the highest priority of the central bank. Other functions from the bank's previous mandate such as guaranteeing stable financial system as well as encouraging sustainable economic development became secondary aims. The inflation target was set at 9% and the main instrument of the central bank became interest rates (National Bank of Georgia, 2009, p. 8). However, the underdevelopment of the lari market limited the effectiveness of this instrument (National Bank of Georgia, 2009, p. 34). The Georgian central bank was restricted from intervening in the FX market, other than when a temporary inflow of too much capital would cause short-term exchange rate volatility, or to increase international reserves (Baiashvili, 2015, p. 55). The Georgian central bank used the following monetary policy instruments – refinancing loans, overnight loans and deposits, treasury notes, and minimum reserve requirements (National Bank of Georgia, 2009, p. 44) (see Eradze, 2022a).

The above-mentioned changes were in line with the general requirements of inflation targeting – the elimination of nominal indicators such as GDP or exchange rates; the prioritization of price stability as the key aim; the prohibition of fiscal dominance; and the independence of central banks, as well as their transparency and accountability. However, such a concentration on inflation usually eliminates focusing on other aims, such as encouraging employment or supporting investments (Epstein, 2001, pp. 3–6). Moreover, exchange rates are left to be determined by the market (Acosta-Ormaechea & Coble, 2011, p. 3). Key preconditions for inflation targeting are: a sustainable financial policy, a developed financial system, and an independent central bank (Mkhatvrishvili, 2016, p. 19), all of which could not possibly have been met by Georgia.

In the 1970s and 1980s, the focus had already shifted from full employment to low inflation in the Global North. A worldwide shift to inflation targeting since the 1990s outlined a close linkage between financialization and central banking, as inflation targeting regimes are directly linked with the interests of financial investors in price stability (Karwowski & Centurion-vicencio, 2018, p. 16). The central bank of New Zealand was the first to adopt inflation targeting in 1990, followed by further industrial and emerging economies (Epstein, 2001, pp. 3–4). Interest rates started to play a key role after exchange rates were no longer under a common Bretton Woods system of monetary management. The shift towards inflation targeting and its connection with 'scientific expertise' further supports the depoliticization process of finance (Gabor, 2010, pp. 810–811). Though inflation targeting is associated with increasing levels of price stability and employment, empirical evidence is diverse in terms of measuring the impact of inflation targeting on inflation levels or its expectations (Epstein, 2001, p. 9). There is no big difference in the rates of reduction of inflation among industrialized countries with and without inflation targeting regimes. A link between inflation targeting and positive trends in employment has also hardly been proved empirically (Epstein & Yeldan, 2008, p. 134). The same applies to a positive correlation between the levels of inflation and economic growth (McNamara, 2002, p. 57).

Inflation targeting is interlinked with floating exchange rates, which reduces central banking to 'setting the policy interest rate' (Epstein & Yeldan, 2008, p. 138). The exchange rate becomes subordinated to inflation control as a policy instrument. Moreover, in the presence of inflation targeting, exchange-rate management and a free capital account does not function (Kaltenbrunner & Painceira, 2017, pp. 453–454). Thus, under inflation central banks not only disregard important indicators as growth and unemployment, but also start to ignore dollarization, if their country faces this issue. They not only give up on the exchange rate as a policy tool and stop interventions on the currency market (ideally), but also stay passive when there is a currency crisis, until the inflation level is threatened.

Scholars make a connection between the inflation targeting regime and financialization, linking the idea of inflation targeting to rentier interests (Epstein, 2001, pp. 4–5). Inflation targeting with its focus on interest rates encourages and enables speculation. Furthermore, the disregard of exchange rates from policies disturbs the improvement of competitiveness and increases the vulnerability of short-term capital flows (Gabor, 2010, p. 821). Attracting foreign capital and providing guarantees to international investors explain the motives for introducing inflation targeting in Georgia. The shift to inflation targeting in Georgia should be analysed in the context of the double crisis (2008–2009). The government wanted to attract international investors, as foreign capital was the key to the functioning of Georgian economy. Inflation targeting could offer investors a guarantee of price stability and an independent central bank. It was also no simple coincidence that the Liberty Act was initiated in the same year (2009), as a green light for investors (see Eradze, 2022a).

When low inflation becomes the key priority for a central bank, one of the first questions that arises is to what extent the central bank can influence price stability in countries like Georgia. The Georgian National Bank identifies the following drivers for inflation: the increase of prices of key products like sugar or petrol on international markets; the oversupply of money; an external shock that might hinder production and increase prices; indirect costs like an increased value added tax (VAT); the nominal exchange rate and level of competition in certain sectors of economy (as oligopolies and monopolies might lead to increase in prices) (National Bank of Georgia, 2008a, pp. 18–20) (Figure 8.3). Georgia has a high non-core inflation rate as it relies on oil and food imports (Economic Policy Research Center, 2012, p. 21; National Bank of Georgia, 2010a, p. 20). Inflation in food prices is often more volatile, persistent, and higher than that of other goods. Therefore, developing countries attribute food prices a relatively large share of the consumption basket (for Georgia it was 30% in 2012) (Economic Policy

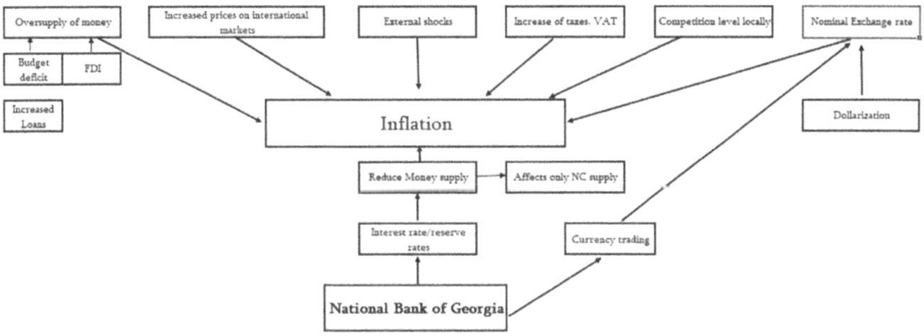

Figure 8.3 Inflation
Source: Author's illustration, based on (National Bank of Georgia, 2008a, pp. 18–23).

Research Center, 2012, pp. 31–32; National Bank of Georgia, 2010a, p. 20). Remittances also influence inflation, as money recipients acquire more purchasing power. This money is mostly spent on imported goods in Georgia, as it is spent more for consumption than for investment or savings. Furthermore, as remittance recipient families often exchange dollars to laris, they influence the increase of demand on the lari. Further sources of inflation can be fiscal deficits and external state debts. Fiscal deficits are directly linked with increased foreign debt as they are mostly financed through borrowing (Economic Policy Research Center, 2012, pp. 24–26).

Thus, if the main aim of the central bank is to control inflation, which factors of those aforementioned can it really influence? The Georgian central bank has no influence over increases of prices on international markets, exogenous shocks, or taxes. Its influence on competition in the domestic market is also limited. The NBG cannot affect remittances and FDI. Thus, the key factor that it could influence is the nominal exchange rate and this indicator has a crucial meaning for an import-dependent country like Georgia. Yet, currency stability is neither the primary aim of the Georgian central bank, nor is the exchange rate its main policy tool (see Eradze, 2022a). Moreover, the central bank of Georgia faces further issues in fighting inflation. As 80% of products in the consumer basket are imported, the NBG can address price changes or imported inflation to a limited extent only. Charaia and Papava suggest that the calculation of inflation be changed: 'according to their consumer basket made up exclusively of imported goods and services' (Charaia & Papava, 2017, p. 99). An inflation targeting regime faces more challenges in developing countries compared to developed countries as it is meant mostly to tackle demand-driven inflation (Economic Policy Research Center, 2012, p. 30).

Thus, the introduction of an inflation targeting regime in 2009 clearly prioritized price stability aims over exchange-rate stability. Yet, the plausibility and effectiveness of an inflation targeting regime for a highly dollarized and import-dependent country like Georgia is highly questionable.

Monetary policy 2009–2012: the pressure of dollarization and inflation targeting

> [W]hile capital flows can bring great benefits, they can also overwhelm countries with damaging cycles of crescendos and crashes [...]. If the flows are coming through the banking system, then macro-prudential tools make sense - such as tightening conditions for housing loans or having banks hold more capital. In other circumstances, temporary capital controls might prove useful.
>
> (Christine Lagarde 2012 cited in Independent Evaluation Office of the International Monetary Fund, 2015, p. 16)

Under inflation targeting, the exchange rate should float and the main policy tool for central banks should be interest rates. The central bank should influence exchanges rate only if their fluctuation creates issues for price stability (Epstein & Yeldan, 2008, p. 138). Empirical research shows that developing and emerging economies with inflation targeting regimes have been influencing exchange rates during fluctuations. However, a combination of inflation targeting, exchange-rate management, and a liberalized capital account is not successful and can be self-defeating (Kaltenbrunner & Painceira, 2017, p. 454). The currencies of developing countries are attractive for investors from the core in times of high liquidity, but short-term capital flows influence the exchange rate. In times of uncertainty, most investors prefer to invest in high quality and less risky assets, causing capital flight from emerging economies. Thus, the key defensive strategy for peripheral states is to accumulate FX reserves or to strengthen the national currency through export-led economic growth (Andrade & Prates, 2013, pp. 400–401). The IMF also recommends interventions in exchange rates although inflation should remain the prior aim for central banks (Kaltenbrunner & Painceira, 2017, p. 458).

It is widely acknowledged that a large majority of countries that officially claim to have a floating exchange rate do not let their currencies freely float. Mostly, such a discrepancy is caused by the volatility of households and firms to changes in the exchange rate, as they are indebted in foreign currency. Two common instruments used by central banks in the case of exchange-rate fluctuations are: the policy rate adjustment and FX interventions. It turns out that when the indebtedness of firms and households in foreign currency is high, central banks intervene more often to influence exchange-rate developments (Kliatskova & Mikkelsen, 2015, pp. 3–5). Thus, the effectiveness of the interest rate as the only policy tool for central banks in developing countries is rather questionable, especially where the rate of dollarization is high, and the volatility of the exchange rate has a direct impact on firms and households indebted in a foreign currency.[4]

The major developments on the Georgian FX market after 2009 demonstrate the general drawbacks of inflation targeting. Two main transmission channels for the Georgian central bank are: interest rate and exchange-rate channels. In the first case, the monetary policy rate can influence interest rate and the level of investments that can affect GDP growth and prices. However, different studies conducted in 2007–2008 confirm the weakness of this channel for Georgia (as well as for developing and transition countries in general). A high level of dollarization and the underdevelopment of financial and inter-bank markets, combined with their excess liquidity, create challenges for the effectiveness of the interest rate channel. The limits of the use of interest rates as a policy tool were demonstrated for example, in 2010, as NBG restricted monetary policy due to expectations of inflation. Even though lending in the national currency declined, banks switched to foreign currency lending as the central bank could not influence interest rates of foreign currency loans directly. Here, the NBG had to raise minimum reserves requirements for money resource in foreign currency (from 5% to 15%) and introduced reserves for loans issued to non-residents in foreign currency in order to tackle the issue (National Bank of Georgia, 2011b, pp. 55–56) (see Eradze, 2022a).

As for the exchange-rate channel, monetary policy can affect the level of savings in the national currency and the exchange rate that influences the level of exports and prices. In an import-dependent country like Georgia the linkage between the exchange rate and prices on imported goods is direct, as the appreciation of the national currency leads to decreasing prices of imported goods. Therefore, the exchange-rate channel is important for transition countries due to their import dependence and high levels of dollarization (Bluashvili, 2013, p. 62) (Figure 8.4). Yet, the impossible trinity of price and exchange-rate stability with free capital flows makes countries prioritize either exchange-rate stability or inflation aims (National Bank of Georgia, 2008a, p. 18). Inflation targeting regime provides a clear answer to which of the two aims Georgian central bank has to follow as a primary priority. In this way, exchange-rate stability becomes subordinated to price stability aims.

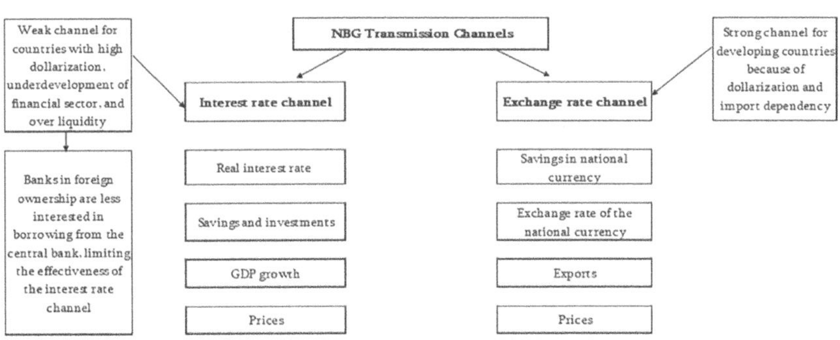

Figure 8.4 Monetary policy transmission channels of the Georgian central bank
Source: Author's illustration, based on Bluashvili (2013).

The 2009 annual report of the National Bank of Georgia revealed the first limitations of monetary policy under inflation targeting. The high level of dollarization made the interest rate channel weak for Georgia. Also, the influence of exchange rates on inflation was strong (National Bank of Georgia, 2009, p. 37). Therefore, the replacement of the exchange rate channel by the interest rate channel raises questions on its plausibility in the Georgian context. The shift to inflation targeting not only weakened the central bank institutionally, but also limited its leverage over monetary policy. Moreover, foreign ownership and easy access to foreign currency demotivated Georgian commercial banks from using the refinancing laws of the NBG; this further weakened the interest rate channel. Due to the excess liquidity of the banking sector in 2009–2010, banks were not interested in refinancing loans of the central bank in the national currency (National Bank of Georgia, 2010c, p. 65). Thus, the effectiveness of the interest rate channel was challenged by two interrelated major obstacles in Georgia: dollarization and the easy access to foreign currency by commercial banks.

In 2010, the Georgian central bank initiated several changes to make refinancing in the national currency more attractive for banks. It created a new instrument – the permanent refinancing loan, which gave banks more guarantee and trust (issued without auction). The rate of interest for permanent refinancing was defined as 1% plus the refinancing rate of the central bank. Furthermore, in 2010, the NBG set a 5% reserve requirement for money borrowed abroad (which did not exist until then) and made it more expensive for banks to borrow abroad (National Bank of Georgia, 2010c, pp. 78–79). In the same year, the NBG raised the minimum reserve requirement for foreign currency money from 5% to 15% to restrict the policy on foreign currency resources for banks. Afterwards, Georgian commercial banks participated more actively in the refinancing market (National Bank of Georgia, 2011c, pp. 45–46). Most of the money that Georgian banks attracted from abroad between 2007 and 2010 came from international financial institutions, with the rest coming from non-resident banks (National Bank of Georgia, 2010c, p. 72).

Inflation targeting weakened the Georgian central bank by replacing its role with commercial banks at the currency market (as argued in Eradze, 2022a). Due to the shift to inflation targeting, the currency market mechanism was replaced by currency auctions in Georgia, which reduced the intervention of the central bank in the currency market. In comparison with 2008, the share of the NBG in buying and selling foreign currency declined four times in 2010–2011 (National Bank of Georgia, 2011c, p. 11). Thus, commercial banks became the main actors of the currency market (Bakhtadze et al., 2012, p. 26). Before March 2009, currency trading occurred on the Tbilisi Interbank Currency Market, operated by seven commercial banks and the NBG. Later, more actors were represented on the Georgian currency market, including investment funds and legal entities or individuals. The exchange rate was mostly influenced by interbank trading in Bloomberg

(Anguridze et al., 2015, p. 13) (Figure 8.5). In the first half of 2009, the share of the NBG intervention on the market was between 75% and 85%, whereas in the second half of the year it declined to 5% to 20%. Georgian banks could trade with currencies at the Bloomberg inter-bank currency market (National Bank of Georgia, 2009, p. 47). However, in case of oversupply of foreign currency, the central bank was still the one that bought money, as the main guarantor of market liquidity (Bakhtadze et al., 2012, p. 26).

This change on the currency market was considered as a positive step by the central bank in terms of avoiding speculation (National Bank of Georgia, 2011c, p. 57) and the improvement of the inter-bank currency market (National Bank of Georgia, 2009, p. 47). Yet, after the shift towards exchange auctions, the volatility of the lari exchange rate increased (National Bank of Georgia, 2010d, p. 80). Despite the limitations of central bank interventions in the FX market, it is difficult to stay away from influencing the exchange rate for highly dollarized countries like Georgia (Figure 8.6). The dilemma is whether to sell a certain amount of reserves to avoid currency depreciation and to ease the debt burden in foreign currency or not to intervene when the national currency devaluates and hope that it will positively affect export competitiveness.

The shift to inflation targeting and the limitation of policy tools to interest rates made clear to the Georgian central bank that its power was declining. It was probably no mere coincidence, that in 2010 the larization programme was initiated by the central bank of Georgia to improve the effectiveness of monetary policy (National Bank of Georgia, 2011c, pp. 9–10). In 2010, the NBG enforced a strict monetary policy by increasing interest rates, as well as requesting reserves for loans issued to non-residents, also in foreign currency. The main aims of the National Bank were to develop domestic financial

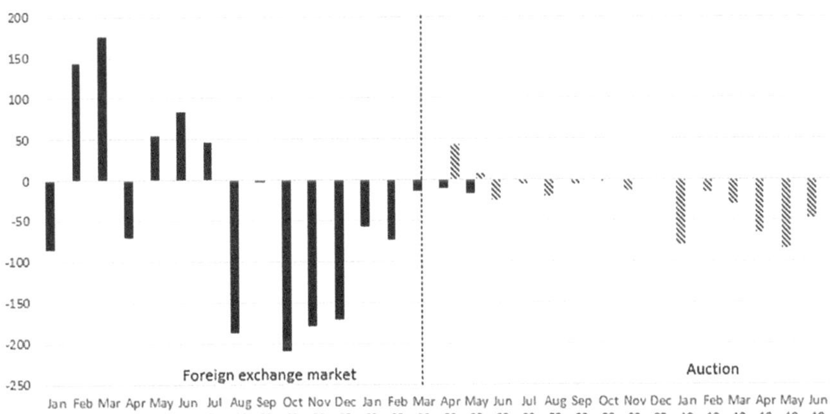

Figure 8.5 Central bank purchases at FX market, 2008–June 2010, in million lari
Source: National Bank of Georgia (2022).

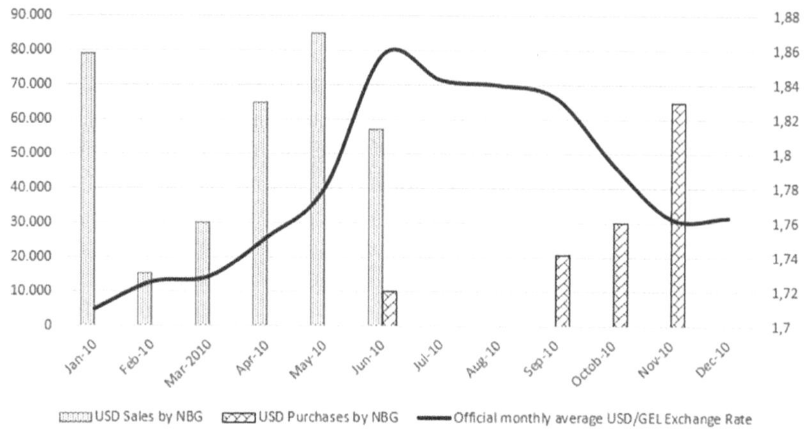

Figure 8.6 Dynamics of Trade on the NBSG's Foreign Exchange USD/GEL Auctions 2010, in thousand USD

Source: National Bank of Georgia (2022).

markets by increasing the liquidity of the money market and developing the long-term market yield curve. These measures were important for increasing the effectiveness of the monetary policy (National Bank of Georgia, 2010d, pp. 9–10).

Thus, the introduction of inflation targeting weakened the central bank's institutional power and created barriers to its monetary policy. Not only was exchange-rate stability subordinated to price stability aims, but the scope of central banking was also limited. If earlier, the National Bank was the main actor in the FX market, inflation targeting limited this role. Furthermore, the interest rate channel was weak and ineffective due to high dollarization, as it could only affect the lari market. In addition, commercial banks showed little interest in refinancing the loans of the NBG, as they had easy access to foreign capital due to the foreign ownership of banks. The policy space of the Georgian central bank was under the double pressures of dollarization and inflation targeting aims.

The original sin of dollarization

One of the key themes in central banking is the accumulation of international reserves, which should serve as self-insurance for countries in case of a crisis. Empirical data shows that countries increase their FX reserves after adopting inflation targeting, which, in fact, they should not need to do, as an inflation targeting regime assumes that central banks do not intervene in exchange-rate markets (Epstein & Yeldan, 2008, pp. 137–138). The amount of reserves is identified according to the following criteria: reserves to imports (mostly three months of imports should be covered), short-term external debt (covering all debt), and money supply (20% of the money supply). The last indicator requires the highest amount of reserves and is most often used for international capital investments (Painceira, 2009, p. 17).

Developing countries have to increase their reserves in foreign currency to be ready for fluctuations in currency exchange rates. However, the increase in reserves is accompanied by rising domestic debt if the country concerned has a current account deficit. This means that these countries are more or less forced to borrow money for keeping reserves (instead of using them for investments) in order to follow an inflation targeting regime. The US dollar is usually used as the reserve currency (Painceira, 2009, pp. 13–16). Poor countries like Georgia, usually finance international reserves through loans from international institutions. However, most of this debt is in foreign currency; 95% of Georgian foreign debt was denominated in foreign currency in 2015 (Mkhatvrishvili, 2016), that leads to the well-known issue of original sin (see Eichengreen & Hausmann, 1999). According to Eichengreen, Hausmann, and Panizza, original sin is 'the inability of a country to borrow abroad in its own currency' (Eichengreen et al., 2007, p. 122). International reserves can also be denominated in Special Drawing Rights, which is an asset created by the IMF in 1969. However, the value of these assets is also based on the basket of 'key' currencies: the US dollar, the euro, the Chinese renminbi, the Japanese yen, and the British pound sterling (International Monetary Fund, n.d.).

Thus, reserves are accumulated in the currencies of developed countries, resembling the core–periphery relations in the international monetary system, where 'the core has the exorbitant privilege of issuing the currency used as international reserves and a tendency to live beyond its means' (Eichengreen, 2004, p. 1). The periphery has to ensure export-led growth through the undervaluation of its exchange rate and to accumulate reserves in foreign currency. This kind of power relations explains how the United States could afford a strong currency alongside a constant current account deficit (Eichengreen, 2004, pp. 2–4).

Besides currency hierarchy, another kind of power asymmetry is being established in debt relations. As Georgia mostly borrows from IOs, a clear debtor–lender relation is being produced. For example, in 2008, the main sources of reserves were central bank purchases on the interbank market, money earned through privatization, and by managing international reserves (National Bank of Georgia, 2008a, p. 32). In 2009, reserves were filled through an IMF tranche and from WB and Asian Development Bank loans, as well as from privatization (National Bank of Georgia, 2009, p. 11). In 2011, the main sources of reserves were currency interventions, WB loan, EU grants, other loans, and grants of international institutions and donor states to the ministry of finance (National Bank of Georgia, 2011c, p. 11). Reserve accumulation through borrowing leads to domestic debt due to sterilization to tackle the impacts of foreign capital inflow on inflation. When central banks increase FX reserves for the sake of stabilization, the monetary base increases. As the foreign capital inflow can cause the appreciation of the exchange rate, central banks try to sterilize to avoid this effect. However, central banks usually pay more on their domestic liabilities than receiving profit from FX reserves (Helleiner, 1997, p. 7). Developing countries usually invest reserves abroad, so that this capital is not used productively. Usually, FX reserves are being invested in low-risk assets of developed countries (often these assets are US treasury securities). Considering such capital flows, despite capital inflow to developing countries, net capital inflows are often negative (Painceira, 2009, pp. 12–13). Georgia also invests reserves in state and international organization bonds or keeps them at the banks with the best ratings. For example, in 2006, most of the reserves were invested in government bonds of Germany, Belgium, France, as well as in assets issued by international banks (National Bank of Georgia, 2006e, pp. 44–46) (see Eradze, 2022a).

Thus, accumulation of reserves for Georgia has two major negative implications – first, the money for reserves is usually borrowed due to current account deficit, which means an increase in external debt; second, this debt is denominated in foreign currency that encourages the persistence of dollarization. The accumulation of reserves would not be so problematic if Georgia did not have a current account deficit.

Credit boom: living beyond one's means

The post-revolution government wanted to build a minimal state, which would not take over social responsibilities such as providing public health insurance, housing, or education. A minimal state also meant the weakening of regulations for the financial sector that had been enabling it to set the rules of the game. Thus, on the one hand, the enhanced need for financing the social and economic needs of the population as well as the increased income of certain parts of the population met a loosely regulated financial sector, which had easy access to foreign money and was keen on issuing credits. As a result, a credit boom took off in 2005, where household indebtedness, in particular, was increasing. In 2006, the share of retail loans was 29% of total loans (National Bank of Georgia, 2006e, p. 66). The key to this story was the high rate of home ownership in Georgia (over 90%). Housing was used as a safe collateral for retail loans, which later led to the homelessness of thousands of insolvent borrowers.

Household credit: democratizing finance or creating social insecurity?[5]

Increasing household debt has been becoming prominent throughout the world, including in the CEE countries since the early 2000s (Backé & Zumer, 2005, p. 94; Beck & Brown, 2015, pp. 467–468; Duenwald et al., 2005, p. 3; Enoch, 2007, pp. 3–7; Sõrg & Tuusis, 2009, p. 4). From 2001 to 2006, household debt growth rate in new European Union (EU) member countries was 40% compared to 11% rate of older EU countries. Most of the debt comprised mortgages (Beck et al., 2010, p. 2). The existence of foreign banks in Central and Eastern Europe has been related to increased household debt, especially in foreign currency (Mihaljek, 2007, pp. 277–279). As banks were privatized and the financial system reformed, trust also increased in this sector (Backé & Zumer, 2005, p. 95; Duenwald et al., 2005, p. 12). For example, while in Bulgaria the stability of exchange rate was guaranteed by the currency board and the high interest rates on local currency loans encouraged foreign currency lending, in Ukraine the pegged exchange rate had triggered an increase in foreign currency loans to households (Backé & Zumer, 2005, p. 94; Duenwald et al., 2005, p. 14) (see Eradze, 2022b).

Credit expansion has been pursued as a natural outcome of economic growth, the development of the financial sphere, and an increase of income (see Detragiache et al., 2006; Duenwald et al., 2005; Kiss et al., 2006; Sõrg & Tuusis, 2009). Furthermore, access of households to credit has been framed as the democratization of finance (Erturk et al., 2007), or financial deepening (Beck et al., 2010, p. 3). Yet Ronas-Tas (2009) and Comparato (2015) focus on systemic reasons for increasing household borrowing such as the retreat of the state from the social sphere. Although credit growth has been linked with economic growth and macroeconomic stability; questions arise about the sustainability of these developments in CEE (Backé et al., 2006, p. 112). Scholars have been concerned about loan procedures. Questions gave arisen about the provision of full information to customers about interest rates, exchange-rate fluctuations, or the meaning of collateral (Enoch, 2007, p. 9). Moreover, foreign-owned banks are characterized by aggressive marketing strategies for consumer loans that have widened household indebtedness (Mihaljek, 2007, pp. 277–279).

A credit boom in a society with inadequate financial education and experience is related to risk, especially when the financial sector is under-regulated and commercial banks set rules on the market. Dating back to the 1920s in the USA, consumer credits are now spread all over the world. The development of consumer loans, especially after World War II, is related to the emergence of consumer finance and a change in banking activities (Ronas-Tas, 2009, p. 154). Consumer theory is much older, taking roots in the Marginalist school of thought in the nineteenth century, perceiving humans as utility maximizers (Santos et al., 2014, pp. 57–58). Since the 1950s, consumption credit has increased significantly, but also 'raised the issue of household solvability and implied the dynamic stabilization of household incomes' (Sapir, 2013). There was no real experience of consumer credit in communist countries. Lending usually occurred via state saving banks and the rarely available credits were accessible to employers for their employees. In this way employers guaranteed that the loan would be repaid through monthly payments. In addition, people tried to avoid going into debt or spending more than what they had earned. Therefore, the public did not have experience with retail banking and a culture of consumption credit was also absent as the new banking system emerged. The first commercial banks had no information about the credit histories of citizens after the collapse of communism. Besides, banks could not expect the state to help them to collect bad credits, neither could they rely on the court system. Thus, banks used social ties and connections to identify 'good' borrowers and started lending money to elites. Later, some banks decided to expand the pool of customers through collateralized lending (Rona-Tas & Guseva, 2014, pp. 91–94). Advertising played an important role in the spread of consumption through loans (Santos et al., 2014, pp. 70–71).

The major issue with foreign currency loans in the region is unhedged borrowing. For example, in 2010, over 80% of private sector loans in Belarus, Latvia, and Serbia were in foreign currency. Bulgaria, Hungary, and Romania demonstrated a similar trend (Brown & De Haas, 2012, p. 59). Furthermore, credit expansion can lead to macroeconomic and financial instabilities (Duenwald et al., 2005, p. 17), as it might cause the rise of prices and wages and negatively influence the international competitiveness of exports in the case of a stable nominal exchange rate. Thus, credit expansion can damage the balance of trade (as in Romania and Bulgaria) (Duenwald et al., 2005, p. 20). A credit boom creates risks in terms of increasing aggregate demand, where the borrowed money is often used for consuming imported goods which, in turn, negatively influences the current account (Barisitz, 2005, pp. 79–80).

Though borrowing in foreign currency has proved to be a common trend among households of the CEE countries, the awareness of exchange-rate risk has been rather low, which has led to herd behaviour and increased risks for the economy (Barrel et al., 2009, p. 12). Institutions like the IMF have warned about exchange-rate risks in relation with foreign currency borrowing. Several countries have reacted to this danger through regulations (Rosenberg & Tirpák, 2008, p. 3). For example, Hungarian, Latvian, and Polish banks were forced to fully inform the customers about exchange-rate risks related to foreign currency loans. Croatia, Kazakhstan, and Romania made it more difficult to borrow in a foreign rather than local currency, whereas in Ukraine it was forbidden in 2008 to issue mortgages in foreign currency to households (Brown & De Haas, 2012, p. 60). Some other measures related to foreign currency loans include: interest rate caps, the conversion of foreign currency loans into national currency, and the buying of debt by the state (Józon, 2015, p. 94). Yet, macroprudential regulations are not sufficient to tackle the rising levels of household debt, as this is mostly caused by the retreat of neoliberal states from social provision (see Eradze, 2022b).

A credit boom in a neoliberal state

Credit expansion started after the Rose Revolution in Georgia as a result of state deregulation policies and the increase of demand for loans. Before 2003, only small banks provided short term (<1 year) loans for individuals that had to be fully collateralized. These were not consumer loans but rather small business loans, mostly for retail or building a house. Loans to individuals made up 45% of the loan portfolio; 70% loan issuers were small banks, as bigger banks showed less interest in retail lending instead specializing in financing corporate borrowers (Amaghlobeli et al., 2003, p. 53).

The expansion of credit to the private sector started in 2005 (Figure 8.7 and Figure 8.8). In comparison with 2004, the volume of loans to the private sector increased by 83% in 2005, reaching 15% of GDP (it was 10% GDP in 2004). In particular, retail loans and credits to construction business increased. The 2006 report of the IMF highlighted the first signs of credit boom in Georgia (International Monetary Fund, 2006, p. 9). These trends continued in 2006–2007 as well (National Bank of Georgia, 2006c, pp. 31–32, 2007c, p. 11). During the credit boom, short-term loans, especially, were on the rise, interest rates were decreasing, and de-dollarization was taking place (the de-dollarization trend was soon reversed though). In 2004 only 15% of loans were in national currency, but in 2005, their share reached 25% (International Monetary Fund, 2006, pp. 10–11). With credit expansion, the share of long-term credits was also increasing. In 2006, almost 70% bank loans were long term (National Bank of Georgia, 2006e, p. 63). Yet, long-term loans (longer than ten years) were related to higher exchange-rate risks, as they were mostly denominated in foreign currency (National Bank of Georgia, 2007c, pp. 12–13), and higher persistence of dollarization (see for data in 2004 and 2005, National Bank of Georgia, 2006d, pp. 10–11).

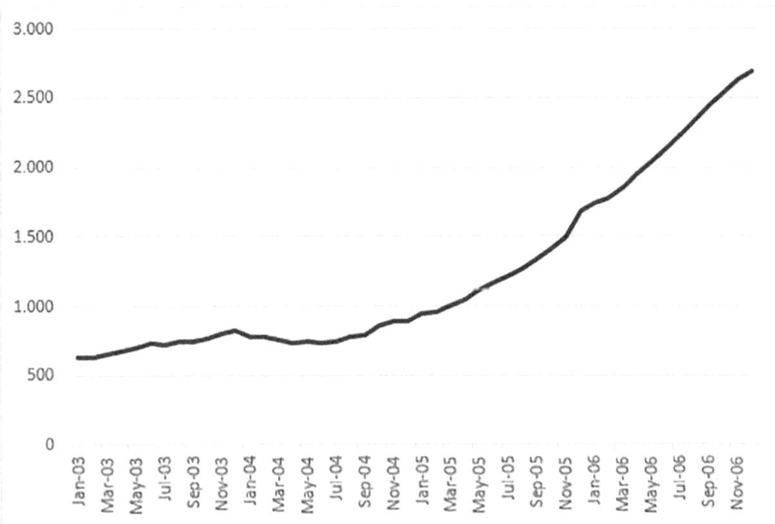

Figure 8.7 Volume of Loans (MLN GEL), 2003–2006
Source: National Bank of Georgia (2022).

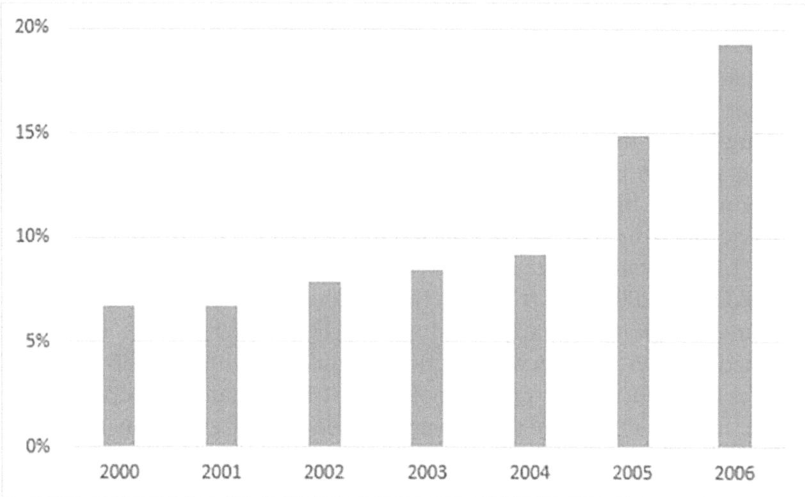

Figure 8.8 Loan to GDP ratio, 2000–2006
Source: National Bank of Georgia (2022).

A remarkable trend of the credit boom was increased lending to households in comparison with judicial entities. For example, in the second half of 2007, loans to individuals increased by almost 80%, whereas credit to legal entities increased by 53% (National Bank of Georgia, 2007c, pp. 12–13). Thus, households were turning into the spotlight of banks. Mostly consumer loans and mortgages experienced growth. Long-term consumer loans increased by almost 97% in 2006 in comparison with the previous year (National Bank of Georgia, 2006e, p. 64). In Georgia, consumer loans were on the rise during the credit boom with a high share of foreign currency lending: In 2005, the volume of consumer loans increased two-fold (National Bank of Georgia, 2006c, p. 14) and kept increasing at the highest rate, after the double crisis of 2008–2009. In 2006 consumer loans made up more than 29% of total loans (National Bank of Georgia, 2006a, p. 57). In 2011, consumer loans were the fastest growing loans with a growth rate of 120% (National Bank of Georgia, 2011a, p. 31).

The credit boom occurred in six major banks. Commercial banks cited the increased level of deposits, the creation of a credit information bureau, and the emergence of demand for loans to finance investment or consumption as the main drivers for the boom (International Monetary Fund, 2006, p. 12). Furthermore, the removal of limitations on bank ownership shares in 2006 increased the rate of foreign ownership and the access of banks to foreign money. The IMF named political and macroeconomic instabilities as the major reasons for the delays in the development of the Georgian financial system before the Rose Revolution. As the demand for money had been very low, money supply and the level of monetization had reduced as well, which negatively influenced the balance sheets of commercial banks. Furthermore, a large amount of money was kept outside banks. Therefore, the legalization of economy, the reform of the tax system, and increases of income triggered credit expansion after the revolution (International Monetary Fund, 2006, pp. 14–15).

The main source of money for banks was deposits in foreign and national currencies (International Monetary Fund, 2006, pp. 10–11). Yet, the volume of loans exceeded deposits, as banks had borrowed money abroad. The inflow of foreign capital was rather high, creating a risk of fast outflow of capital (National Bank of Georgia, 2006c, p. 35). The 2007 financial stability report of the NBG explains credit expansion by an increase of foreign capital in the banking sector. Banks issued loans in foreign currency despite the demand for national currency credits (National Bank of Georgia, 2007c, p. 11) because they had access to foreign money. In 2010, the borrowed (abroad) money by banks made up 7% of GDP; 77% of money was borrowed from international financial institutions and 13% from parent companies (National Bank of Georgia, 2010c, p. 76).

Foreign currency loans were increasing faster than those in the national currency. According to the National Bank of Georgia, such a trend was caused by the oversupply of banks in foreign currency. These developments had a direct influence on dollarization. Though loan dollarization was decreasing till the end of 2006, in 2007 the trend was reversed, and it reached 72.7% by the end of the year (National Bank of Georgia, 2007c, p. 14). Furthermore, deposit dollarization was significantly lower than loan dollarization at this point due to the access of Georgian banks to foreign currency (National Bank of Georgia, 2007c, p. 16). Interest rate differentials also played a significant role in foreign currency lending, as borrowing in foreign currency was cheaper (Figure 8.9). This trend continued after the 2008–2009 crisis as well. The spread between the interest rates on loans in foreign and national currency was especially high from 2007 to 2010 (Anguridze et al., 2015, p. 33), encouraging borrowing in foreign currency.

According to the IMF, credit expansion in Georgia was caused by increased confidence in the financial system and improved governance, as well as a better chances of doing business and an increase in demand for consumer goods and real estate (International Monetary Fund, 2006, pp. 10–11). However, this is not the complete story. The credit boom in Georgia was directly linked to the neoliberal state. The turning away of the government from social responsibilities and its radical deregulation policies triggered higher demand for credit and enabled money supply for banks in foreign ownership. Moreover, the credit boom was embedded in the FDI-led accumulation regime, which provided economic growth, but did not create jobs and did not reduce income inequalities or poverty. Thus, there was a gap between the average income of the population and their needs or desires, which also existed before the revolution. Yet, the post-Rose Revolution

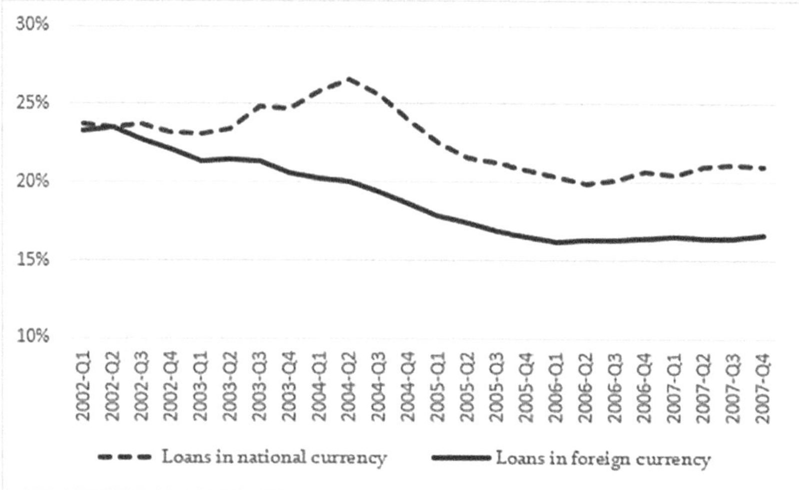

Figure 8.9 Interest rates for loans in national and foreign currencies, 2002–2007
Source: National Bank of Georgia (2022).

accumulation regime and neoliberal state opened doors to foreign capital and the possibility of meeting these needs by credit appeared for households. The deregulation of finance further accelerated mass lending policies, but also shifted the power towards creditors and created risks for borrowers.

Changes in law and the abolition of certain regulations, such as seizing collateral, made it easier for banks to issue loans (International Monetary Fund, 2006, p. 14). Furthermore, a debtors' register was created. The abolition of personal insolvency law made it easier for banks to reclaim the loans (Economic Policy Research Center, 2014, p. 6). Fines on delayed loan payments were not regulated by law either, even for force-majeure situations (Economic Policy Research Center, 2014, p. 20). In 2007, the interest rate ceiling for loans was abolished (Charaia, 2018) and commercial banks could change interest rates on loans without advance notification (Participant 6, personal communication, 30 May 2017). Furthermore, there was no general guideline about income–interest rate ratio for borrowers, as each bank could decide how conservative they would be in issuing loans (Participant 4, personal communication, 3 May 2017). In 2008, a special agency was created to ensure the takeover procedure of collaterals; the police were also involved in this process (Nikolaishvili, 2017). In the same year, Georgian banks started to set up separate firms for selling non-performing loans (National Bank of Georgia, 2010d, p. 73).

The deregulation of banking practices created favourable conditions for financial institutions to issue loans, encouraged a credit boom, and created risks for borrowers, as well as for the whole financial system. In addition, the central bank of Georgia was not regulating all financial institutions (for example, online lending platforms) and, even if it had restricted regulations, it could not guarantee the stability of the financial system. A common explanation for the limited regulatory power of the central bank among policymakers during has been that the national bank was concerned only with institutions that took deposits to protect depositors' rights. There was a belief that interest rates on loans could not be the object of regulation because they should be set by market competition (Participant 4, personal communication, 3 May 2017; Participant 5, personal communication, 29 May 2017; Participant 21, personal communication, 13 April 2016). However, it is puzzling to imagine a central bank as a protector of depositors' rights only, disregarding other consumers who take loans from online platforms or microfinance organizations, for example. Even though the central bank of Georgia was aware of risks of increased lending to households, it did not undertake any measures to avoid the accumulation of these risks. The 2006–2009 financial system development strategy of the NBG discussed the development of a fair consumption credit system (National Bank of Georgia, 2006d, p. 37). In the 2007 annual report, the NBG was warning about the impacts of the credit boom, as there was a risk of delivering improper information to borrowers. In addition, the underdevelopment of credit bureaux and the absence of relevant legal framework created obstacles for collecting and providing proper information about creditors (National Bank of Georgia, 2007c, p. 13). The IMF also called for an improvement in creditor rights, court procedures, and information access for the development of a sustainable financial system in 2006. The Fund warned that the rapid credit expansion could have caused financial instabilities, as had occurred in CEE countries (International Monetary Fund, 2006, pp. 16–17). However, the Georgian central bank did not react to the credit boom in time. Until 2011, there was not even a department for consumer rights at the National Bank.

Thus, the credit boom in Georgia was characterized by increased lending to households, especially in foreign currency. It was mostly financed by the money that Georgian banks had borrowed abroad. Although the first years of the credit boom encouraged de-dollarization, from 2007, the trend was reversed. During this period, the dollarization rate of loans remained higher than that of deposits. Bfore the revolution dollarization mostly had been driven by deposits in foreign currency, but after 2003 the opposite was the case. The credit boom was accompanied by high inflation, leading to the reduction of real interest rates. As the value of the lari was increasing due to foreign capital inflow, foreign currency loans were rather more accessible than national currency loans (National Bank of Georgia, 2010c, p. 49). Furthermore, increasing consumption credits had a negative impact on the current account of the country. A significant part of household loans was used for financing imported consumer goods which widened the current account deficit. The consumption saving ratio in 2004–2005 was respectively on average 87%–6% and 89.6%–3.6% (National Bank of Georgia, 2006c, p. 11).

The credit boom continued until the crisis of 2008. Problem loans started to increase in 2008 and the share of negative portfolio[6] reached 40% in 2009 (National Bank of Georgia, 2010a, p. 63). Yet, banks revived lending in 2010 due to excess liquidity (National Bank of Georgia, 2010c, pp. 62–64). The competition was so high among banks that interest rates on loans started to decline (National Bank of Georgia, 2011b, p. 46). This enabled banks to increase their loan portfolios again after the crisis (National Bank of Georgia, 2010d, p. 69). In 2011, loans increased by 29.4% in comparison with 2010; the volume of loans even exceeded the level prior to the crisis (National Bank of Georgia, 2011c, pp. 69–70). Loan dollarization reached 72%, while deposit dollarization was 65% in 2011 (National Bank of Georgia, 2011b, p. 49). Retail loans still presented a significant share of total loans (31%) in 2010 (National Bank of Georgia, 2010d, p. 61); consumer loans and mortgages were increasing at fast rates along with the energy and construction sectors (National Bank of Georgia, 2010a, p. 60).

The first signs of over-indebtedness were visible soon after the 2008 crisis. After 2010, the amount of sold collateral (real estate) grew and housing accounted for 25% of this collateral (National Bank of Georgia, 2010d, p. 72). Various studies and surveys demonstrate that most people were facing financial problems and were trying to cope with them by taking loans. According to a 2010 United Nations Children's Fund (UNICEF) study, two-thirds of the surveyed households named the repayment of loans as one of the causes of economic hardship (UNICEF, 2010, p. 5). A 2011 saving behaviour survey[7] showed that only 14% of the surveyed population managed to save money on a monthly basis, while 66% spent money almost immediately, and 34% confirmed that they could afford major purchases only through credit (ACT Research, 2011, p. 6); 70% of total surveyed people named low income as the main obstacle to saving (ACT Research, 2011, p. 8). Only 38% saved their money in a bank, while 47% chose another place for it (ACT Research, 2011, p. 26). Also, for 69% of the surveyed population, currency stability was more important than the interest on savings (ACT Research, 2011, p. 35). 82% of the surveyed population belonged to low income families, 17% to middle income and only 1% to the high income group (ACT Research, 2011, p. 55). The 2013 UNICEF welfare research showed that 44% households had borrowed money. Many of them had a loan from more than one source. More than 70% of these households borrowed money from banks and pawn shops, almost 17% from friends and family, and the same amount from shops and pharmacies. The number of people who borrowed from friends and family had decreased since 2009 and the number of those taking bank and pawn shop loans had increased (UNICEF, 2013, p. 149). The issues connected with the loan repayment continued and intensified. In 2014 35% of customers were poor and had financial issues. They faced difficulties repaying the loans that they had taken for everyday needs, education, food, etc. (*Caucasus Business Week*, 2014). In January 2014, there were 107,805 people in the debtors' register, who could not repay their loans and against whom the ministry of justice had started legal procedures (Economic Policy Research Center, 2014, p. 14).

Thus, the credit boom started in Georgia in 2005 due to major improvements in the political and macroeconomic situation, which, however, did not improve the socio-economic situation of the population and thereby created the need for loans. Collateralized lending enabled the shift of focus towards households. Changes in legislation in favour of financial institutions further encouraged the process. Increased foreign ownership of banks provided money in foreign currency to Georgian banks, encouraged foreign currency lending, and shifted exchange-rate risks towards borrowers. Yet not only the level of dollarization increased throughout the credit boom, but also the questions of solvency of many households arose.

Mortgages: housing as a safe collateral and attractive investment

Mortgages constituted a significant share of retail loans, which were characterized by a high rate of dollarization and that resembles the housing policy of a neoliberal state. A high level of home ownership turned into one of the drivers of the credit boom in Georgia, as housing was often used as a collateral for different kinds of loans. The housing ownership rate of 93% in Georgia is higher than EU average of 70% (Colliers International, 2015, p. 6). Thus, not only did mortgages increase, but the share of loans collateralized by the real estate also rose in 2006–2013 (20% in 2013) (Economic Policy Research Center, 2014, p. 11). Long-term loans, in particular, were collateralized by real estate; the rate of dollarization was also higher in such loans (National Bank of Georgia, 2011a, p. 35). The increased usage of housing as a collateral is significant in two respects – it influences consumption and makes home prices an important channel for monetary transmission (Cardelli et al., 2008, p. 2). Thus, if before the Rose Revolution Georgian banks did not have much knowledge about collateral-based lending (International Monetary Fund, 2001, p. 64), this changed after the Revolution. Legal reforms played a significant role here in terms of creating guarantees for creditors to seize collateral in the case of inability of borrowers to repay their loans. A 2009 change in the civil codex stated that a debtor would remain indebted in case of default, if the collateral was insufficient to cover the debt (Economic Policy Research Center, 2014, p. 6). Moreover, forceful evictions of indebted borrowers from their homes became possible with the help of the police (Qashakashvili & Janiashvili, 2018, p. 82).[8]

Post-revolution developments in the real-estate market influenced the level of dollarization in two ways: first, as price of real estate (for sale or for rent) was set in dollars, this had a significant influence on price dollarization; second, prices in dollars and better access to long-term loans in foreign currency triggered demand for mortgages in foreign currency. As real estate prices increased dramatically after the revolution, households needed more money to buy property and the volume of mortgages also increased.

Moreover, housing turned into a profitable means of investment in Georgia. Thus, the housing boom was not only caused by the demand for housing for living, but also for investment purposes (Participant 8, personal communication 7 June 2017).

An increase in mortgages has been a common trend in CEE countries as well (Mihaljek, 2007, p. 276). These countries have witnessed credit bubbles partially due to mortgage booms, triggered not only by the cultural aspects of home ownership, but also by easy access to loans and special state subsidies for housing credit (Andresan-Grigoriu & Moraru, 2015, pp. 121–122). Furthermore, such booms were accompanied with increases in housing prices that also led to an increase in mortgages (Backé & Zumer, 2005, p. 96). Until the 1980s, mortgage markets were under strict regulation in developed countries; after that deregulation took place in terms of lifting of lending and deposit rate ceilings and of credit controls (Cardelli et al., 2008, p. 2).

Georgia also experienced dramatic price increases in real estate. In 2006, prices for residential estate increased by 34% and in 2007 by 28% (National Bank of Georgia, 2007c, p. 17). A peak in prices in residential (four times more expensive in comparison with 2005) and commercial real estate was reached in 2008, but this then started to decrease due to the crisis (National Bank of Georgia, 2010c, p. 14). Furthermore, the average household size was changing in Georgia; on average the number of people living in one household decreased by 11% between 2005 and 2015 (Colliers International, 2015, p. 6). Demand for housing also increased due to the purchases of Georgian diaspora (Salukvadze, 2016, p. 8).

Alongside the price boom the share of mortgages in all credit also increased, reaching 19% in July 2007. Furthermore, the level of dollarization among mortgages was very high. In 2007, 84% of mortgages were issued in dollars (National Bank of Georgia, 2007c, p. 17). By 2010, the share of real estate loans (not only mortgages, but also loans providing for the development and management of real estate, or for producing and trading construction materials) was more than 31% of total loans (National Bank of Georgia, 2010c, p. 15). Buying real estate became popular as a means of investment, as profits earned through rents were greater than returns on deposits (10–14% annual return in 2014) and were also higher than mortgage interest rates (Biermann & Devdariani, 2015).

The housing boom, which led to the increase in mortgages and supported the process of dollarization, is directly connected with state politics, the deregulation of the construction sector, and the focus on FDI. After the break-up of the Soviet Union, mass privatization of real estate started, as earlier public and cooperative housing had been under the Soviet state. Later, at the end of the 1990s, the privatization of urban land also started. 'A poorly regulated land market was locally described as a 'wild market', emphasizing its violence-based nature' (Salukvadze & Golubchikov, 2016, p. 46). Housing privatization meant giving housing under private ownership to tenants, which encouraged high home ownership rate (of more than 85%)

(Salukvadze, 2016, p. 8). However, the construction of mass housing ceased in the 1990s, whereas 'do it yourself' home extension became widespread. Households were allowed to add balconies, verandas, loggias, etc., to their apartments. This process was completely unregulated, causing violations of security and aesthetics. From the early 2000s, demand for housing started to grow due to the improved macroeconomic situation and the growth of FDI and remittances from Russia. The legal system also became more efficient in terms of housing regulations and registration, and a credit market started to develop to encourage banks for participation. However, Tbilisi had basically no new planning and no one cared about old Soviet rules. The new urban planning was liberal and flexible, and this was further strengthened under the presidency of Saakashvili (Salukvadze & Golubchikov, 2016, pp. 46–47). Saakashvili was keen on supporting post-modern buildings 'as a quick fix in achieving a modernized and globalized image for the capital and, by implication, in linking the whole nation to "European civilization"' (Salukvadze & Golubchikov, 2016, pp. 48–49). This process in the post-revolution period is referred by developers to as 'investor-urbanism'. Despite a new land use cadastral plan of 2009, the city government continued to satisfy the will of investors (Salukvadze, 2016, p. 8). After the revolution, deregulation took place in the construction sector, which encouraged the real estate boom (Zazanashvili & Nikolaishvili, 2017). In 2005, the ministry of urbanization and construction was abolished. A bureaucratic process of acquiring building permission for companies became easier. Banks became actively involved in the process of real estate development and construction, buying bankrupt companies, or establishing new companies. A well-known example is the construction company m^2 which came under the ownership of one the biggest banks – the Bank of Georgia (Nikolaishvili, 2017).

The housing boom in 2007–2008 reached almost the same volume of newly built houses, as in the 1960s–1970s. Yet, the newly built houses were not accessible to the majority of society, with luxury apartments making up 40–50% of all constructions (Salukvadze & Golubchikov, 2016, pp. 46–47). According to the housing affordability index of the ISET institute, it remains unaffordable to buy a flat (Participant 8, personal communication, 7 June 2017). Even the top 20% households in terms of average income reported that they needed most of their money for basic needs, leaving little financial possibility of repaying mortgages (Salukvadze, 2016, p. 10).

Real-estate developers were hit most by the crisis in 2008–2009 and the level of non-performing loans increased especially for construction companies, reaching 54% in 2009. However, mortgages were considered as the least risky in terms of loan performance (National Bank of Georgia, 2011b, pp. 21–22). Tbilisi municipality responded by urging construction companies to buy finished projects at cost recovery price (USD 400 pro m^2) and thereby avoid a crisis (Salukvadze & Golubchikov, 2016, pp. 46–47). Despite a major decline in capital inflows, after the crisis, real estate attracted FDI. The share of real estate in total FDI reached 25% in 2011, while before the crisis it was only 1.5%. If construction and additional services are also considered, then the share increases to 60% of total FDI in 2011 (International Monetary Fund, 2011, p. 12). The share of real estate loans also increased after the crisis and reached 30% of total bank loans in 2010. Mortgages made up almost half of these loans (National Bank of Georgia, 2011a, p. 20). The trend of increasing housing prices continued after the crisis and within 2013 and 2014, the average price for residential properties rose by 11% (Biermann & Devdariani, 2015).

Thus, the housing boom was encouraged on the one hand by the availability of mortgages and, on the other hand, by the construction boom. Yet, the increased demand for housing was caused by a neoliberal state which did not assume social responsibility for providing affordable housing. Moreover, the price boom on the real estate market and the deregulation of the construction sector – the government withdrawing from involvement leaving all responsibility to the good will of investors and developers – made it impossible to buy housing without a credit. These developments had a direct influence on price dollarization and loan dollarization; real estate prices were set in dollars and banks preferred to provide long-term loans such as mortgages in foreign currency.

Conclusion

The financial sector became a key focus of post-Rose revolution reforms in Georgia and its development became the key priority for Saakashvili's government. The deregulation of the financial market opened the way for foreign capital to enter the country. Foreign capital domination soon became visible in the banking sector, as most of the Georgian commercial banks were owned majorly by foreign shareholders. Thus, commercial banks turned into the most powerful actors at the market and foreign capital became the driver of the process of peripheral financialization in Georgia.

The deregulation of banking activities, the development of the legal system, and the improvement of collateral lending practices encouraged commercial banks to choose big corporations and households as their main focus group. Yet, only a few sectors of the economy profited from bank loans such as trade, infrastructure, and energy. Furthermore, SMEs and start-ups barely gained any access to bank credit. Thus, commercial banks were not contributing to the development of real economy through their loan policies; in the absence of development banks, the impact of such policies was crucial for the Georgian economy. These policies indirectly encouraged the persistence of dollarization as the Georgian economy remained dependent on imports and vulnerable to exchange-rate fluctuations.

A further channel of lending policies that aided dollarization was based on foreign currency lending. Easy access to foreign money encouraged the Georgian banks to get engaged with trade activities, issuing foreign currency loans, where the exchange-rate risk was mostly borne by the borrowers (especially in retail lending). Thus, a high level of dollarization persisted in Georgia, especially for long-term loans. Foreign capital was considered the major source of the credit boom in Georgia that started in 2005. During the credit boom, household debt (consumer loans and mortgages), especially, was rising. This development not only led to household over-indebtedness later, but also supported the persistence of dollarization. Consumer loans were mostly used for financing imports that further worsened the trade balance. While mortgages played an important role in the increase in demand for long-term loans in foreign currency, it also encouraged price dollarization on the real estate market.

These developments in the financial sector remained unaddressed by the central bank of Georgia. The financialization of monetary policy weakened the institution. Especially after the shift to inflation targeting in 2009, the NBG was constantly facing dilemmas of dollarization and price stability aims. Exchange-rate stability was not the top priority of the NBG; in currency markets, commercial banks became the main actors. Yet, in 2010, it became clear that targeting inflation through the interest rate channel was ineffective for Georgia. On the one hand, the central bank could influence only the lari market directly; on the other hand, commercial banks were not interested in refinancing loans of the central bank due to excess liquidity in foreign currency. Though a de-dollarization strategy was adopted in 2010, monetary policy remained under multiple constraints and dilemmas of exchange-rate stability, inflation targets, and current account deficit. Monetary policy in Georgia has been on a tumultuous path struggling against the competing interests of international capital, commercial banks, the Georgian government, and IOs. Yet, dollarization has remained uncontested and persisted at high levels.

Thus, financialization strengthened the role of dollar in the Georgian economy and encouraged the persistence of dollarization. Mass lending to households, also in foreign currency, contributed to high levels of loan dollarization while the financialization of monetary policy through the shift to inflation targeting weakened the Georgian central bank institutionally and subordinated exchange rate stability to the aims of price stability. These developments were embedded in the neoliberal state that emerged after the Rose Revolution. The FDI-led accumulation regime and the ambition of the Georgian government to create a financial hub in Georgia led to the subordination of currency stability aims to price stability, free capital flows, and the free usage of foreign currencies. Thus, foreign currency domination remained uncontested and was even further encouraged by these processes. The Georgian state was the main conductor, as well as a vessel of these relations.

Notes

1 Carry trade refers to borrowing money in hard currency at a low interest rate and issuing loans in foreign currency at higher interest rates, without bearing exchange rate risks.

2 For the Georgian case, foreign ownership of banks refers to more than 50% of shares in the hands of foreign investors and institutions.
3 The main claims of this chapter are based on a journal article by the author, 'Financialization of Monetary Policy in a Dollarized Economy: the case of Georgia', which has been published, https://doi.org/10.1093/cje/beac019 at the *Cambridge Journal of Economics.*
4 For example, a 2011 IMF working paper acknowledges the weakness of the interest rate channel for Peru and Uruguay (dollarized countries under inflation targeting regimes), whereas the exchange rate channel appears to be more effective in terms of influencing inflation (Acosta-Ormaechea & Coble, 2011, p. 4).
5 This section is based on a book chapter 'Taming Dollarization Hysteresis: Evidence from Post-socialist Countries', which has been accepted for publication in an edited book.
6 Negative portfolio included non-performing loans, watch loans, negative investments, net write-offs, and repossessed property.
7 The survey was conducted in Tbilisi (100 respondents), other cities (100 respondents) and villages (300 respondents), based on face-to-face interviews.
8 Police led evictions were outlawed in 2016.

References

Acosta-Ormaechea, S., & Coble, D. (2011). Monetary Transmission in Dollarized and Non-Dollarized Economies: The Cases of Chile, New Zealand, Peru and Uruguay (11/87; IMF Working Paper).

ACT Research. (2011). Saving Behavior Assessment Survey in Georgia. Saving Banks Foundation for International Cooperation.

Amaghlobeli, D., Farrell, J., & Nielsen, J. (2003). The evolution of commercial banking in Georgia, 1991–2001. *Post-Communist Economies*, 15(1), 47–74.

Andrade, R. P., & Prates, D. M. (2013). Exchange rate dynamics in a peripheral monetary economy. *Journal of Post Keynesian Economics*, 35(3), 399–416.

Andresan-Grigoriu, B., & Moraru, M. (2015). Country Report Romania. In H.-W. Micklitz & I. Domurath (Eds.), *Consumer Debt and Social Exclusion in Europe* (pp. 117–137). Ashgate Publishing Limited.

Anguridze, O., Charaia, V., & Doghonadze, I. (2015). *Security Problems and Modern Challenges of the Georgian National Currency.* Ivane Javakhishvili Tbilisi State University TSU Center for Analysis and Forecast, Tbilisi.

Backé, P., Égert, B., & Zumer, T. (2006). Credit Growth in Central and Eastern Europe: New (Over)Shooting Stars? *OeNB Focus on European Economic Integration*, 1(06), 112–139.

Backé, P., & Zumer, T. (2005). Developments in Credit to the Private Sector in Central and Eastern European EU Member States: Emerging from Financial Repression—A Comparative Overview. *OeNB Focus on European Economic Integration*, 2(05), 83–109.

Baiashvili, T. (2015). opt'imaluri savalut'o polit'ik'a sakartvelos ek'onomik'isatvis [Optimal Currency Policy for Georgian Economy]. *Ek'onomik'a Da Sabank'o Sakme*, 42–61.

Bakhtadze, L., Barbakadze, K., & Khandashvili, T. (2012). *Pinansuri inst'it'ut'ebi da bazrebi* [Financial Institutions and Markets]. Ivane Javakhishvili State University, Faculty of Economics and Business.

Balls, E., Howat, J., & Stansbury, A. (2018). Central Bank Independence Revisited: After the financial crisis, what should a model central bank look like? (No. 87; Harvard Kennedy School M-RCBG Associate Working Paper Series).

Barisitz, S. (2005). Banking in Central and Eastern Europe since the Turn of the Millennium – An Overview of Structural Modernization in Ten Countries. *OeNB Focus on European Economic Integration*, 2(05), 58–82.

Barrel, R., Davis, P. E., Fic, T., & Orazgani, A. (2009). Household Debt and Foreign Currency Borrowing in New Member States of the EU (No. 23; Economic and Finance Working Paper).

Beck, T., & Brown, M. (2015). Foreign Bank Ownership and Household Credit. *Journal of Financial Intermediation*, 24(4), 466–486.

Beck, T., Kibuuka, K., & Tiongson, E. (2010). Mortgage Finance in Central and Eastern Europe: Opportunity or Burden? (No. 5202; World Bank Policy Research Working Papers).

Beckmann, E., Roitner, A., & Stix, H. (2015). A Local or a Foreign Currency Loan? Evidence on the Role of Loan Characteristics, Preferences of Households and the Effect of Foreign Banks. *OeNB Focus on European Economic Integration*, 1(15), 24–48.

Biermann, F., & Devdariani, S. (2015). Real Estate Prices in Tbilisi: No Bubble, No Trouble. ISET.ge. https://iset-pi.ge/en/blog/392-real-estate-prices-in-tbilisi-no-bubble-no-trouble.

Bluashvili, A. (2013). monet'aruli polit'ikis gadatsemis mekanizmebi sakartveloshi: bolodroindeli dinamik'a [Channels of Monetary Policy in Georgia: latest dynamics]. *Ek'onomik'a Da Sabank'o Sakme*, 1(3), 57–74.

Brabant, J. M.van. (1998). *The Political Economy of Transition: Coming to Grips With History and Methodology*. Routledge.

Brown, M., & De Haas, R. (2012). Foreign banks and foreign currency lending in emerging Europe. *Economic Policy*, January, 57–98.

Capie, F., Goodhart, C., & Schnadt, N. (1994). The development of central banking. In N. S. Forrest Capie, Stanley Fischer, CharlesGoodhart (Eds.), *The Tercentenary Symposium of the Bank of England* (pp. 1–261). Cambridge University Press.

Cardelli, R., Igan, D., & Rebucci, A. (2008). The changing housing cycle and the implications for monetary policy. In *World Economic Outlook: Housing and the Business Cycle*. International Monetary Fund.

Caucasus Business Week. (2014, August 11). 94% of Population of Georgia Enjoy Banking Services: An interview with a research director at "TNS" representation in the South Caucasus George Abramishvili.

Charaia, V. (2018). Vakhtang Charaia – 2007 ts'els khelisuplebam sapinanso seqt'ors neba darto, seskhebi nebismieri sap'rotsent'o ganak'vetiT gaetsat [Vakhtang Charaia – in 2007 the government allowed the financial sector to issue loans at any interest rate]. 1tv.ge.

Charaia, V., & Papava, V. (2017). The Role of Inflation and its Targeting for Low-Income Countries (Lessons from Post-Communist Georgia). *Slovak Republic European Journal of Economic Studies*, 6(2), 96–103.

Colliers International. (2015). Resident Market Report Georgia 2015.

Comparato, G. (2015). The Design of Consumer and Mortgage Credit Law in the European System. In H.-W. Micklitz & I. Domurath (Eds.), *Consumer Debt and Social Exclusion in Europe* (pp. 9–29). Ashgate Publishing Limited.

Crowe, C., & Meade, E. E. (2008). Central Bank Independence and Transparency: Evolution and Effectiveness (No. 119; IMF Working Papers).

Detragiache, E., Tressel, T., & Gupta, P. (2006). Foreign Banks in Poor Countries: Theory and Evidence (No. 18; IMF Working Paper).

Dübel, H.-J., & Walley, S. (2010). *Regulation of Foreign Currency Mortgage Loans – the case of transition countries in Central and Eastern Europe*. World Bank.

Duenwald, C., Gueorguiev, N., & Schaechter, A. (2005). Too Much of a Good Thing? Credit Booms in Transition Economies: The Cases of Bulgaria, Romania, and Ukraine (No. 128; IMF Working Paper).

Economic Policy Research Center. (2012). sabiujeto gadasakhdelebis ruk'a [A map of budget payments 2012].

Economic Policy Research Center. (2014). sakartveloshi arsebuli p'roblemuri seskhebis martva: analizi da rek'omendatsiebi [Managing non-preforming loans in Georgia: analysis and recommendations].

Eichengreen, B. (2004). *The Dollar and the New Bretton Woods System*. University of Berkley.

Eichengreen, B., Hausmann, R., & Panizza, U. (2007). Currency Mismatches, Debt Intolerance, and Original Sin: Why They Are Not the Same and Why It Matters. In S. Edwards (Ed.), *Capital Controls and Capital Flows in Emerging Economies: Policies, Practices and Consequences* (Issue May, pp. 121–170). University of Chicago Press.

Eichengreen, B., & Hausmann, R. (1999). Exchange Rates and Financial Stability. NBER Working Paper Series No. 7418.

Enoch, C. (2007). Credit Growth in Eastern and Central Europe. In C. Enoch & I. Ötker-Robe (Eds.), *Rapid Credit Growth in Central and Eastern Europe: Endless Boom or Early Warning?* (pp. 3–13). Palgrave Macmillan UK.

Epstein, G. A. (2001). *Financialization, Rentier Interests, and Central Bank Policy* (pp. 1–43). Political Economy Research Institute.

Epstein, G. A., & Yeldan, E. (2008). Inflation targeting, employment creation and economic development: assessing the impacts and policy alternatives. *International Review of Applied Economics*, 22(2), 131–144.

Eradze, I. (n.d.). Dollarization Persistence in Georgia in the Prism of State Building. Globalizations.

Eradze, I. (2022a). Financialization of Monetary Policy in a Dollarized Economy: the case of Georgia. *Cambridge Journal of Economics.* https://academic.oup.com/cje/advance-article/doi/10.1093/cje/beac019/6602081?login=true.

Eradze, I. (2022b). Taming Dollarization Hysteresis: Evidence from Post-socialist Countries. In C. Scherrer, A. Garcia, & J. Wullweber (Eds.), *Handbook on Critical Political Economy and Public Policy.* Edward Elgar Publishing Ltd.

Erturk, I., Froud, J., Johal, S., Leaver, A., & Williams, K. (2007). The democratization of finance? Promises, outcomes and conditions. *Review of International Political Economy*, 14(4), 553–575.

European Investment Bank. (2013). Private Sector Financing in the Eastern Partnership and the Role of Risk-bearing Instruments Country Report: Georgia (Issue November).

Gabor, D. (2010). The International Monetary Fund and its New Economics. *Development and Change*, 41(5), 805–830.

Gabor, D. (2011). *Central Banking and Financialization: A Romanian Account of how Eastern Europe became subprime* (J. Hölscher & H. Tomann (Eds.)). Palgrave Macmillan.

Gelaschwili, S., & Nastansky, A. (2009). Development of the Banking Sector in Georgia (No. 36; Statistische Diskussionsbeiträge, Issue 36).

Helleiner, G. K. (1997). Capital Account Regimes and the Developing Countries. In *International Monetary and Financial Issues for the 1990s: Vol.* VIII (pp. 1–26). United Nations.

Independent Evaluation Office of the International Monetary Fund. (2015). The IMF's Approach to Capital Account Liberalization: Revisiting the 2005 IEO Evaluation.

International Monetary Fund. (n.d.). About the IMF. imf.org.

International Monetary Fund. (1998). Georgia: Recent Economic Developments and Selected Issues. https://www.elibrary.imf.org/view/journals/002/1998/099/002.1998.issue-099-en.xml.

International Monetary Fund. (2001). Georgia: Recent Economic Developments and Selected Issues. https://www.elibrary.imf.org/view/journals/002/2001/211/002.2001.ıssue-211-en.xml.

International Monetary Fund. (2006). Georgia: Selected Issues (Issue 06/170). https://www.elibrary.imf.org/view/journals/002/2006/170/002.2006.issue-170-en.xml.

International Monetary Fund. (2011). IMF Country Report: Georgia: Selected Issues (Issue 11/93). https://www.elibrary.imf.org/view/journals/002/2011/093/002.2011.issue-093-en.xml.

International Monetary Fund. (2017). Georgia: request for extended arrangement under the extended fund facility and cancellation of stand-by arrangement - press release; Staff report: And statement by the executive director of Georgia (Issue 17/97). http://www.economy.ge/uploads/files/2017/imf_monetary_found/cr1797_2.pdf.

Jarociński, M., & Jirny, A. (1999). Monetary Policy and Inflation in Georgia 1996–98. *Russian & East European Finance and Trade*, 35(1), 68–100.

Józon, M. (2015). Country Report Hungary. In H.-W. Micklitz & I. Domurath (Eds.), *Consumer Debt and Social Exclusion in Europe* (pp. 85–99). Ashgate Publishing Limited.

Kaltenbrunner, A., & Painceira, J. P. (2017). The Impossible Trinity: Inflation Targeting, Exchange Rate Management and Open Capital Accounts in Emerging Economies. *Development and Change*, 48(3), 452–480.

Karwowski, E., & Centurion-Vicencio, M. (2018). Financialising the State: Recent developments in fiscal and monetary policy. Financial Geography Working Papers No. 11.

Khishtovani, G. (2012). *K'apit'alis bazari sakartveloshi da misi mt'rebi* [Capital Market in Georgia and its Enemies]. Institute for Development of Freedom of Information (IDFI), Tbilisi.

Kiss, G., Nagy, M., & Vonnák, B. (2006). Credit growth in Central and Eastern Europe: Trend, Cycle or Boom? (No. 10; MNB Working Papers).

Kliatskova, T., & Mikkelsen, U. (2015). Floating with a Load of FX Debt? (15/284; IMF Working Papers).

Lashkhi, I., Evgenidze, N., Narmania, D., & Gabedava, M. (2008). *sakartvelos mtavrobis '50 dghiani p'rograma-' analizi da shepasebebi* ['50 Day Program' of the Georgian government - analysis and assessments]. Open Society Georgia Foundation, Tbilisi.

Mcloughlin, C., & Kinoshita, N. (2012). *Monetization in Low- and Middle-Income Countries* (WP/12/160; IMF Working Paper Series).

McNamara, K. R. (2002). Rational Fictions: Central Bank Independence and the Social Logic of Delegation. *The Politics of Delegation*, 25(1), 47–76.

Mihaljek, D. (2007). The Role of Housing Markets and Foreign Owned Banks in the Credit Expansion in Central and Eastern Europe. In C. Enoch & I. Ötker-Robe (Eds.), *Rapid Credit Growth in Central and Eastern Europe: Endless Boom or Early Warning?* (pp. 267–284). Palgrave Macmillan.

Mkhatvrishvili, S. (2016). laris gatsvliti k'ursi da sakartvelos erovnuli bank'is monet'aruli p'olit'ik'is shepasebebi [Exchange course of Lari and the assessment of the monetary policy of the National Bank of Georgia]. *Ek'onomik'a Da Sabank'o Sakme*, 4(1), 5–33.

Mkhatvrishvili, S., Mdivnishvili, T., & Liqokeli, A. (2016). gatsvliti k'ursi da mimdinare angarishis depitsit'i [Exchange rate and current account deficit]. *Ek'onomik'a Da Sabank'o Sakme*, 4(2), 67–84.

Modebadze, G. (2011). Foreign Investment Effects on the Banking Sector in Georgia (No. 32897; MPRA Papers).

National Bank of Georgia. (n.d.). Inflation Targeting. nbg.gov.ge.

National Bank of Georgia. (2004). Ts'liuri angarishi [Annual Report]. https://nbg.gov.ge/publications/annual-reports.

National Bank of Georgia. (2006a). Ts'liuri angarishi [Annual Report]. https://nbg.gov.ge/publications/annual-reports.

National Bank of Georgia. (2006b). Pinansuri stabilurobis angarishi [Financial Stability Report]. https://nbg.gov.ge/publications/annual-reports.

National Bank of Georgia. (2006c). pinansuri st'abilurobis angarishi [Financial Stability Report]. https://nbg.gov.ge/publications/annual-reports.

National Bank of Georgia. (2006d). sakartvelos sabank'o sist'emis ganvitarebis st'rat'egia 2006–2009 ts'lebistvis [Strategy for the Development of the Georgian Banking System for 2006–2009]. https://nbg.gov.ge/publications/annual-reports.

National Bank of Georgia. (2006e). Ts'liuri anagarishi [Annual Report]. https://nbg.gov.ge/publications/annual-reports.

National Bank of Georgia. (2007a). Ts'liuri angarishi [Annual report]. https://nbg.gov.ge/publications/annual-reports.

National Bank of Georgia. (2007b). Pinansuri stabilurobis angarishi [Financial Stability Report]. https://nbg.gov.ge/publications/annual-reports.

National Bank of Georgia. (2007c). Pinansuri st'abilurobis angarishi [Financial Stability Report]. https://nbg.gov.ge/publications/annual-reports.

National Bank of Georgia. (2008a). sakartvelos erovnuli bank'i: z'iritadi mimartulebebi da funktsiebi [National Bank of Georgia: main directions and functions] (1st ed.). https://nbg.gov.ge/publications/annual-reports.

National Bank of Georgia. (2008b). Ts'liuri angarishi [Annual report]. https://nbg.gov.ge/publications/annual-reports.

National Bank of Georgia. (2009). Ts'liuri angarishi [Annual report]. https://nbg.gov.ge/publications/annual-reports.

National Bank of Georgia. (2010a). Ts'liuri angarishi [Annual report]. https://nbg.gov.ge/publications/annual-reports.

National Bank of Georgia. (2010b). Pinansuri stabilurobis angarishi [Financial Stability Report]. https://nbg.gov.ge/publications/annual-reports.

National Bank of Georgia. (2010c). Pinansuri stabilurobis angarishi [Financial Stability Report]. https://nbg.gov.ge/publications/annual-reports.

National Bank of Georgia. (2010d). Ts'liuri angarishi [Annual report]. https://nbg.gov.ge/publications/annual-reports.

National Bank of Georgia. (2011a). Pinansuri stabilurobis angarishi [Financial Stability Report]. https://nbg.gov.ge/publications/annual-reports.

National Bank of Georgia. (2011b). Pinansuri st'abilurobis angarishi [Financial Stability Report]. https://nbg.gov.ge/publications/annual-reports.

National Bank of Georgia. (2011c). Ts'liuri angarishi [Annual report]. https://nbg.gov.ge/publications/annual-reports.

National Bank of Georgia. (2014). Statement of National Bank of Georgia. nbg.gov.ge.

National Bank of Georgia. (2022). https://nbg.gov.ge/en/statistics/statistics-data.

Nikolaishvili, G. (2017). Sp'ek'ulatsiuri sabinao-samsheneblo biznesi sakartveloshi [Speculative housing and construction business in Georgia]. European.ge.

Painceira, J. P. (2009). Developing Countries in the Era of Financialisation: From Deficit Accumulation to Reserve Accumulation (No. 4; Research on Money and Finance Discussion Papers, Issue 4).

Papava, V. (2009). Georgia's economy: Post-revolutionary development and post-war difficulties. *Central Asian Survey*, 28(2), 199–213.

Papava, V. (2010). The 'Rosy' Mistakes of the IMF and World Bank in Georgia. *Problems of Economic Transition*, 52(7), 44–55.

Pistor, K. (2012). Into the Void: Governing Finance in Central and Eastern Europe. In G. Roland (Ed.), *Economics in Transition The Long-Run View* (pp. 134–153). Palgrave Macmillan.

Posen, A. (1995). Central Bank Independence and Disinflationary Credibility: A Missing Link? (No. 1; Federal Reserve Bank of New York Staff Reports).

Priewe, J., & Herr, H. (2005). *The Macroeconomics of Development and Poverty Reduction: Strategies beyond Washington Consensus.* Nomos.

Qashakashvili, N., & Janiashvili, M. (2018). *upleba satanado sackhovrisze: z'iritadi gamots'vevebis analizi* [Right to housing: analysis of main challenges]. EMC.

Rona-Tas, A., & Guseva, A. (2014). *Plastic Money: Constructing Markets for Credit Cards in Eight Postcommunist Countries.* Stanford University Press.

Ronas-Tas, A. (2009). Consumer Credit and Society in Transition Countries. In V. Perez-Diaz (Ed.), *Markets and Civil Society: The European Experience in Comparative Perspective* (pp. 151–179). Berghan Books.

Rosenberg, C. B., & Tirpák, M. (2008). Determinants of Foreign Currency Borrowing in the New Member States of the EU (08/173; IMF Working Papers).

Salukvadze, J. (2016). The Current State of Housing in Tbilisi and Yerevan: a Brief Primer. *Caucasus Analytical Digest*, 87(September), 8–11.

Salukvadze, J., & Golubchikov, O. (2016). City as a geopolitics: Tbilisi, Georgia – A globalizing metropolis in a turbulent region. *Cities*, 52, 39–54.

Santos, A. C., Costa, Vâ., & Teles, N. (2014). The political Economy of Consumption and Household Debt: An Interdisciplinary Contribution. *RCCS Annual Review*, 6(6), 55–82.

Sapir, J. (2013). Credit, indebtedness and economic growth. http://russeurope.hypotheses.org/.

Sattler, M. (2014). *Georgien kompakt: Banken.* Deutsche Wirtschaftvereinigung.

Sharumashvili, N., & Agladze, G. (2013). k'omertsiuli bank'ebis invest'itsiebi arasabank'o sekt'orshi da mati mizanshets'oniloba sakartveloshi [Commercial Banks' Investments in Non-Banking Sector in Georgia and their Appropriaty]. *Ek'onomik'a Da Sabank'o Sakme*, 1(1), 22–29.

Škarica, B. (2014). Determinants of non-performing loans in Central and Eastern European countries. *Financial Theory and Practice*, 38(1), 37–59.

Soldatuk, N., & Zoninashvili, E. (2015). *mtsire da sashualo biznesis dapinansebis khelshets'kh'oba* [Supporting SME Financing]. CreditInfo Georgia.

Sõrg, M., & Tuusis, D. (2009). Determinants of foreign loans in Estonian private sector. *Bank and Bank Systems*, 4(3), 4–11.

Stein, H. (2010). Financial liberalisation, institutional transformation and credit allocation in developing countries: the World Bank and the internationalisation of banking. *Cambridge Journal of Economics*, 34, 257–273.

Steinmo, S. (2008). What is Historical Institutionalism? In D. Della Porta & M. Keating (Eds.), *Approaches in the Social Sciences* (pp. 118–139). Cambridge University Press.

Timm, C. (2013). Economic Regulation and State Interventions: Georgia's Move from Neoliberalilsm to State Managed Capitalism (2013/03; PFH Research Papers).

UNICEF. (2010). rogor umk'lavdebian sakartveloshi bavshvebi da mati ojakhebi pinansuri k'rizisis zegavlenas? k'etildgheobis k'vleva [How do Georgian children and their families cope with the results of the financial crisis? Research on social welfare]. https://www.unicef.org/georgia/media/3676/file/WMS_2009_ge.pdf.

UNICEF. (2013). bavshvebis da mati ojakhebis k'etildgheoba sakartveloshi: sakartvelos mosakhleobis k'etildgheobis k'vleva [Welfare of children and their families in Georgia: Welfare Research]. https://www.unicef.org/georgia/media/1141/file/WMS%20Geo%202013.pdf.

World Bank. (2002). Global Development Finance: Financing the Poorest Countries. https://documents.worldbank.org/en/publication/documents-reports/documentdetail/876431468140678171/analysis-and-summary-tables.

Zazanashvili, N., & Nikolaishvili, G. (2017). *satskhovrisit uzrunvelkh'opis p'olit'ik'a: saertashoriso gamotsdileba da sakartvelos realoba* [Housing policy: international experience and Georgian reality]. Urban Lab.

Part IV

The politicization of dollarization

> When an ox-cart turns over, only then one will see the road.
>
> (Georgian Proverb)

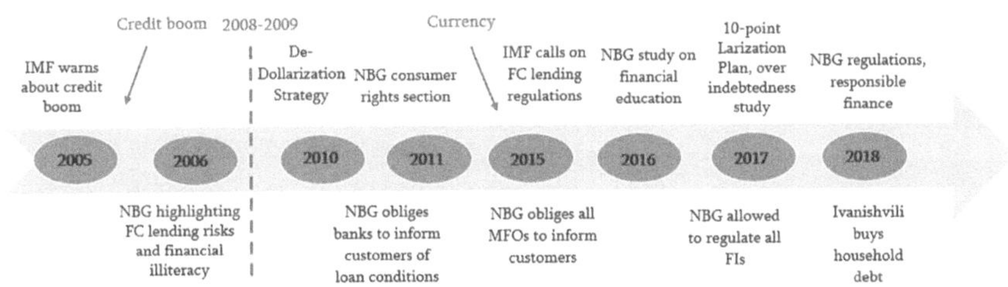

Figure T3 Timeline 3: The politicization of dollarization
Source: Author's illustration.

DOI: 10.4324/9781003240174-12

9 The politicization of dollarization: the currency crisis unfolding

The king is dead, long live the king!

Saakashvili's presidency had been challenged since 2008. Although the government recognized its mistakes in 2008 and initiated reforms to support the poor, the negative attitudes of the public were getting stronger. Among the main causes of the decreasing popularity of Saakashvili's government were poverty, the lost war with Russia (2008), and violations of human rights. Yet, a scandal on human rights abuses determined the fate of the parliamentary elections in 2012. Videos of prison torture became public shortly before the elections and thousands of Georgians went to the streets to protest against the inhuman treatment of prisoners (*The Guardian*, 2012). It was becoming clear that Saakashvili's party did not have a chance of winning the upcoming elections. At this point, a new political force was evolving around a Georgian billionaire, Bidzina Ivanishvili, who was well known for his philanthropy, but who had preferred to remain behind the scenes until 2011. His political party Georgian Dream (created in 2011) soon turned into the dominant opposition force (Fairbanks, 2014, p. 155). Although Ivanishvili had been a major supporter of Saakashvili after the Rose Revolution (Aprasidze, 2016, p. 111), Saakashvili's government had lost his sympathy, as well as the unconditional support it had previously enjoyed from the West. Western countries placed significant pressure on Saakashvili to allow a peaceful transfer of power through elections (Lebanidze, 2018, p. 4) after Georgian Dream won the parliamentary elections of 2012 (Cohen & Benovic, 2016, p. 2).

The new government promised to free the public from government pressure, ensure the protection of human rights, and to improve the social welfare system (see (Article 42 of the Constitution et al., 2015, p. 4). In 2013 Ivanishvili announced his resignation from politics after he had achieved his major aim – of ending Saakashvili's authoritarian regime in Georgia:

> I have kept my promise – Georgia is free from a violent regime, the state institutions are free from pressure. [...]. That's why I quit the Prime Minister's Post and now I am quitting politics too [...]. We have eventually put an end to an authoritarian regime.
>
> (Ivanishvili, cited in Civil.ge, 2013)

DOI: 10.4324/9781003240174-13

Yet, quitting politics turned out to be a symbolic gesture, as Ivanishvili did not just remain an active citizen (as he claimed), but kept governing from behind the curtains without having any official post; some even referred Georgia as a 'monarchy' (Navarro, 2018). Ivanishvili's informal power has been an open secret to everyone (Aprasidze, 2016, p. 112), despite his denials of being a shadow ruler (Lomsadze, 2018).

Ivanishvili's ideals of democracy and European values (Civil.ge, 2013) did not differ much from Saakashvili's state-building agenda. Yet, foreign policy towards Russia turned milder and closer relations with the EU outweighed friendship with the USA (see Macfarlane, 2015; Zasztowt, 2013). Though Saakashvili's government had also tried to improve relations with Russia in its final years, Ivanishvili had different links with Russia, where he had made his fortune; he had given up Russian citizenship only in 2011 (Zasztowt, 2013, pp. 3–4). If Saakashvili and his party members were well connected with the US, this was not the case with Georgian Dream (Macfarlane, 2015, pp. 5–6). Nevertheless, Ivanishvili's party did not change Georgia's pro-western foreign policy. A key example of cooperation with the EU was the signature of an Association Agreement providing for a Deep and Comprehensive Free Trade Area (DCFTA) in 2014 (Perchoc, 2017).

A major difference between the United National Movement (Saakashvili's party) and Georgian Dream lay in their ideology. Though Georgian Dream comprised different forces from liberal to nationalist and mercantilist, the party claimed to be centre-left (Aprasidze, 2016, p. 111). However, its policies were often eclectic and partially neo-liberal. Nevertheless, the shift of focus towards social welfare differentiated the new government from Saakashvili's party's ideals. In 2014, a socio-economic development strategy for the period to 2020 was adopted that focused on three main areas – the competitiveness of the private sector, the development of human resources, and accessibility to finance (Government of Georgia, 2014, p. 12). It was based on three core principles – development of the real economy, inclusive growth, and ecological sustainability (Government of Georgia, 2014, p. 3). Thus, at least on paper, economic development goals included social and ecological aspects. This way of thinking differed from the post-revolution economistic growth imperative. The 2020 government strategy criticized aims of short-term and the foreign direct investment (FDI)-led economic development approach of the previous government. In addition, the new government criticized the belief that FDI would naturally lead to knowledge and technology transfer, as most investments were directed to sectors that did not increase employment, poverty did not decline, exports did not increase, and the trade deficit widened during Saakashvili's presidency (Government of Georgia, 2014, pp. 9–11). However, this critique remained in written and spoken words throughout the governance of the Georgian Dream, as the government followed more or less the same path regarding foreign capital, that Saakashvili's government had done (see Eradze, 2020, 2021).

Georgian Dream cared about social justice along with economic growth and aimed at reducing unemployment, as well as improving the social benefit system (Government of Georgia, 2014, p. 5). The 2020 strategy considered increases of social benefits, pensions, and affordable healthcare (Government of Georgia, 2014, pp. 50–52). In a 2016 open letter, Ivanishvili highlighted that one of the primary aims of his party was to achieve an economic development that would benefit every citizen (News.On.ge, 2016). Yet the perception of the state and its relation to the markets did not change. Minimal government intervention was promoted, to guarantee security of private property and freedom of private sector (Government of Georgia, 2014, p. 4).

There was also no fundamental change in terms of macroeconomic and monetary policy. The government aimed at fiscal consolidation, price stability, keeping government debt below 40% of GDP, and increasing the share of debt held in national currency, as well as a reduction of the current account deficit. The current account deficit should have been reduced through fiscal consolidation, the flexibility of exchange-rate regime, and an increase in exports. The government supported the independence of the central bank and a flexible exchange rate (Government of Georgia, 2014, pp. 13–16). Larization was also part of this strategy, but without specific measures being elaborated (Government of Georgia, 2014, pp. 58–60).

Georgian Dream initiated reforms in healthcare, education, the tax system,[1] labour, and welfare (Cohen & Benovic, 2016, p. 1). In 2014–2015, almost one-third of the state budget was spent on social purposes (Economic Policy Research Center, 2015, p. 91). In 2013, a universal healthcare system was introduced, offering state health insurance to almost 90% of the population. In the same year, the labour code was changed to improve workers' rights. For example, employers were prohibited from dismissing workers without providing a reason (Cohen & Benovic, 2016, pp. 16–18). Yet, a number of issues remained unsolved in terms of protecting workers' rights, mostly due to the lack of enforcement of the legal changes (Human Rights Education and Monitoring Center, 2015, p. 59). Despite the aforementioned changes, the poverty rate remained high and unemployment persisted as a key issue (Cohen & Benovic, 2016, pp. 21–24). A survey conducted by the National Democratic Institute (NDI) and the Caucasian Research Resource Centre (CRRC) in 2016 demonstrated that almost 40% of the surveyed population thought the country was going in the 'wrong direction'. Moreover, negative attitudes towards general developments had increased, especially since 2014. More than one-half of the respondents claimed they had to spend more and 40% had reduced consumption due to the devaluation of the lari. Rising prices ranked as the second most important problem, after unemployment (Civil.ge, 2016).

Thus, despite changes in the social welfare system, as well as easing the authoritarian pressure on the public, Georgian Dream did not manage to initiate systemic or structural change in terms of development. Social policies were not backed up by economic transformation. Although the new government promoted inclusive and sustainable growth, its aims often remained on paper and Georgia remained a neoliberal state. The shift of focus towards developing the real economy occurred without a reassessment of monetary policy or the functions of the central bank. Though larization was defined as one of the priorities of the government, no specific changes were enforced until the currency crisis.

Currency crisis and its discontents

Dollarization would have most likely remained an unseen and unheard phenomenon had the currency crisis not broken out in Georgia. The lari crisis soon emerged as a major economic and political challenge for the government, as it also uncovered a wide range of structural socio-economic problems that had accumulated over the years. The rapid depreciation of lari (by 37% to the dollar in 2015) rang warning bells first in the pockets of households and then in the minds of politicians. People began to protest in the streets and the credibility of commercial banks as well as that of the Georgian central bank started to decrease. Dollarization was becoming politicized. Yet, political and public debates were polarized and focused on finding a scapegoat – avoiding a fundamental historical analysis of the problem.

The currency crisis unfolding

The lari started to lose its value at the end of 2014 and, in 2015, a currency crisis broke out (Figure 9.1). On 5 May, the lari reached its historical lowest point since 1998; 1 USD equalled 2,3303 lari (Anguridze et al., 2015, p. 13). Between 2015–2017, the Georgian Lari lost 50% of its value to the US dollar. The GDP growth rate of 2.7%, in 2016 was the worst indicator since the 2008–2009 crisis (World Bank, 2018, p. 6).

Various explanations including conspiracy theories appeared regarding the currency crisis. Yet, a combination of external shocks and internal issues were the main drivers for the crisis. The currency depreciation in Georgia coincided with and was preceded by the Russian–Ukrainian conflict, decreasing oil prices (affecting remittances from Russia and Azerbaijan negatively), declining economic growth rates in neighbouring countries, and restrictions in Armenian and Azerbaijani customs policies (Anguridze et al., 2015, p. 19). Falling oil prices negatively influenced Azerbaijan and Kazakhstan - two important trading partners of Georgia. Turkey was also experiencing problems due to the conflict in Syria. The quantitative easing policy of the US Federal Reserve (FED) in 2014 was leading to the appreciation of the dollar. Furthermore, the Greek economy was suffering in 2014–2015, which negatively influenced the remittances sent by Georgian migrant workers there (National Bank of Georgia, 2015c, p. 9). Money transfers from abroad declined by 23% (in US dollar terms), especially from Russia and Greece (World Bank, 2018, p. 6), as these are the two biggest

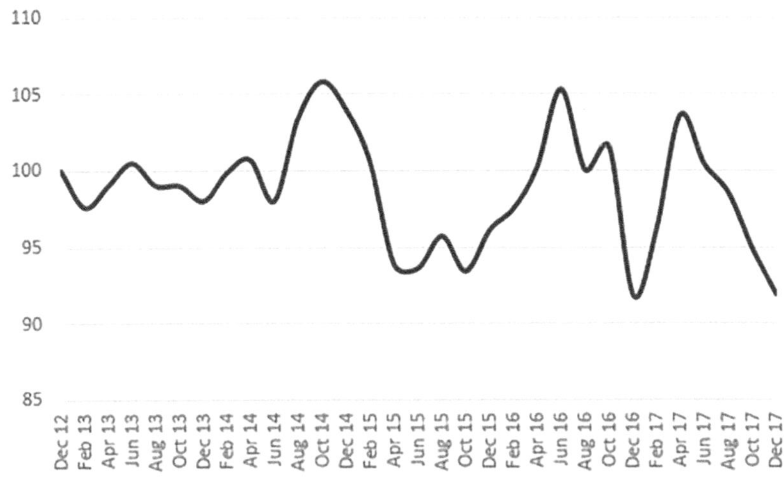

Figure 9.1 Index of the real effective exchange rate (Dec. 2012=100)
Source: National Bank of Georgia (2022).

countries in terms of remittance volume (National Bank of Georgia, 2015c, p. 25). Remittances played an important role in the Georgian economy at that point, as their level even exceeded the volume of FDI in 2010–2014 (Anguridze et al., 2015, pp. 23–25).

Georgia was also losing export competitiveness despite currency depreciation, as the currencies of neighbouring countries were experiencing a larger depreciation than the Georgian lari, and the import prices of these countries' export goods were becoming cheaper. Exports declined by 23% in 2015 (World Bank, 2018, p. 6). Demand for re-exported cars in Armenia and Azerbaijan[2] also fell (Anguridze et al., 2015, p. 22). Declining exports negatively influenced current account balance and the stability of the lari. Most of the currencies in the South Caucasus and Central Asia were overvalued at that time (Horton et al., 2016, p. v). The lari was overvalued by 10%–12% (International Monetary Fund, 2017, p. 11). The trade deficit for goods played the most significant role in the negative balance of payments in 2015 (the balance for services was positive).[3] Tourism had a key importance among services (National Bank of Georgia, 2015b, pp. 15–16). As for the capital account, capital transfers declined from 2011 to 2015 and, in 2015 decreased by 43% compared to the previous year. During these years, the biggest share of transfers was directed towards the government (in 2015 96.3% of transfers). In the financial account, FDI[4] played the most important role, which was rising until 2014 and declined slightly in 2015 (by 10%). FDI remained the most important source for financing the current account in 2015 (National Bank of Georgia, 2015c, pp. 25–26).

In addition to the external and geopolitical aspects, issues in fiscal and current account balances further weakened the lari. The 2015–2016 state budget in Georgia had a larger deficit than planned, as social expenditure was high and transfers to state-owned enterprises increased twice in 2015 (World Bank, 2018, pp. 6–7). The Georgian Dream government significantly increased social expenditures (as described above) that caused an increase in national debt – taxation revenues did not increase, and the government could not introduce changes in taxation due to the Liberty Act, as it prohibits Georgian governments from introducing new taxes or increasing existing taxes them without a referendum (Perchoc, 2017, pp. 4–5). Moreover, in 2014–2015 significant shares of the budget were spent towards the end of the year, negatively influencing the exchange rate of the national currency and the international reserves of the central bank (Economic Policy Research Center, 2015, p. 92). Besides increased government spending, the loose monetary policy of the Georgian central bank also influenced the exchange rate negatively. Since 2011 the NBG had been reducing the refinancing interest rate and the lari supply was increasing (Anguridze et al., 2015, p. 33). One of the factors that also influenced the value of the lari in 2015 was the repayment of corporate debt by commercial banks, negatively affecting the portfolio investment balance (National Bank of Georgia, 2015c, pp. 25–26).

Thus, the currency crisis was triggered by external shocks, but the structural causes of the crisis lay in the underdeveloped structure of the Georgian economy. As the IMF also argued, external shocks 'unveiled structural weaknesses (narrow production base, high under- and unemployment, and skill mismatches)' (International Monetary Fund, 2017, p. 6), and the Georgian government took too much time to react too to the depreciation of the lari (International Monetary Fund, 2017, p. 24).

What does it take for dollarization to become visible?

The lari crisis had a negative impact on prices, as well as on the foreign currency debt of the government, companies, and households. The current account balance deteriorated, poverty levels increased, and overall public attitudes towards the government turned significantly negative. The currency crisis soon evolved into a crisis of political legitimacy, clearly demonstrating the political economic character of dollarization.

Changes in the nominal effective exchange rate affected prices on imported products negatively, for example, medicine became more expensive (National Bank of Georgia, 2015c, p. 8). The share of imported inflation was especially high in 2015 (International Monetary Fund, 2017, p. 22). Prices for consumer goods (especially durable consumer goods, which are usually imported) and services were increasing in 2015 (National Bank of Georgia, 2016c, p. 41). Yet, the Georgian central bank managed to maintain inflation within its target limit of 5% in 2015–2016 (though inflation was increasing in 2015, it started to decrease in 2016). Other than the depreciation of the lari, the increase of value added tax (VAT) on alcohol and tobacco, as well as increases in electricity prices negatively influenced price stability in 2015. The effects of these factors were lower in 2016 (National Bank of Georgia, 2016c, p. 36). However, core inflation was higher than headline inflation, and it even exceeded the 5% target in 2015 (6.9%) due to declining oil prices. Nominal effective exchange-rate fluctuations have a significant influence on inflation in Georgia due to the high share of imported and mixed products in the consumer basket (more than 40% in 2015) (Figure 9.2). Yet, declining oil prices minimized the negative pressure of imported inflation on price stability. Though the share of food and non-alcoholic beverages is high in the consumer basket (31%), it did not influence inflation significantly. As the trading partners of Georgia were also experiencing currency devaluation, imported products were becoming cheaper. On the supply side, the increase of production intermediary costs (due to the depreciation of the lari and the indebtedness of businesses in foreign currency) negatively influenced price stability. Furthermore, the restriction of monetary policy decreased demand, and positively influenced inflation from the demand side (National Bank of Georgia, 2015c, pp. 34–37).

Increases in prices led to a reduction of imports (by 16.5% in 2015), mostly consumer goods (in 2015) (National Bank of Georgia, 2015c, p. 10) and intermediary products (in 2016) (National Bank of Georgia, 2016c, p. 27). Yet, imports did not decrease to scale, as was expected (Participant 15, personal communication, 3 May 2017). These developments led to a deterioration in the current account balance: the deficit increased from (-)5.8% in

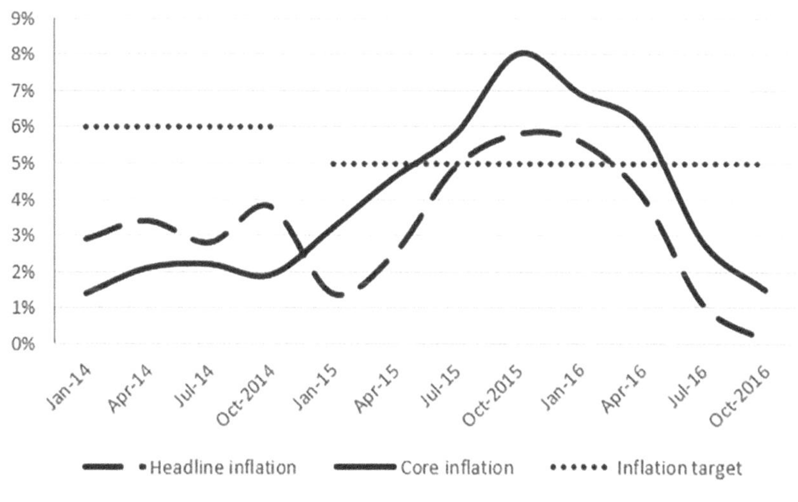

Figure 9.2 Headline and core inflation, 2014–2016
Source: National Bank of Georgia (2022).

2013, to (-)12% of GDP in 2015. The current account balance was further worsened in 2016 (-12,8% to GDP) though the services balance remained positive, thanks to tourism (National Bank of Georgia, 2016b, pp. 15–16).

Lari depreciation made investors hesitant to invest in Georgia (Namchavadze, 2015). Although industry and trade experienced downward trends, the construction sector was growing (15% growth), mostly due to the construction of the Baku-Ceyhan gas pipeline and other government-financed infrastructure projects, as well as private construction (National Bank of Georgia, 2015c, p. 11). Capital transfers further decreased by 9% in 2016 (National Bank of Georgia, 2016b, p. 34).

Indebtedness in foreign currency was rising at the household, corporate, and state levels, illustrating a downside of dollarization. Even though the absolute volume of external debt did not increase in terms of USD between November 2014 and February 2015, it increased by 1.4 billion lari due to currency depreciation (Namchavadze, 2015). Georgia's external debt grew from 81% of GDP in 2014 (National Bank of Georgia, 2015a) to 108% of GDP in 2015. Government debt made up 29% of the total foreign debt, inter-company debts 20%, and commercial bank debts 19.6% (National Bank of Georgia, 2016b, pp. 44–45). Almost 95% of Georgian foreign debt was denominated in foreign currency (National Bank of Georgia, 2015b, p. 46). Foreign debt increased by 4% in comparison with the 2015 level, though the debt of the NBG decreased by 8.6% and that of commercial banks by 2.8%. The non-government and non-financial sectors experienced the highest rates of debt increase, that is, by more than 20%; inter-company debt also increased by almost 17% (National Bank of Georgia, 2016b, pp. 15–16).

The depreciation of the lari negatively affected producers who had to repay interest on their foreign currency loans, and the intermediary costs of production increased creating significant pressure on inflation (National Bank of Georgia, 2015c, p. 8). Yet, the most vulnerable groups hit by the currency crisis were households who were indebted in foreign currency. In 2015, consumer loans had the highest share in retail lending (42%), followed by mortgages (36% retail loans) (National Bank of Georgia, 2015c, p. 79). In 2015, Georgia demonstrated one of the highest levels of foreign currency debt in the non-financial private sector among emerging economies, with around 55% to GDP, out of which one-half was domestic debt (Kliatskova & Mikkelsen, 2015, p. 7). Household debt to GDP was 15% in 2013, and by 2018 this indicator had doubled and reached 30%, mostly due to currency devaluation (Society and Banks, 2018). One-third of the household borrowers spent more than 50% of their income on paying interest in 2015 (International Monetary Fund, 2015a, p. 18); this was a clear indication of over-indebtedness. In the 2015 report, the IMF named the significant share of non-resident deposits and dollarization-related risks among the most important issues for the Georgian financial system. In terms of dollarization, banks faced two major problems – the solvency of its unhedged borrowers and the inability of the Georgian central bank to support commercial banks in dollars in case of a crisis (International Monetary Fund, 2015b, p. 5). The first risk was important also in terms of transmitting exchange-rate shocks to GDP, though the ratio of household debt to GDP (27%) might not have seemed high at first sight. More than 90% of those indebted in foreign currency earned money in the national currency and were not hedged against currency risks. In addition, the reliance of banks on non-resident deposits created a liquidity risk, in case customers would lose confidence (International Monetary Fund, 2015b, pp. 11–12).

The currency crisis not only causes a sharp increase in dollarization related risks, but also contributed to the further increase of dollarization. People were converting lari deposits into foreign currency due to insecurity (Namchavadze, 2015). The process of larization was challenged in 2015 (National Bank of Georgia, 2015c, p. 11). Deposit dollarization increased in 2015, reaching 70% (National Bank of Georgia, 2015c, p. 93). Despite lari depreciation and the increase of exchange-rate risk, interest rates on foreign currency loans did not increase, as banks had excess liquidity in foreign currency. For corporate, SME, and retail loans, the interest rates on lari loans had increased since the start of the currency crisis (National Bank of Georgia, 2015c, pp. 75–76). Loan dollarization was declining in 2013–2014, yet started to rise in 2015 and remained at over 60%in 2015–2017, while the deposit dollarization rate exceeded 70% by 2017 (International Monetary Fund, 2017, p. 25) (Figure 9.3).

Retail loans were still increasing at the highest rate (40% of the total loans) in 2016 (National Bank of Georgia, 2016c, pp. 82–83). Consumer loans

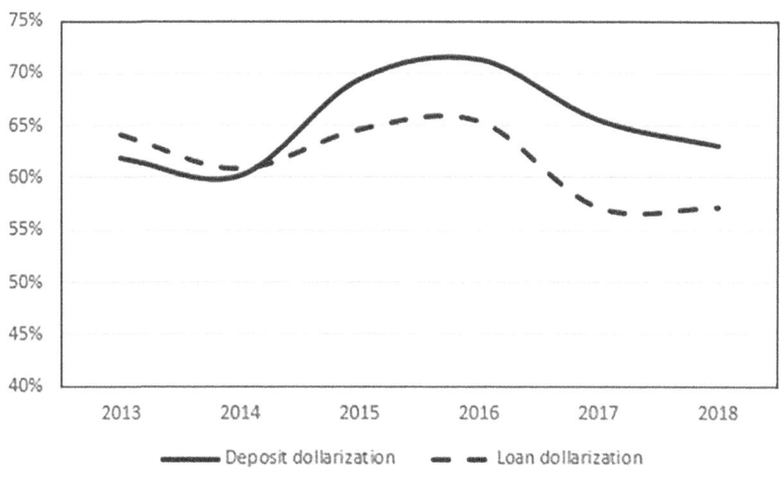

Figure 9.3 Loan and deposit dollarization, 2013–2018
Source: National Bank of Georgia (2022).

(17.6% of the total loans) and mortgages (16,4% of total loans) maintained significant shares in retail loans (National Bank of Georgia, 2016c, p. 85). The level of dollarization in corporate and SME borrowing was more than 70%, while more than 50% of the retail loans were denominated in foreign currency in 2016 (National Bank of Georgia, 2016c, p. 88) (Figure 9.4).

Despite the high indebtedness of households and corporations in foreign currency and the increase of loan-servicing burdens after the depreciation of the lari, negative portfolios (non-performing loans, watch loans,[5] negative investments, net write-offs, and repossessed property) did not increase significantly at commercial banks. Within a year of the currency crisis, negative loans (watch loans and non-performing loans) increased just slightly (to 13.6% of total loans); the share of non-performing loans (NPLs)[6] was 7.4%. Corporate loans had the highest share of negative loans (National Bank of Georgia, 2015c, p. 80). Such a development can be explained, on the one hand, by the limitation of the central bank data to commercial banks only and, on the other hand, through the tactics of commercial banks to improve their balance sheets. Banks were selling NPL portfolios to make their balance sheets look better (Participant 20, personal communication, 12 April 2016). Small private companies were set up that bought NPL portfolios and tried with by means – threat calls, falsifying court decisions, public shaming – to get the money back from borrowers (Participant 25, personal communication, 15 April 2016; Participant 27, personal communication, 20 April 2017).

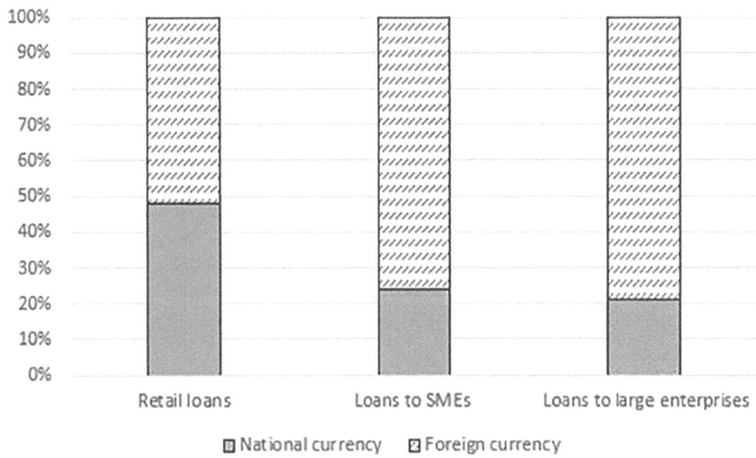

Figure 9.4 Currency composition of loans across segments, 2016
Note: Interbank loans are not included).
Source: National Bank of Georgia (2022).

Commercial banks were profiting from the devaluation of the lari from increased interest rates on foreign currency loans and rising commission fees. Income from currency trading also increased. Yet, returns on equity (ROE) decreased by 0.6%, due to the high risk of loans lost on foreign currency loan portfolios (National Bank of Georgia, 2015c, p. 99). In 2015, the biggest share of income (70% of total income) for banks originated from interest rates, followed by other non-interest income, commission, and fees (10%). However, trading income, based on currency conversion, was not a significant part of the total income (International Monetary Fund, 2015b, p. 10).

Thus, the outbreak of the lari crisis in 2015 had severe implications for producers, households, and the government that were indebted in foreign currency. Moreover, the increase in prices due to currency depreciation negatively influenced the purchasing power of the Georgian public and devalued lari exacerbated the current account deficit. Households were the major losers of the crisis, as it directly influenced their well-being, poverty was increasing and over-indebtedness was slowly making itself visible. Yet, commercial banks gained from the exchange rate fluctuations. They kept lending in foreign currency due to excess liquidity – clearly showing that banks in foreign ownership are not always sensitive to developments in local markets. Thus, the currency crisis aggravated the issue of dollarization and most importantly, paved a way towards its problematization.

Dollarization as a political issue: looking for a scapegoat

High indebtedness in dollars and the upcoming parliamentary elections of 2016 were making the depreciation of the lari a topic of political debate in Georgia. There were protests against high interest rates and forceful evictions (due to loan defaults) (Kachkachishvili, 2015; TV Free, 2015). Trust in banks was declining. In 2008, 53% of the surveyed population trusted banks, but in 2015, the share fell to 27%. While in Tbilisi distrust was doubled, in rural regions it almost tripled (Caucasus Research Resource Center, 2016). Protests due to the evictions of indebted households had soared since 2013, as the amount of seized collateral had already increased notably in 2009–2013 (National Bank of Georgia, 2010, p. 72, 2017a, p. 92).[7] These borrowers faced the threat of homelessness and sometimes turned to radical measures of protest in order to attract the attention of the government (see Ambebi.ge, 2016; BM.GE, 2016; ipn.ge, 2013).

The Georgian government adopted an anti-crisis plan to deal with currency depreciation. It aimed at reducing state expenditure, acquiring revenue through privatization, supporting the export sector, decreasing taxes on profits, and improving the investment climate in the country (Namchavadze, 2015). On 25 February 2015, the minister of economy, Kvirikashvili, presented a privatization plan, which included the selling off of a building of the ministry of economy and a former building of the central bank (Civil.ge, 2015c). It was an irony of life – that the privatization of the building of the ministry of economy and a former building of the central bank should have saved the national currency. The helplessness of the government against the lari crisis was acquiring symbolic expression. In 2016, fiscal consolidation was initiated as a response to the currency crisis (World Bank, 2018, pp. 6–7). Among other measures, the costs of the universal healthcare system should have been reduced by focusing on the most vulnerable only (World Bank, 2018, p. 49). The Georgian government was obeying the austerity imperative of international organizations and hoped to solve the crisis through decreased social spending. Yet, these measures only further aggravated the existing socio-economic issues.

The currency crisis was well used by media and opposition parties to blame the government for causing the lari crisis and for not having a plausible solution (Anguridze et al., 2015, pp. 15–17; New Posts, 2016). Yet, Ivanishvili tried to frame the devaluation of the lari as nothing dangerous at the initial stage, as it had not affected prices. He blamed the opposition party, the United National Movement (Saakashvili's former party) and the TV station Rustavi 2 for exaggerating and dramatizing the issue (Civil.ge, 2015a). The central bank president, Giorgi Kadagidze, also claimed that the panic was causing the further depreciation of the lari (Babych & Mosiashvili, 2014).

At a later stage, criticism was levelled not only towards the government, but also the central bank, as the NBG considered interventions at the FX market through selling reserves as counterproductive (National Bank of Georgia, 2015c, p. 56). Thus, the Georgian central bank maintained a

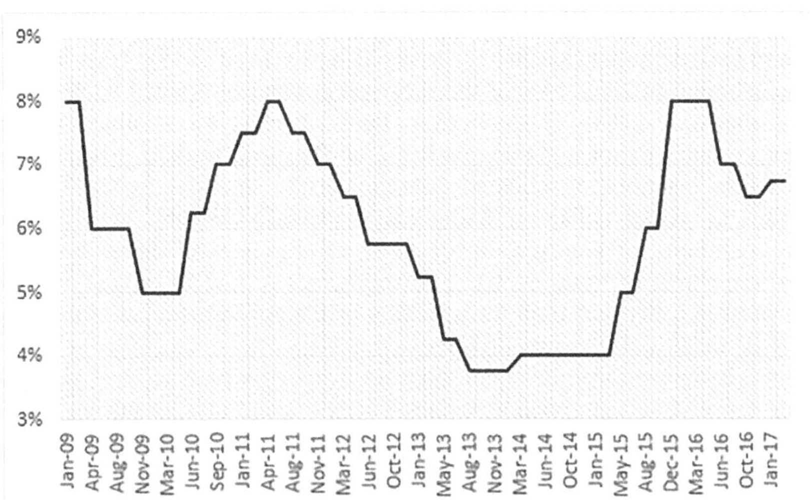

Figure 9.5 Monetary policy rate, 2009–2017
Source: National Bank of Georgia (2022).

floating exchange rate and intervened in the currency market on a very limited scale to send signals against panic (National Bank of Georgia, 2015c, p. 58). Here the subordination of exchange rate stability to price stability under inflation targeting was clearly manifested. The National Bank was not ready to intervene into the currency market unless price stability was challenged.

Moreover, the central bank restricted the monetary policy rate, as according to the NBG, a loose monetary policy was not a good strategy for Georgia due to its high rate of dollarization (Figure 9.5). Also, as production costs had increased, prices might have risen significantly. Therefore, in order to tame the inflation, the NBG restricted monetary policy to reduce the demand for loans in the lari (the policy rate increased from 4% to 8%) (National Bank of Georgia, 2015c, pp. 9–10). Thus, while the central bank of Georgia was trying to stay faithful to inflation targeting aims, its strict monetary policy was negatively affecting demand and economic growth (see Eradze, 2022). Yet, such a policy was in tune with austerity measures planned by the government. The procyclical policy of the NBG further increased the level of loan dollarization by raising interest rates and making lari loans more expensive than foreign currency loans.

Government–central bank blame games

At the beginning of the currency crisis, the government and NBG worked together to find a solution. In February 2015, Prime Minister Gharibashvili was highlighting successful cooperation with the central bank (Civil.ge, 2015b). Nevertheless, the situation changed very quickly, as public pressure increased, and the government started to disapprove of central bank policies. Ivanishvili publicly blamed the president of the NBG, Kadagidze, for driving the country into a crisis. The core of his criticism addressed the central bank's hesitation over selling international reserves to influence the exchange rate. Moreover, he outlined the fact that Kadagidze had been appointed during Saakashvili's presidency (Civil.ge, 2015d). Kadagidze responded that he did not want to get involved in political debates and the central bank would not repeat the mistakes of the 1990s (referring to the hyperinflation of 1992–93). He considered it useless to spend reserves, as the drivers of the depreciation of the lari were the declines in tourism, exports, and remittances. In his opinion, the solution was rather the reduction of taxes, the limitation of bureaucracy, and the creation of jobs to increase income (Kharadze, 2015). The IMF was calling on the NBG to improve its communications in relation to the inflation-targeting regime (International Monetary Fund, 2015c, p. 9). Thus, Kadagidze was passing the responsibility of crisis management to the government.

Central bank policy decisions were contested not only due to pressure from the public and government, but also from the IMF. According to an interviewee from the ministry of economy, one of the points of disagreement between the IMF and the Georgian government during the crisis was over the export competitiveness–Lari stability dilemma (Participant 13, personal communication, 21 April 2017). The IMF believed in the positive impacts of lari depreciation on export competitiveness, though the Georgian authorities were hesitant about using the exchange-rate channel in external adjustment. For the Georgian government, structural changes were more important than currency depreciation to reduce the current account deficit (International Monetary Fund, 2015c, p. 10). According to an interviewee from the central bank, the lari's depreciation against the dollar does not have such positive effects for Georgian exports as textbooks teach; Georgia's trading partner is not the United States. However, if the lari were to depreciate against the Turkish lira, then this could have a positive effect on the balance of trade. In addition, in a dollarized economy currency depreciation has negative impacts for consumers and businesses who are indebted in foreign currency (Participant 4, personal communication, 3 May 2017) (Figure 9.6) (see Eradze, 2022).

In May 2015, parliamentary members of Georgian Dream initiated a legal change to remove the supervisory function from the NBG. This was one more attempt by the Georgian government to gain further control over the central bank (previous attempts had occurred in 2006 and 2008). An independent agency should have been established which would have been responsible to the parliament and been led by a board of seven members, including the president of the central bank. The president of Georgia opposed this idea, as it was considered as a political decision and an interference of politics in the economic sphere (Civil.ge, 2015e). A political dimension of this initiative was clear, but there were also supporters of the central bank within the government in this conflict, especially at the ministry of finance (Participant 21, personal communication, 13 April 2016).

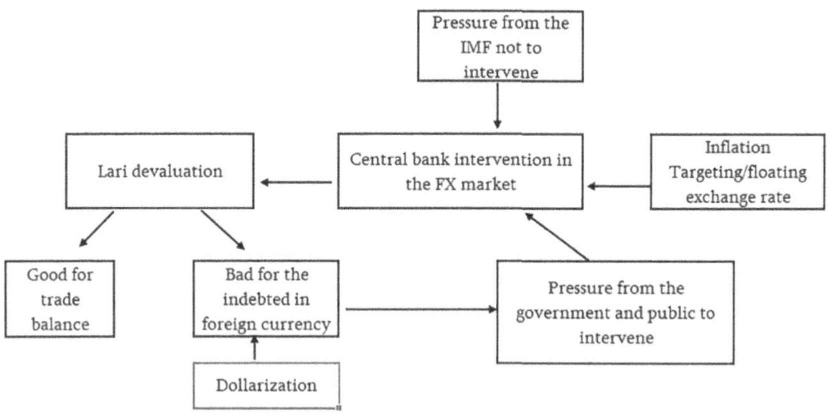

Figure 9.6 Lari depreciation and central bank dilemmas
Source: Author's illustration.

Ivanishvili supported the initiative to remove the supervisory function from the central bank, as it would increase the independence of commercial banks from the NBG (Civil.ge, 2015f). Opposition party members, business associations, the American chamber of trade and industry, the EU-Georgia Business council, the banking association, etc. were against the law (Kunchulia, 2015). Even though the Georgian president used his veto against this change, it was overridden by a majority in the parliament (Gogua, 2015) and the law was accepted in June 2015. The WB representative in Georgia, Henry Kerali, was unhappy with the decision, highlighting the conditions of the Association Agreement and the importance of the independence of the central bank (Evgenidze, 2015). So was the IMF country representative in Georgia, Azim Sadikov (Civil.ge, 2015g). The Fund warned Georgia that they would stop the ongoing project, if the government would not stop pressure on the central bank (Participant 15, personal communication, 3 May 2017).[8] International organizations (the IMF, the WB, the EBRD) sent a letter to the Georgian government on 24 June 2015 and explained why it was a bad idea to remove the supervisory body from the NBG. They considered that the central bank should have been responsible for both monetary and financial stability (Civil.ge, 2015h). In May 2015, NGOs in Georgia (Transparency International Georgia, the Economic Policy Research Center, Open Society Georgia Foundation, the Civil Development Agency, Society and Banks, the Georgian Reforms Association, the Georgian Farmers Association) also addressed the Georgian government in an open letter in which they opposed the idea of removing the supervisory body from the central bank. They feared that such a change would damage Georgia's international reputation (Transparency International Georgia et al., 2015). Though a supervisory agency was created in October 2015, it worked only for two days, as the constitutional court of Georgia recognized the change in the Organic Law as unconstitutional. Thirty-nine opposition Parliament members (from the UNM and the Free Democrats) had addressed the constitutional court on this issue (Voice of America, 2015). Thus, the independence of the Georgian central bank turned into a matter of divided interests at both the local and international levels. While the president of the country, as well as the ministry of finance, opposition parties, local NGOs, business associations, and international organizations defended the NBG's independence, Ivanishvili and the majority in the parliament opposed it.

As Kadagidze's term expired in 2016, a new president, Koba Gvenetadze, was appointed at the central bank. Later, the National Bank of Georgia loosened monetary policy and reduced the refinancing interest rate from 8% to 6.5% (National Bank of Georgia, 2016c, pp. 11–12). The NBG was now intervening into the currency market to avoid the further depreciation of the lari (International Monetary Fund, 2017, p. 3).

The above-described rivalry between the NBG and the government was one of the first clear signs that the currency crisis and dollarization had become a political issue. Yet a scapegoat was needed, especially shortly before the 2016 parliamentary elections. The trustworthiness of the central bank over the inflation targeting regime and its hesitation to spend international reserves provided grounds for blaming the NBG for the crisis. Thus, the price stability–exchange-rate dilemma triggered a political crisis in Georgia. Nevertheless, the core reason behind central bank policy decisions – its mandate of inflation targeting – was not questioned. The NBG was acting within its mandate and therefore it was this very mandate that needed to be examined. The government-central bank conflict wasted the currency crisis in 2015 without reconsidering monetary policy or financial stability; it remained at a superficial politically motivated level of dispute. Yet, this dispute also clearly showed that central bank independence had many supporters in and outside the country, from local NGOs and business associations to international organizations and the president of Georgia.

Financial education as a scapegoat

NBG was not the only scapegoat for the lari crisis; financially uneducated borrowers also turned into a favourite explanation for the high indebtedness of households. The lack of financial education became a favourite argument of experts, businessmen, and politicians, including a candidate for minster of finance, Dimitri Qumsishvili (Banks and Finance, 2016). This way the focus was shifted towards borrowers and the importance of structural factors, such as the responsibility of banks, was forgotten. Moreover, picturing financial education as a solution inherently assumes that households have access to full information. Yet, this was not the case in Georgia and the aggressive credit policies of commercial banks had encouraged the rise of household debt. Most of the banks were not informing customers about effective interest rates, as they were not sure that their competitors would do the same (Participant 9, personal communication, 10 May 2017; Participant 10, personal communication, 7 June 2017; Participant 12, personal communication 18 May 2017). The effective interest rate was not included in contracts until 2011. Often banks tried to attract customers through advertising 0% credit (Khaliani, 2012). Moreover, loans were issued without checking the income of lenders; there were no relevant regulation on this matter. In the beginning of the credit boom, people had positive expectations and little experience with credit. Sometimes they even thought that a credit card was a gift. Yet, for sales managers it was preferable not to tell customers all the relevant information, as their bonus depended on the number of loans issued (Participant 20, personal communication, 12 April 2016).

Even though the central bank had highlighted exchange-rate risks for customers as early as 2006 (National Bank of Georgia, 2006, p. 5), the central bank only introduced new rules that ordered commercial banks to provide relevant information to customers (households) in 2011 (National Bank of Georgia, 2011a, p. 58). The 2011 NBG report revealed that commercial banks did not always provide full information to customers, as their main goal was to sell products. Therefore, the new rule obliged banks to include such information in loan contracts as the effective interest rate, all costs related to deposits or credits, the exchange-rate risk (Article 3), commission fees, fines and a complaints procedure. Banks had to write the following sentences in the contract: 'foreign currency loan places a customer under significant risk' and 'changes in the exchange rate might increase the payments in Lari significantly' (K'omertsiuli Bank'ebis Mier Sabank'o Momsakhurebi Gats'evisas Momkharebisatvis Inpormatsiis Mits'odebis Ts'esi [Rule for Commercial Banks on Providing Mandatory Information for Consumers], 2011) (Article 3, point 9 and 10, author's translation). The same formulations applied to deposits in foreign currency. Furthermore, banks had to establish a special procedure for receiving complaints and then report on them to the central bank (K'omertsiuli Bank'ebis Mier Sabank'o Momsakhurebi Gats'evisas Momkharebisatvis Inpormatsiis Mits'odebis Ts'esi [Rule for Commercial Banks on Providing Mandatory Information for Consumers], 2011). In 2011, a new division for consumer rights was established at the central bank (National Bank of Georgia, 2011b, pp. 59–60). The NBG could impose sanctions on commercial banks in cases where these rules were violated (K'omertsiuli Bank'ebis Mier Sabank'o Momsakhurebi Gats'evisas Momkharebisatvis Inpormatsiis Mits'odebis Ts'esi [Rule for Commercial Banks on Providing Mandatory Information for Consumers], 2011) (Article 8).

Research conducted by the Georgian central bank in cooperation with the Sparkasse Foundation for International Development in the South Caucasus (SBFIC) in 2012 outlined significant violations of the new rules. The situation did not improve significantly in 2015 either; commercial banks were still not providing full information to their customers (National Bank of Georgia, 2015c, pp. 110, 113). According to the interview with SBFIC in Georgia, quite often staff at banks themselves were not informed of the new rules (Participant 12, personal communication, 8 May 2017). Another study of Client Voices, in 2016, demonstrated that 28% of the surveyed customers of microfinance organizations had no information on the interest rate of their loans (Center for Financial Inclusion, 2016). In 2015, the NBG started working on a strategy for financial education with the involvement of international experts. The strategy was oriented towards providing information to banks, the public, and SMEs. The central bank also called for a proper regulation of the credit bureau (National Bank of Georgia, 2015c, pp. 115–116).

Full access to information and financial education cannot be a solution when loans are badly needed. Households might be ready to accept any loan conditions if they are in desperate need for credit. This was the case in Georgia, where the rise of demand for retail loans was largely conditioned by poverty. Moreover, interest rate differentials for loans in national and foreign currencies had a significant influence on borrowing decisions. Even those who were aware of the risks often chose a foreign currency loan because of the lower interest rates (Participant 10, personal communication, 7 June 2017; Participant 6, personal communication, 30 May 2017). A 2016 study of the National Bank of Georgia revealed that 45% respondents had borrowed money because their income was insufficient to meet expeniture. However, more than 40% borrowed money from friends, while 39% applied to banks for credit (Sonar Ltd, 2016, pp. 2–4). In addition, at the time of the survey, more than one-half of the households had a loan (Sonar Ltd, 2016, p. 20). More than 32% of respondents faced difficulties in making financial ends meet (Sonar Ltd, 2016, p. 42). A study among clients of microfinance organizations demonstrated that the income to debt ratio was 37%, and more than 20% respondents had had to reduce their food consumption to repay debt (Center for Financial Inclusion, 2016).

The currency crisis was unveiling clear signs of over-indebtedness in Georgia. A 2017 central bank research NBG on over-indebtedness showed that although the risk for financial institutions and financial stability was legal (at the time), there was a danger of over-indebtedness. Small loans were concentrated among the households with lowest income, who struggled to repay their debt. The Georgian central bank highlighted the lack of awareness about financial risks among borrowers and the need of new regulations for the loan market. In 2017, the NBG was allowed to regulate all financial organizations and a department for consumer rights and financial education was created (National Bank of Georgia, 2017d, pp. 15–17). The year 2018 was announced as the year for financial education by the central bank president (National Bank of Georgia, 2017d, p. 19). In the same year, the NBG introduced a corporate governance codex for commercial banks (BM.ge, 2018f).

Thus, financial education turned out to be a scapegoat for explaining household indebtedness in foreign currency. Even though financial education is important, its role was overstated in the aftermath of the currency crisis, and was used as a means of shifting the responsibility from structural causes to individual borrowers. As one of the interviewees from the WB representation in Georgia pointed out, financial education is a good thing to have, but one does not have to be educated; central banks should be caring about consumer rights (Participant 15, personal communication, 3 May 2017). Moreover, financial education cannot prevent households from borrowing when loans are the only means of solving their urgent problems. Although the Georgian central bank started to tighten regulations regarding lending practices, the new rules appeared way too late. Households were already highly indebted in foreign currency and the central bank initiatives were rather aimed at avoiding future problems.

Over-indebtedness unravelled

The problem of household debt was too big to squeeze in a small bottle and label it as a conspiracy, the incompetence of the central bank, or a lack of financial education. In 2017, the government started to criticize commercial banks and blame them for driving the country into poverty. The main driver of such a change in discourse was the acknowledgement of poverty and over-indebtedness. The lari crisis led to the unfolding of various socio-economic issues and consequently, led to a political crisis.

During this author's interviews in 2017, experts, central bank staff, and financial institutions opposed any kind of interest rate ceilings or any interference of the government to stopping the eviction of indebted households. Such interventions were considered as a limitation of business's rights, as neither the government nor anyone else should have tried to take over responsibilities that borrowers had taken through signing a loan contract. There was a fear of creating the wrong incentives. Also, the private sector or banks could not and should not have carried exchange-rate risks, as they risked insolvency or leaving the market (Participant 20, personal communication, 12 April 2016). A further common argument against regulations was that lending would be shifted towards informal markets (Participant 24, personal communication, 22 April 2016). The Georgian financial market was considered as underpenetrated and underbanked (Participant 23, personal communication, 22 April 2016). A wave of regulations in 2017–2018 most likely surprised and disappointed supporters of market efficiency and a minimal state, as the government started to intervene in the 'sacred' financial sector.

In 2017, the Georgian government introduced a four-point plan that aimed at fast economic development through reforms in four areas: education, economy, infrastructure, and governance. Some of the key economic initiatives included reforms in capital markets, the pensions system, public private partnerships, deposit insurance, larization, and insolvency law (there is no private insolvency law in Georgia) (Ministry of Economy of Georgia, 2017, p. 2). The establishment of a pension fund as well as capital market reform was motivated by the need to create long-term money resources in the lari and to encourage the process of larization (Ministry of Economy of Georgia, 2017, p. 18). Thus, the national currency played a central role in the general economic development plan of the government. Yet, the pensions reform implemented in Georgia (a pensions law entered into effect in January 2019), is based on an accumulative pensions system without elements of solidarity, where employers, employees, and the government pay 2%[9] of taxable salary each (in total 6% of the salary is accumulated into the pension fund) (Law of Georgia on Funded Pensions, 2018) (Article 3). This saving should be added to the basic monthly pension (75 USD in 2019). The pensions agency is an independent institution (Law of Georgia on Funded Pensions, 2018) (article 4), supervised by a supervisory board.[10] Yet its investments are under the regulation of the Georgian central bank (Article 5). Investment board members are elected by the Georgian parliament (Article 12) (Law of Georgia on Funded Pensions, 2018). Thus, the main aim of the pensions fund is to invest accumulated pensions in corporate bonds and financial assets of private companies. The Georgian government perceives the pensions reform as a major tool for the development of capital markets and the creation of long-term savings in the national currency (Karelidze, 2018). Though a pension reform is badly needed in Georgia, it is rather doubtful whether the setting up of an investment pensions fund is the right solution. Investments carry risks that might threaten the welfare of the elderly population. The pensions agency does not provide clear information about whether participants of the pension scheme are insured against loses[11] (Pension Agency, 2019). In addition, it is rather unclear how this system would support the development of the local capital market if investments can be made outside Georgia that might lead to capital outflow.

The four-point plan of the Georgian government fully complied with the IMF recommendations from the 2017 Extended Fund Facility (EFF) programme that issued 210.4 million SDR for Georgia. 'The [EFF] program includes [...] higher and more inclusive growth, focusing on improving education; investing in infrastructure; making the public administration more efficient; and improving further the business environment' (International Monetary Fund, 2017, p. 2). Yet, the IMF was explicitly calling for de-dollarization as early as 2015. The Fund recommended that the Georgian central bank reduce foreign currency lending to unhedged borrowers, especially for short-term loans and introduce loan-to-value or debt-service-to-income ratios (International Monetary Fund, 2015a, pp. 4–5).

In 2017, the government and the central bank adopted a ten-point Larization plan with three major aims: to increase accessibility to long-term lari loans; to tackle currency risks; and to establish prices in lari. Loans up to 100,000 lari had to be issued in the national currency only[12] and foreign currency reserve norms became more strict for commercial banks in accordance with IMF recommendations. Furthermore, a strategy for capital market development was initiated. The pensions reform was also part of the larization programme. A one-time conversion of foreign currency loans was allowed for households with government subsidy.[13] Payment to interest (PTI) and loan to value (LTV) indicators were introduced for household loans. Prices had to be announced in lari and a special program was launched to encourage real-estate transactions in the national currency (National Bank of Georgia, 2016c, pp. 61–63). Furthermore, several important legal changes were made in the civic codex in 2017 – a ceiling for the annual effective interest rate was set at 100% for all loans and a maximum amount of sanctions for delayed payments was defined (National Bank of Georgia, 2017c). PTI and LTV ratios were also suggested by the IMF in 2017 as a means of strengthening the financial system (International Monetary Fund, 2017, p. 4). Larization reforms were mostly planned by the government in consultation with IOs and a few local experts, but the private sector was not involved. However, they did not express protest nor initiative around these themes (Participant 11, personal communication, 8 June 2017). The NGO sector was also not involved in developing the ten-point de-dollarization plan (Participant 17, personal communication, 1 June 2017).

Though these rules were important, they carried a risk of superficiality as they did not address the core issue. For example, the law on prices in lari is not working, as most construction companies change prices in lari in accordance with the lari-USD exchange rate on the day of payment.[14] Thus, no shift has occurred in the minds of people and businesses and the exchange risk continues to be carried by consumers. Furthermore, the extent to which the deepening of financialization by developing the capital market and investment pensions funds can save the lari in the long term is rather questionable.

Political discourse changed in 2018 as government officials recognized over-indebtedness and started to criticize commercial banks publicly. In a 2018 interview, Ivanishvili highlighted the issue of over-indebtedness[15] and explicitly blamed two big banks for leading the country into poverty (Tsintsadze, 2018). In April 2018, Finance Minister Mamuka Bakhtadze also made a statement that Georgian banks and their expensive loans for businesses were not supporting the economic development of the country (bpn.ge, 2018). The finance minister not only criticized banks for creating barriers to economic development, but also talked about the issue of over-indebtedness (BM.ge, 2018a). Mamuka Bakhtadaze named over-indebtedness as a major cause of poverty in Georgia. According to him, 30% of the economically active population (630,000 people) were on a blacklist and were not economically active. Therefore, it was important to bring these people back to the labour market for inclusive growth (BPI.ge, 2018). This statement of the finance minister shows the main motivation of the government to deal with over-indebtedness – the government wanted to return hundreds of thousands of people to market again to achieve economic growth.

Ivanishvili's and Bakhtadze's statements were preceded by a United Nation's Children Fund (UNICEF) report that triggered a broader discussion on over-indebtedness and the alarming poverty rates in Georgia. The main message of the report was that poverty had increased in Georgia in recent years and especially since the lari crisis. Though the real income of households had increased in 2015–2017 and income inequality decreased, poverty had still increased since 2015; 21.7% of the population and 27.6% of children lived under a general rate of poverty in 2017. According to the UNICEF, the main drivers for such a trend were slower economic growth and increase in consumer prices (food, transport, tobacco, alcohol) due to the devaluation of the lari (UNICEF, 2018, pp. 8–14). More than 43% of the surveyed population declared that their economic condition had worsened in comparison with the previous year due to increased prices. For many of them credit (mostly bank loans) was one of the important sources of income (UNICEF, 2018, p. 22). The share of loans to income (for households) had been mostly increasing since 2010 and at the beginning of 2015, reached more than 25% (in 2010, it had been around 11%–12%). According to the IMF, 680 out of every 1,000 adults had a loan in Georgia in 2015, ranking very highly in the world in such terms. In 2016, 2.4 million individual loan contracts existed (Khundadze, 2018); the population of Georgia is 3,7 million. Around one-third of the retail borrowers spent more than one-half of their income on interest payments of loans (International Monetary Fund,

2015a, pp. 18–19). In 2016, every seventh family in Georgia lived beyond the subsistence minimum (Kakulia et al., 2017, p. 5). The 2018 WB report also highlighted alarming poverty rates in Georgia – 20% of the population lived in poverty ($1.90 a day), while almost 50% of the population were on the verge of poverty (World Bank, 2018, p. 10). According to the WB report, one of the key causes of poverty was high expenditures on health care (World Bank, 2018, p. 14).

These socio-economic developments influenced public attitudes. According to a public opinion survey of the International Republican Institute (2017), unemployment and economic crisis occupied the first two places among the top problems of the surveyed population (Center for Insights in Survey Research, 2017, p. 19). Furthermore, 69% felt that the economic situation had regressed since 2013 (Center for Insights in Survey Research, 2017, p. 24). The share of the population thinking that the country was going in the wrong direction, had increased from 12% in 2012 to 65% in 2017, while the share of people with positive thoughts on general developments was decreasing (Center for Insights in Survey Research, 2017, p. 26). Unfulfilled promises, the economic crisis, inflation, and unemployment dominated the top answers on the government's biggest failures (Center for Insights in Survey Research, 2017, p. 32). Also, the Georgian Orthodox Church was the most favourably regarded institution (88% considered as favourable) next to the Georgian army (86%) and only 21% considered the National Bank favourably (for 50% it was considered unfavourably and 37% did not have an opinion on that matter) (Center for Insights in Survey Research, 2017, p. 38). An anti-bank public discourse was strengthening. Many considered banks as robbers and not as their partners; the negative attitudes of people towards financial institutions were increasing (Participant 24, personal communication, 22 April 2016; Participant 26, personal communication, 20 April 2016).

Thus, the pressure of poverty and over-indebtedness did not let the Georgian government ignore the elephant in the room any longer. International organizations were also calling for regulatory measures to tackle these issues. These factors triggered a change in the discourse and the government publicly blamed commercial banks for the crisis, having found a new scapegoat. However, this shift was neither preceded by discussions on a fundamental rethinking of the functioning of the economy or the financial sector nor caused by concerns of the government about the over indebted population. The government was worried rather about economic growth and therefore cared about the blacklisted hundreds of thousands members of the labour force, who had no incentive to work.

The government responds to over-indebtedness

The Georgian government soon realized that something had to be done about over-indebtedness to address pressure from the public and the international community. One of the clear demonstrations of the government reaction was the official return of Ivanishvili to party politics. Even though he had left politics in 2016 (once again), with the promise that he would not return unless there was a Doomsday, in 2018, he was asked by Prime Minister Kvirikashvili to take over the political leadership. Ivanishvili was elected as Georgian Dream party chairman once again (Democracy and Freedom Watch, 2018).

In 2018, minister of finance Mamuka Bakhtadze called for structural changes to promote economic development and named the following areas of reform: the development of a capital market, pensions reform, public private partnerships, responsible finance, and the attraction of technology transfer-oriented FDI (Ambebi.ge, 2018). Furthermore, a state guarantee fund was supposed to be set up to support exports and help SMEs, especially, to find financial resources (BM.ge, 2018d). The NBG also initiated new rules with a focus on responsible finance. A major change was manifested in limiting the issuance of loans without a proper analysis of consumer repayment capacities. The amount of loans without such an assessment should not have exceeded 25% of a bank's regulatory capital (from 7 May 2018). However, this requirement did not apply to loans that were collateralized by real estate or precious stones (the amount of loans collateralized through real estate without payment capacity assessment should not have exceeded 15% of a bank's regulatory capital and Loan to Value Ratio for this kind of loans was set at 50%). Furthermore, according to the EU association agreement, Georgia had to introduce the assessment of the repayment capacity of borrowers before September 2019 (National Bank of Georgia, 2018a). These changes were approved at the end of 2018 and entered into force in January 2019 (National Bank of Georgia, 2018b). The ceiling of the annual effective interest rate decreased from 100% to 50% in 2018 and the rules of calculation for fines and delayed payments were changed. In addition, banks could not take over any property if it was not indicated as collateral in the loan contract (Khundadze, 2018).

The new regulations were not welcomed by everyone. One of the two biggest banks, TBC bank, publicly expressed its dissatisfaction with the new regulations (Netgazeti, 2018a). The Bank of Georgia was also demanding more time for implementing the changes (BM.ge, 2018c). This position of commercial banks was shared by the business association of Georgia (BM.ge, 2018b), business and banking associations, Georgian chamber for international trade, associations of microfinance organizations, EU – Georgia business council, Georgian employers' association, SME association, and farmers' association (BM.ge, 2018i). Local, financial, and business elites did not welcome restrictions on loan policies.

Yet, the initiative was supported by IMF representation in Georgia, (see BM.ge, 2018e), the WB regional office (see BM.ge, 2018d) and the regional representative of EBRD (BM.ge, 2018h). Bakhtadze also declared in his June 2018 speech that the changes were not only his idea, but they were also supported by international partners (Ambebi.ge, 2018). Fitch Ratings also positively assessed the 2018 changes in banking regulations (BM.ge, 2018g). Thus, while local, financial, and economic forces opposed the regulations; IOs supported and even initiated the changes. This clearly demonstrates how the international community can stand with national public interests, despite the opposition of local and international and capital.

A culmination of the currency crisis and the politicization of dollarization was the purchase of the debts of 600,000 Georgian citizens (around 16% of the total population) by Ivanishvili's charity fund Qartu at the end of 2018, immediately before the presidential elections. If previously foreign currency loans and dollarization had not been topics of election debate in Georgia, during the 2018 presidential elections they became so. The Georgian Dream candidate Salome Zurabishvili struggled in the first round against the opposition party (United National Movement) candidate Grigol Vashadze. Former president Saakashvili had also announced a plan of dealing with currency depreciation issues a couple of months prior to the elections. He wanted to follow the example of Orbán's policies in Hungary and set the exchange rate of loan repayments at 1.65 USD, the initial exchange rate of the lari to the dollar at the time of borrowing. Furthermore, Saakashvili wanted to create a special registry for doubtful loans, freeze some NPLs for two years, and allow citizens to repay these loans gradually after two years (Netgazeti, 2018b).

In November 2018, the prime minister announced that Ivanishvili's Qartu Fund was buying the debt of 600,000 Georgians, who were on the black-list (due to loan defaults) and had not repaid their debt for at least a year. Also, the amount of loans taken by individual borrowers should not have exceeded 2,000 lari (Civil.ge, 2018). The sum paid by Qartu was announced to be 1.5 billion lari, though the calculation was not transparent. Georgian NGOs (TI, ISFED, and GYLA) assessed such a decision as bribing electoral votes. They also criticized opaque negotiations between the financial sector and the Georgian government (Tabula, 2019).

The purchase of debt by Ivanishvili shortly before the second round of presidential elections not only demonstrates the entanglement of political and economic spheres, but also highlights the power of currency and financial issues in governance. However, the measures of the government and the central bank, described above, did not tackle the core reasons of over-indebtedness. They only treated the symptoms and enforced new rules to avoid similar problems. Yet, why did the government start regulating and criticizing the financial sector and why did it buy the debt? The government could not escape the triple pressure of indebted households, international organizations, and the fear of losing elections. The Georgian Dream government had to pay for the misdeeds of previous governments, which had allowed financial institutions to flourish without rules and which had not perceived dollarization as a threat. The persistence of poverty over decades and accumulation of household debts (also in foreign currency) could no longer be ignored. Yet, the logic behind tackling over-indebtedness and taming the financial system was very much economistic. It aimed at returning insolvent borrowers to the labour or consumer markets to achieve economic growth; this should have guaranteed the long-term stability of the financial system. The economic growth imperative was guiding the new wave of regulations and de-dollarization policies.

Conclusion

The lari crisis shed light on the structural socio-economic issues of the country – poverty, unemployment, over-indebtedness, and unlocking the debate on dollarization and weak currency. The trajectory of the politicization of dollarization passed through the recognition of household over-indebtedness and poverty as a problem. This process was accompanied by polarized debates based on finding scapegoats – from the government to the central bank, financially uneducated borrowers, and commercial banks. The burden of assuming responsibility was too heavy. Still, the government and the central bank could not escape the introduction of new rules to tame dollarization and limit the freedom of lending institutions.

Despite the new regulations and laws, a fundamental rethinking of economic and monetary policy did not occur in Georgia. This can be explained by the continuation of neoliberal policies after the government change in 2012. Even though the Georgian Dream administration put more emphasis on social welfare and justice, its perceptions of the state and of state – market relations remained the same as under Saakashvili's government. No fundamental change occurred in the development path or economic structure of the country either. Foreign currency domination would have most likely stayed unaddressed by the Georgian Dream government had the currency crisis not happened.

It is important to set fair rules of the game in loan policies – such as responsible finance – to avoid further indebtedness, but the issue of a weak currency must be addressed, as well. It is crucial to question the mission and functions of the central bank, as well as economic development trajectories and the interplay of fiscal and monetary policies. Development of the capital market or enforcing a financialized pension reform cannot provide a solid basis for de-dollarization. These changes only strengthen the dependency of the Georgian economy on foreign capital and financial actors, instead of lifting it from its peripheral positioning in the global structure. A strong currency cannot exist without a strong economy and stable political system.

Notes

1 In 2013 a tax-free threshold was increased from 300 to 500 lari as the monthly salary (Cohen & Benovic, 2016, p. 8). However, it was abolished in 2015, in the aftermath of the currency crisis (International Monetary Fund, 2015c, p. 8).

2 In 2014, Azerbaijan was the most important trading partner for Georgia (19% of exports), followed by Armenia, Russia, and Turkey (Economic Policy Research Center, 2015, p. 94).

3 One of the most important imported products in 2015 was medicine for Hepatitis C, followed by oil products, cars, and copper. The service account balance had been positive since 2011 (National Bank of Georgia, 2015b, p. 26).
4 The biggest share of FDI (more than 37%) was diverted to transport and communication, followed by the financial sector (11.4%), energy (10.8%) and industry (9.9%) (National Bank of Georgia, 2015c, pp. 25–26).
5 The NBG defines watch loans as a loan that is 'adequately protected, but is potentially weak' (National Bank of Georgia, 2017b, Article 6).
6 Non-performing loans include substandard, doubtful, and loss loans, according to the Georgian central bank. NPLs are part of negative portfolio.
7 Despite the lack of accurate data on the size of seized housing as collateral, it is estimated that almost one-half of these loan contracts were made on informal loan markets (Society and Banks, 2017, p. 3).
8 Finally, the IMF three-year Extended Fund Facility was approved in April 2017 and 210.4 million SDRs were allocated to Georgia to support reforms (International Monetary Fund, 2017, p. 2).
9 The government pays 2% for annual salaries less than 24,000 lari and 1% for salaries not exceeding 60,000 lari. Those who earn more than 60,000 lari annually do not receive government assistance in the pensions fund (Article 3).
10 The board has four members: the Minister of Finance; the Minister of Economy and Sustainable Development; the Minister of Internally Displaced Persons from the Occupied Territories, Labour, Health and Social Affairs; the Chairperson of the Investment Board (Article 10).
11 In the section of questions and answers of the pension agency website, the answer to the question about insurance is that risks are minimized through diversified investments (https://www.pensions.ge/public-information/faq). This answer can be interpreted as indicating that there is no insurance for participants.
12 In 2018, this ceiling was increased to 200,000 lari and the change became applicable not only to households, but to legal entities, as well (BM.ge, 2018).
13 Loans could have been converted at the exchange rate of the day of operation minus 20 Tetri. The difference was covered from the state budget. This option was given to all households who had taken a loan before January 2015, if the loan did not exceed 100,000 USD and if their annual income did not exceed 100,000 lari (NBG, 2017).
14 As an example one can see the price policy of one of the real-estate developers, Jikia House (Jikia House, 2019).
15 During the author's interviews, in 2017, there was no publicly available statistical data on household over-indebtedness.

References

Ambebi.ge. (2016, July 8). ip'otek'it dazaralebulta armia mtavrobas up'irisp'irdeba [Victims of mortgaged property against the government]. https://www.ambebi.ge/article/169414-ipotekit-dazaralebulta-armia-mtavrobas-upirispirdeba/.

Ambebi.ge. (2018, June 20). "Ch'arbvalianoba akhrchobs kveq'anas" – rogor ap'irebs kveq'anashi sigharibis dadzelvas Mamuka Bakhtadze ["Over-indebtedness is a huge issue" – how does Mamuka Bakhtadze want to solve poverty].

Anguridze, O., Charaia, V., & Doghonadze, I. (2015). *Security Problems and Modern Challenges of the Georgian National Currency.* Ivane Javakhishvili Tbilisi State University TSU Center for Analysis and Forecast, Tbilisi.

Aprasidze, D. (2016). Consolidation in Georgia: Democracy or Power? In *Institute for Peace Research and Security Policy at the University of Hamburg (IFSH) (Ed.), OSCE Yearbook 2015* (pp. 107–115). Nomos.

Article 42 of the Constitution, Agency, C. D., Economic Policy Research Center, Georgia's Reforms Association, Georgian Young Lawyers' Association, Green Alternative, Human Rights Center, & Human Rights Education and Monitoring Center. (2015). Two Years in Government: Georgian Dream's Performance Review: October 2012–December 2014. https://transparency.ge/en/post/report/two-years-government-georgian-dream-performance-review.

Babych, Y., & Mosiashvili, N. (2014). *laris zamtris bluzi sheshpotebis mizezi?* [Winter blouse of Lari. A reason for concern?]. ISET Policy Institute.

Banks and Finance. (2016). Ganatlebis simts'iris gamo mosakhleobas arahejirebuli seskhebi akvs [Population has unhedged loans due to lack of education]. bfm.ge.

BM.ge. (2016, April 7). ip'otek'arebi p'remiertan shekhevdras itkhoven [Money-lenders request a meeting with the prime minister]. https://www.bm.ge/ka/article/ipotekarebi-premiertan-shexvedras-itxoven/2741/.

BM.ge. (2018a, April 18). shemosavlebis dadst'urebis gareshe seskhebis gatsema modad iktsa [It has become a trend to issues loans without verifying income]. https://www.bm.ge/ka/article/quotshemosavlebis-dadasturebis-gareshe-sesxebis-gacema-modad-iqcaquot/18570/.

BM.ge. (2018b, April 27). BAG-.is imedi makvs, rom ervnul bank's p'ozitsiebs sheatsvlevinebs [I hope that BAG will make the central bank change its positions]. https://www.bm.ge/ka/article/bag-s-imedi-aqvs-rom-erovnul-banks-poziciebs-sheacvlevinebs/18894/.

BM.ge. (2018c, April 30). BOG akhali regulatsiebis gadadebas itkhovs [BOG requires postponing of new regulations]. https://www.bm.ge/ka/article/bog-axali-regulaciebis-gadavadebas-itxovs/18963/.

BM.ge. (2018d, May 10). Erovnuli bank'i shesanishnavad artmevs tavs sabank'o sek-t'oris zedmakhedvelobas [Central bank fullfills its banking supervisory functions perfectly]. https://www.bm.ge/ka/article/quoterovnuli-banki-shesanishnavad-artmevs-tavs-sabanko-seqtoris-zedamxedvelobasquot/19371/.

BM.ge. (2018e, May 18). Seb-is initsiat'ivebs mkhars vuch'ert, tumtsa dialogi unda gagrdzeldes [We support the Georgian central bank, but dialogue should continue]. https://bm.ge/ka/article/quotseb-is-iniciativebs-mxars-vuchert-tumca-dialogi-unda-gagrdzeldesquot/19726/.

BM.ge. (2018f, July 27). Erovnulma bank'ma k'omerstiuli bank'ebistvis k'orp'or-atsiuli martvis k'odeksis p'roekt'i gamoakveq'na [Central bank published corporate governance codex for commercial banks]. https://www.bm.ge/ka/article/erovnulma-bankma-komerciuli-bankebistvis-korporaciuli-martvis-kodeqsis-proeqti-gamoaqveyna/23070/.

BM.ge. (2018g, September 12). FITCH. sabank'o sekt'oris akhal regulatsiebs dade-bitad vapasebt [FITCH: we assess new banking regulations positively]. https://www.bm.ge/ka/article/fitch-sabanko-seqtoris-axal-regulaciebs-dadebitad-vafasebt-/24384/.

BM.ge. (2018h, September 12). P'asukhismgebliani dak'redit'ebis p'rintsip'is shemo-gheba sak'maod k'argi idea [It's quite a good idea to adopt responsible finance principles]. https://www.bm.ge/ka/article/quotpasuxismgebliani-dakreditebis-principis-shemogeba-sakmaod-kargi-ideaaquot/24392/.

BM.ge. (2018i, October 17). Biznes gaertianebebis ertoblivi gantskhadeba seb-is daa-nonsebul regulatsiebze [A statement of the business association on central bank announced regulations]. https://www.bm.ge/ka/article/biznes-gaertianebebis-ertoblivi-gancxadeba-seb-is-daanonsebul-regulaciebze-/25692/.

BPI.ge. (2018, May 29). Mamuka Bakhtadze: sigharibis gamomts'vevi tamashis usamartlo ts'esi sruldeba [Mamuka Bakhtadze: unfair rules of the game, that caused poverty, are ending].

bpn.ge. (2018, April 12). Mamuka Bakhtadze: is sap'rotsent'o ganak'vetebi, rats chvens sit'emashia, biznesis dats'q'ebis shanss ar idzelva [Mamuka Bakhtadze: interest rates in our financial system does not allow starting businesses]. https://www.bpn.ge/article/44414-mamuka-bakhtadze-qis-saprocento-ganakvethebi-rac-chvens-sistemashia-biznesis-datsyebis-shanss-ar-idzlevaq/.

Caucasus Research Resource Center. (2016). Trends in the Data: Declining trust in the banks in Georgia. crrc-caucasus.blogspot.com.

Center for Financial Inclusion. (2016). "Client Voices" at the Georgian Parliament. Center for Financial Inclusion. https://www.centerforfinancialinclusion.org/client-voices-at-the-georgian-parliament.

Center for Insights in Survey Research. (2017). Survey of Public Opinion in Georgia. https://www.iri.org/wp-content/uploads/legacy/iri.org/iri_poll_presentation_georgia_2017.03-general.pdf.

Civil.ge. (2013, November 24). Ivanishvili: 'I Quit Politics, But Remain Active Citizen'. https://civil.ge/archives/186857.

Civil.ge. (2015a, January 30). Bank Chief: Tightening Monetary Policy, Cutting of Growth Forecast Needed. https://old.civil.ge/eng/article.php?id=28012.

Civil.ge. (2015b, February 21). PM: Govt to Cut Growth Forecast, Reduce Administrative Spending. https://old.civil.ge/eng/article.php?id=28070.

Civil.ge. (2015c, February 25). Govt Vows to Set up Privatization Amid GEL Depreciation. https://old.civil.ge/eng/article.php?id=28081.

Civil.ge. (2015d, February 26). Ivanishvili Blames GEL Fall on Central Bank. *Civil.ge*. 1–2. https://civil.ge/archives/124416.

Civil.ge. (2015e, May 24). President's Office Warns Against Bill on Banking Supervisory Agency. https://old.civil.ge/eng/article.php?id=28295.

Civil.ge. (2015f, June 4). Ivanishvili Backs Controversial Bill on Banking Supervisory Agency. https://civil.ge/archives/124652.

Civil.ge. (2015g, June 5). C. Bank Chief Calls to Stop 'Mudslinging Campaign'. https://old.civil.ge/eng/article.php?id=28328.

Civil.ge. (2015h, June 27). IMF, WB, EBRD, ADB Warn Georgia Against Removing Banking Supervision from NBG. https://civil.ge/archives/124709.

Civil.ge. (2016, April 11). NDI-Commissioned Public Opinion Survey. https://old.civil.ge/eng/article.php?id=29096.

Civil.ge. (2018, November 19). Government Announces Deal to Write off Bad Debts. https://civil.ge/archives/266476.

Cohen, A., & Benovic, I. (2016). *Georgian Dream Meets Reality: The Coalition's First Term and Future Reform Prospects*. Institute for the Analysis of Global Security.

Democracy and Freedom Watch. (2018, April 26). Ivanishvili to make political comeback, will head Georgia's ruling GD. https://dfwatch.net/ivanishvili-make-political-comeback-will-head-georgias-ruling-gd-50262.

Economic Policy Research Center. (2015). Economy. In *Two Years in Government: Georgian Dream's Performance Review: October 2012–December 2014* (pp. 90–97).

Eradze, I. (2020). Corona Pandemic as an Amplifier of Socio-Economic Crises in Georgia. *Caucasus Analytical Digest*, 115(May), 3–7.

Eradze, I. (2021). Imbalanced foreign trade, debt, and investment in developing countries: The case of Georgia (Issue June). https://eu.boell.org/en/2021/06/16/imbalanced-foreign-trade-debt-and-investment-developing-countries-case-georgia.
Eradze, I. (2022). Financialization of Monetary Policy in a Dollarized Economy: the case of Georgia. *Cambridge Journal of Economics*. https://doi.org/10.1093/cje/beac019.
Evgenidze, N. (2015). khelisupleba erovnuli bank'is dasust'ebaze uars ar ambobs [The governemnt is weakening the central bank]. Radio Liberty.
Fairbanks, C. H. (2014). Georgian democracy: Seizing or losing the chance? *Journal of Democracy*, 25(1), 154–165.
Gogua, G. (2015). P'rezident'is vet'o daidzlia [President's veto was overcome by the parliament]. Radio Liberty.
Government of Georgia. (2014). sakartvelos sotsialur-ek'onomik'uri ganvitarebis st'rat'egia sakartvelo 2020 [Strategy of Social-economic development of Georgia 2020]. https://www.gov.ge/files/382_42949_233871_400-1.pdf.
Horton, M., Samiei, H., Epstein, N., & Ross, K. (2016). *Exchange Rate Developments and Policies in the Caucasus and Central Asia*. International Monetary Fund.
Human Rights Education and Monitoring Center. (2015). Labor Rights. In Georgian NGOs (Ed.), *Two Years in Government: Georgian Dream's Performance Review: October 2012–December 2014* (pp. 59–61).
International Monetary Fund. (2015a). Georgia: Financial Sector Assessment Programm. Macroprudential Policy Framework – Technical Note (Issue 09). https://www.elibrary.imf.org/view/journals/002/2015/009/002.2015.issue-009-en.xml.
International Monetary Fund. (2015b). Georgia: Financial Sector Assessment Programm. Stress Testing the Banking Sector – Technical Note. https://www.elibrary.imf.org/view/journals/002/2015/007/article-A001-en.xml.
International Monetary Fund. (2015c). Georgia: First Review Under the Stand-By Arrangement and Request for Modification of a Performance Criterion (Issue 15). https://www.elibrary.imf.org/view/journals/002/2015/017/article-A001-en.xml.
International Monetary Fund. (2017). Georgia: request for extended arrangement under the extended fund facility and cancellation of stand-by arrangement – press release; Staff report: And statement by the executive director of Georgia (Issue 17/97). http://www.economy.ge/uploads/files/2017/imf_monetary_found/cr1797_2.pdf.
ipn.ge. (2013, July 25). p'arlament'shi ip'otek'arebi da ip'otek'iT dazaralebulebi daup'irisp'rdnen [Money lenders and victims of housing collaterilized lending against each other in the parliament]. https://www.interpressnews.ge/ka/article/247952-parlamentshi-ertmanets-kerzo-ipotekarebi-da-ipotekit-dazaralebulebi-daupirispirdnen/.
Jikia House. (2019). Sheni sakhli jikiaze: gasaq'idi binebi [Your house as Jikia: Flats for sale]. jikiahouse.ge.
Kachkachishvili, T. (2015). Ip'otek'uri seskhit dazaralebulta motkhovnebi utsvlelia [Mortgage lenders are not changing their requests]. Radio Liberty.
Kakulia, M., Kapanadze, N., & Qurkhuli, L. (2017). Kronik'uli sigharibe da shemosavlebis utanabroba sakartveloshi: ek'onomik'ur-st'at'ist'ik'uri k'vleva [Chronic poverty and income inequality in Georgia: economic-statistical research]. Georgian Foundation for Strategic and International Studies & Friedrich Ebert Stiftung, Tbilisi. https://gfsis.org.ge/ge/publications/view/2509.
Karelidze, T. (2018). *Georgia's divisive pension reform splits opinion*. Emerging Europe.
Khaliani, T. (2012). Bank'ebis nulp'rotsent'iani ut'op'ia [Zero % Utopia of Banks]. Liberali.ge.
Kharadze, N. (2015). Vin aris damnashave laris mimart [Who is to be blamed for Lari]. Radio Liberty.

Khundadze, T. (2018). *Opinion: Bank reforms touted by Georgia's Prime Minister – to-be could spell the end of predatory lending*. OC Media.
Kliatskova, T., & Mikkelsen, U. (2015). Floating with a Load of FX Debt? (15/284; IMF Working Papers).
K'omertsiuli bank'ebis mier sabank'o momsakhurebis gats'evisas momkhmareblisatvis inpormatsiis mits'odebis ts'esi [Rule for commercial banks on providing mandatory information for consumers] (2011) (testimony of National Bank of Georgia).
Kunchulia, L. (2015). erovnuli bank'i, p'arlament'i, lari da gant'evebis vatsi [Central bank, parliament, Lari and a scapegoat]. Radio Liberty.
Lebanidze, B. (2018). Making Georgia's democracy work: Western political conditionality and domestic agendas of Georgian political parties (No. 10; Georgian Institute of Politics Policy Brief).
Lomsadze, G. (2018). Billionaire's big talk on his big plans for Georgia: Ivanishvili holds on forth on his behind-the-scenes decision making. eurasia.net.
Macfarlane, N. S. (2015). *Two Years of the Dream: Georgian Foreign Policy During the Transition*. Chatham House.
Ministry of Economy of Georgia. (2017). 4 P'unkt'iani gegma - qveq'nis sts'rapi ganvitarebistvis [4 point plan for the fast development of the country]. Ministry of Economy.
Namchavadze, B. (2015). laris gaupasurebis gavlena sakartvelos sotsialuri-ek'onomik'uri ganvitarebis st'rat'egeia "sakartvelo 2020"-ze [Influence of Lari depreciation on socio-economic development strategy 2020]. IDFI.ge.
National Bank of Georgia. (2006). pinansuri st'abilurobis angarishi [Financial Stability Report]. https://nbg.gov.ge/en/publications/financial-stability-reports.
National Bank of Georgia. (2010). Ts'liuri angarishi [Annual report]. https://nbg.gov.ge/en/publications/annual-reports.
National Bank of Georgia. (2011a). pinansuri st'abilurobis angarishi [Financial Stability Report]. https://nbg.gov.ge/en/publications/financial-stability-reports.
National Bank of Georgia. (2011b). Ts'liuri angarishi [Annual report]. https://nbg.gov.ge/en/publications/annual-reports.
National Bank of Georgia. (2015a). Gross external Debt of Georgia. nbg.gov.ge.
National Bank of Georgia. (2015b). sakartvelos sagadasakhdelo balansi [Current account balance of Georgia]. nbg.gov.ge.
National Bank of Georgia. (2015c). Ts'liuri angarishi [Annual Report]. https://nbg.gov.ge/en/publications/annual-reports.
National Bank of Georgia. (2016a). Ts'liuri angarishi [Annual Report]. https://nbg.gov.ge/en/publications/annual-reports.
National Bank of Georgia. (2016b). sakartvelos sagadasakhdelo balansi [Current account balance of Georgia].
National Bank of Georgia. (2016c). Ts'liuri angarishi [Annual Report]. https://nbg.gov.ge/en/publications/annual-reports.
National Bank of Georgia. (2017a). Ts'liuri angarishi [Annual Report]. https://nbg.gov.ge/en/publications/annual-reports.
National Bank of Georgia. (2017b). Decree N 117/04 of the Governor of the National Bank of Georgia on approving the Regulation on Assets Classification and the Creation and Use of Reserves for Losses by Commercial Banks. nbg.gov.ge.
National Bank of Georgia. (2017c). Erovnuli bank'is gantskhadeba [National Bank Statement]. nbg.gov.ge.
National Bank of Georgia. (2017d). Ts'liuri angarishi [Annual Report]. https://nbg.gov.ge/en/publications/annual-reports.

National Bank of Georgia. (2018a). Sakartvelos erovnuli bank'i k'omertsiuli bank'ebistvis p'asukhismgebliani dak'redit'ebis motkhovnebis shemoghebaze atskhadebs [Georgian central bank on reponsible finance requirements for commercial banks]. nbg.gov.ge.

National Bank of Georgia. (2018b). Sakartvelos erovnulma bank'ma pizik'ur p'irebze seskhebis gatsemis ts'esi daamt'k'itsa [Georgian central bank approved rules for issuing loans to households]. nbg.gov.ge.

National Bank of Georgia. (2022). https://nbg.gov.ge/en/statistics/statistics-data.

Navarro, L. (2018). *Georgian Shadow Democracy in the Age of Illiberalism*. Foreign Policy Research Institute.

Netgazeti. (2018a, April 27). Akhali regulatsiebi bank'ebisa da mik'rosapinansoebis akt'ivobas sheamtsirebs – Vakhtang Butskhrikidze [New regulations will decrease the activities of micro finance organisations – Vakhtang Butskhrikidze]. https://netgazeti.ge/news/271700/.

Netgazeti. (2018b, May 28). Dzveli seskhis 1,65 k'ursit gadaxda da 'saech'vo valis 2 ts'lit gaq'inva – saak'ashvilis dap'irebebi [Repaying debts with old exchange rate of 1.65 and freezing 'doubtful loans' for 2 years – Saakashvili's promises]. http://netgazeti.ge/news/280701/.

New Posts. (2016, January 20). ertiani natsionaluri modzraoba mtavrobas ek'onomik'uri k'rizisidan gamosvlis gegmas stavazobs [UNM offers the government a plan out for the crisis]. www.newposts.ge/?l=G&id=97352.

News.On.ge. (2016, May 30). Biz'ina ivanishvilis ghia ts'erili [Bidzina Ivanishvili's Open Letter].

Law of Georgia on Funded Pensions (2018) (testimony of Parliament of Georgia).

Pension Agency. (2019). Khshirad dasmuli k'itkhvebi [Frequently asked questions]. Pensions.ge.

Perchoc, P. (2017). *Georgia: European engagement in an unstable environment*. European Parliamentary Research Service.

Society and Banks. (2017). *dasak'utrebuli uz'ravi konebis mimokhilva* [A review of seized real estate collateral] (pp. 1–5). Society and Banks.

Society and Banks. (2018). Sazogadoeba da bank'ebi" akhal sabank'o regulatsiebs apasebs [Society and Banks assesses new banking regulations]. Sab.ge.

Sonar Ltd. (2016). Financial Literacy and Financial Inclusion Study. National Bank of Georgia.

Tabula. (2019, November 19). NGO-ebi: valebis chamots'eris initsiat'iva amomrchevelta up'retsendent'o masst'abis shesadzlo mosq'idva [NGOs: debt annulation is a widescale bribing of electorate]. www.tabula.ge/ge/story/140016-ngo-ebi-valebis-chamotseris-iniciativa-amomrchevelta-uprecendento-masshtabis-shesadzlo.

The Guardian. (2012, September 19). Georgia prison guards' captured on video torturing prisoner'.

Transparency International Georgia, EPRC, OSGF, & et.al. (2015). Arasamtavrobo organizatsiebis gantskhadeba erovnuli bank'is shesakheb k'anonshi dagegmili tsvlilebis shesakheb [NGOs' statement on the legal planned changes about the Central bank]. Georgian Reform Association.

Tsintsadze, M. (2018). Int'erviu bidzina ivanishviltan [Interview with Bidzina Ivanishvili]. 1tv.ge. https://1tv.ge/video/aqtualuri-tema-maka-cincadzis-stumaria-bidzina-ivanishvili-partia-qartuli-ocnebis-tavmjdomare/.

TV Free. (2015, July 14). Bank'ebi chven gvekheba [Banks concern us].

UNICEF. (2018). Mosakhleobis k'etildgheobis k'vleva 2017: mok'le mimokhilva [Population Welfare Research 2017: short overview].

Voice of America. (2015, October 13). sapinanso zedamkhedvelobis saagent'om mkholod ori dghe imushava [Financial supervision agency worked for two days only]. http://www.amerikiskhma.com/a/georgiaconstitutionalcourtdecision/3003730.html.

World Bank. (2018). Georgia from Reformer to Performer. https://openknowledge.worldbank.org/handle/10986/29790.

Zasztowt, K. (2013). Georgian Dream's Foreign Policies: An Attempt to Change the Paradigm? (3 (51); The Polish Institute of International Affairs Policy Paper).

10 Conclusion

Rising public and private debt during the Covid-19 pandemic points at the perils of increased borrowing in foreign currency for households, firms, and the state. The pandemic has made it clear that peripheral economies are especially vulnerable to external shocks. The global inequality gap is widening, inflation is on the rise and weak currencies are experiencing devaluations. The existing crisis further aggravates power asymmetries between the Global North and the Global South, as well as among world currencies. Dollarization-related issues cannot be solved sustainably without understanding the embeddedness of dollarization within the state and within global power relations. However, rethinking of the state is not happening, neither at the global nor at national levels.

The pandemic gave hope to many all over the world that a major rethinking of state and state-market relations would take place. Yet, this hope did not find any echo in Georgian policy making. Neither ante- nor post-crisis plans of the government, nor the academic and public discourses led to questioning of the neoliberal state in Georgia. Ideas about transforming the economic structure (expressed at the beginning of the pandemic) have faded away, while the mandate of the central bank has not been examined. The architecture of the global financial system and currency hierarchy is also resistant to fundamental changes. While countries from the Global South try to avoid socio-economic disaster through holding external debts in foreign currency, the level of dollarization is rising, and these states become even more vulnerable to economic and financial shocks.

Georgia's public debt is on the rise, its share to GDP has increased from 40% in 2019 to 60% in 2020. Most of this debt is denominated in foreign currency (International Monetary Fund, 2021, p. 9). As the Georgian government tries to tackle the current socio-economic crisis through additional foreign borrowing,[1] the importance of a strong currency and a well-developed local money market becomes clear. Although the National Bank of Georgia has been actively intervening in the FX market during the pandemic to counteract the depreciation of the lari (National Bank of Georgia, 2021a, pp. 56, 68), it remains trapped in between price and currency stability aims.[2] The level of inflation (12%) has reached a ten-year peak and the IMF has

DOI: 10.4324/9781003240174-14

called for a strict monetary policy and a decline in fiscal spending (see International Monetary Fund, 2021). This will negatively influence the socio-economic recovery of Georgia, as the country is still in deep economic and political crisis.

Even though awareness of dollarization-related issues has increased in Georgia, there is a lack of understanding of the issue in connection with the overall political, institutional, historical, cultural, and social questions. Moreover, a direct linkage between the peripheral position of the Georgian economy and the weakness of its national currency is either forgotten or ignored. The Georgian political elite still pictures the world market as a place of fair and equal games in which countries like Georgia can have free trade on equal conditions with states such as China.[3] Yet, an acknowledgment of asymmetrical global power relations is crucial for the political and economic discourse. Fairy tales about the success of small and open economies (that are underdeveloped) through free-trade relations or liberalized markets cannot remain legitimate for long. Concepts such as financialization remain unknown in Georgian policymaking and academic circles.[4] A technocratization discourse of central bank policies is dominant, making the critique of this institution and its mission difficult. Yet, Georgia's historic experience of banking and central banking (for example during the First Republic of Georgia, 1918–1921), that could have brought about the questioning of the normalized views on the financial system, has been forgotten. This is closely connected with the understanding and functioning of the state itself. While Georgia remains a neoliberal state and neoclassical economics is hegemonic in Georgian academia, and disciplines like political economy are absent, there can be no expectation of a fundamental rethinking of the economy or central banking occurring.

Narrow economistic thinking and the disregard of asymmetrical global power relations cannot fix the current crisis; nor can it illuminate such a complex phenomenon as foreign currency domination. The persistence of dollarization is rooted in state building narratives, dominant discourses on development, as well as in accumulation regimes and governance practices. Currency issues are not purely economic, they are always linked with socio-economic, historical, and cultural processes; they are an integral part of politics. Therefore, this book has traced the roots, persistence, and politicization trajectories of dollarization alongside a historical analysis of the Georgian state, at the local and global levels.

The history of dollarization shows that foreign currency domination is rooted in socio-political and economic processes at the national and international levels. Transition policies (with an agenda of liberalization) since the early 1990s not only opened the doors of the Georgian economy to the world market, but also to international currencies. Thus, it was no wonder that a currency such as the US dollar was welcomed in a highly unstable environment. The hyperinflation of 1993 finally decided the supremacy of the dollar over the Russian ruble in Georgia. This experience shaped the first attitudes of Georgians towards a national currency (the coupon was a temporary currency at that point) and negatively influenced societal trust in the national currency. Prior to the introduction of the Georgian lari (1995), the dollar played a significant role in the Georgian economy. Although the Georgian currency was quite successful in the beginning, the 1998 Russian crisis caused its depreciation and an immediate rise of dollarization of loans and deposits. These trends proved to be hard to reverse and dollarization persisted.

A patrimonial bureaucratic state, which emerged after the break-down of the Soviet Union, disregarded the question of dollarization, whereas the shadow accumulation regime well integrated and used the dollar as the main means of transaction. The Georgian political elite was neither concerned about currency issues nor did they have enough knowledge and experience on these matters throughout the 1990s. The economic policy space in general was disregarded. Discourses on nationalism, territorial integrity and foreign policy had a priority on the policy agenda. The nationalism discourse also accepted foreign currency dominance, as its focus was rather ethnic in nature, and did not acknowledge economic matters as an object of nationalist feelings. This is understandable in a newly independent country that was involved in wars and conflicts. Yet, even after the stabilization of the political situation (from the mid-1990s), political, economic, and financial power groups were focused on private rent-seeking goals, disregarding the interests of Georgian society. Georgian civil society was too occupied with democratization issues to pay attention to foreign currency domination.

Thus, a bureaucratic, patrimonial hybrid state was not acknowledging dollarization as an issue; this phenomenon was beyond its scope of knowledge and interest. Nevertheless, it was not just the lack of knowledge or ignorance of currency issues that encouraged dollarization, but that the hegemony of the dollar well served the rent-seeking interests of elite groups and links between economic and political power groups were rather inseparable throughout the 1990s. A flourishing shadow economy fully embraced the dollar as its main currency. The emerging financial system, which was idle and fed by central bank loans, profited from speculative practices and had nothing to lose from a high rate of dollarization. Moreover, commercial banks contributed to dollarization by strengthening the distrust of the population through their speculative practices. Thus, dollar hegemony was not contested in Georgia since independence. International organizations (especially the IMF) were slowly acknowledging the issue of dollarization (from the late 1990s), but they were hesitant to admit the role of liberalization and deregulation policies in this issue and shifted the responsibility towards the Georgian government.

The Rose Revolution of 2003 marked a new beginning for the Georgian state. For the first time since independence, institutions were taking shape and the economy was recovering, but dollarization remained uncontested and persisted at high levels. State building and the development narratives of the new government did not perceive dollarization as an issue. Saakashvili's government aimed at building a 'modern', democratic, minimal state. Economic growth through libertarian economic reforms and the eradication of bureaucratic structures were hoped to transform Georgia into an 'European' state. The regulatory role of the state was reduced to a minimum and even the abolition of institutions like the central bank was discussed. A neoliberal understanding of the state, a libertarian approach to the monetary policy, and the readiness of the post-revolution government to pay any price for integration into the global market, explain why a weak national currency was not perceived as a key problem.

These views were fully compatible with the approach to economic development, which aimed at achieving GDP growth through FDI. The free circulation of a foreign currency was one of the preconditions for creating a foreign capital friendly environment. Moreover, the accumulation of foreign capital in the banking sector directly encouraged lending in foreign currency and supported the persistence of dollarization. Even though macroeconomic stability was achieved and the economy was growing, nothing changed in the sectoral composition of the economy. The Georgian economy was still struggling with high trade and current account deficits, making the lari vulnerable to regional and global developments. Dollarization created barriers for the development of the production sphere and of small and medium-sized businesses in Georgia. Georgian civil society was still occupied with questions of foreign policy and democracy, and did not focus on socio-economic problems. Furthermore, Saakashvili's authoritarian governance weakened civil society groups and reduced spaces of criticism. Therefore, the possibilities of criticism on any matter, including dollar hegemony, shrank to a minimum. Thus, macroeconomic stability and low inflation did not turn out to be enough for de-dollarization in Georgia.

The rise of the financial sector after the Rose Revolution (2003) and the inflow of foreign capital encouraged the persistence of dollarization. The process of peripheral financialization, which had roots in the 1990s transition policies, was directly encouraged and enabled by the deregulation policies of the post-revolution government. The main actors of the process were the commercial banks, most of which were under foreign ownership after the revolution, and the driving force of the process was foreign capital. Finance became the most successful and fast growing sector of the Georgian economy, but it was not contributing to the development of other economic sectors. Georgian banks had easy access to foreign currency and actively issued loans mostly in US dollars due to the absence of regulations on foreign currency lending. Households became the major focus group for commercial banks, which led to a credit boom (2005–2007, renewed in 2010) and consequently household over-indebtedness. Increasing demand for retail loans was largely caused by the minimal state agenda and retreat of the Georgian government from the social sphere, in areas such as health, education, and housing. For example, the absence of housing politics and the price boom in the real estate market largely contributed to the increasing level of foreign currency mortgages, as well as the dollarization of real estate prices. Moreover, the credit boom after the revolution was also linked with the increased daily needs of households, which they could not pay from wages. The post-revolution accumulation regime did bring economic growth, but alongside this, unemployment and poverty rates, as well as income inequality, increased. Thus, the diminished role of the state in social welfare and its policies of deregulation not only created demand for retail loans, but also provided the supply of loans, which finally led to the credit boom and the over indebtedness of households.

The central bank of Georgia did not and could not respond to the ongoing processes in good time. Its policy space was limited due to the high level of dollarization and because of political pressures. After the transition to an inflation-targeting regime in 2009, the central bank became even weaker institutionally. Its main mission was to watch the level of inflation, even though several factors hindered the central bank from fulfiling even this narrow mandate. Exchange rate stability became subordinate to price stability and the National Bank of Georgia faced a challenge of an impossible trinity of free capital flows, price, and exchange rate stabilities. Furthermore, the major instrument of control possessed by bank, control over interest rates, was ineffective not only due to dollarization, but also because of the foreign ownership of banks. Most banks in Georgia had access to foreign capital, and they were not interested in lending from the central bank. Moreover, the National Bank of Georgia was a permanent object of attack by the government, which tried to maintain control over central bank policies and even questioned the need of this institution. Thus, inflation targeting encouraged international investors after the double crisis of 2008–2009, but negatively influenced the process of de-dollarization and further weakened the Georgian central bank.

The currency crisis of 2015–2016 finally let the dollarization genie out of the bottle, and unravelled structural socio-economic issues that had accumulated over the years, upon increased debt burden and prices. A trajectory of politicization of dollarization was affected by increased poverty and household over-indebtedness. The currency crisis soon turned into manifold conflicts and blame games among and between the government, central bank, and commercial banks and led to a crisis of political legitimacy. The importance of dollarization was becoming visible. Public pressure, as well as the recommendations of IOs (the IMF, WB) pushed the Georgian government and the central bank towards de-dollarization. These developments showed that neither the government, nor economic and financial forces, would have questioned the phenomenon in the long run had a crisis not broken out. Despite the government change in 2012, key values and especially views of development remained the same. The role of foreign capital and the subordination of currency stability aims to inflation targets were not questioned. Dollar hegemony was still profitable for commercial banks and for economic sectors such as real estate and construction, and for international investors. Thus, it took public pressure and the compulsion of IOs to tackle dollarization.

Despite the introduction of new regulations and de-dollarization measures in Georgia after 2018, a fundamental questioning of the financial system and central bank policies has not occurred. The Georgian government wanted short-term responses to put the fire out, while IOs started to worry about dollarization because they could see long-term risks for the stability of the global financial system. Therefore, neither the motives of the government nor international organizations emerged from the concerns of the broader society. Although regulations were adopted regarding financial education and responsible finance, no fundamental rethinking of monetary policy, the financial sector, or the overall economic development and state has occurred. New laws and rules have treated symptoms of dollarization, whereas its root causes have remained untouched.

Strong currencies cannot exist without strong state institutions, public trust in the government, and a well-developed economy. Foreign currency domination is directly rooted in the functioning of the state and its solutions should also be analysed at the level of political and civil society, as well as that of the regime. The organization of the state and its relationship to markets can support or discourage the usage of foreign currencies. For example, the retreat of neoliberal states from social provision directly encourages the rise of demand for household loans, while the deregulation of finance shifts the balance of power towards creditors and enables them to lend in foreign currency. Therefore, de-dollarization measures do not address monetary and fiscal policies or commercial banks alone, but it should lead to the rethinking of such questions as: what is a state? How does the political interact with the economic? What kind of policy spaces does a country have? How much agency does the state have? What threats and chances does the country face in the global market? Answers to these questions address the well-being of the society and should not be outweighed by the rent-seeking interests of political and financial groups at local and global levels.

This book looked for plausible answers to explain dollarization and understand the Georgian state. It unravelled the importance of discourses on development and the state within political and civil society, that either see foreign currency domination as a matter of concern or completely disregard it. This research unveiled the embeddedness of foreign currencies within the accumulation regimes of dollarized states and their role in ensuring the rent-seeking aims of financial and political elites. It also highlighted the importance of global players, liberalized foreign capital flows and the process of financialization in causing and tackling the questions of dollarization, as dollarization is embedded in the international currency hierarchy and open current accounts. I hope that this work will contribute to the rethinking of dominant discourses in dollarization literature and policy space, evoke new questions, and start new debates on the role of currencies, central banks, or monetary politics.

Notes

1 The Loan to GDP ratio increased significantly in 2020, mostly due to the depreciation of the lari (National Bank of Georgia, 2021b, p. 52)
2 The interest rate differential between loans in foreign and national currency has been increasing since 2014, while it remained more or less the same for SMEs and corporate loans (in 2020 the spread increased here too) (National Bank of Georgia, 2021a, pp. 96–97).
3 In 2017, Georgia signed a free trade agreement with China.
4 In 2017, most of the interviewees (both in policymaking and expert circles) had never heard the term financialization and those who had heard it, defined it in positive terms.

References

International Monetary Fund. (2021). Eighth Review under the Extended Fund Facility Arrangement – press release; and staff report (Issue 21/79).
National Bank of Georgia. (2021a). Annual Report 2020. https://nbg.gov.ge/en/publications/annual-reports.
National Bank of Georgia. (2021b). pinansuri st'abilurobis angarishi [Financial Stability Report]. https://nbg.gov.ge/en/publications/financial-stability-reports.

11 Annex 1

A methodological note

The main methodological claim of the book is the application of state theory to the analysis of dollarization. In this respect, the research goes beyond a purely economic understanding of this phenomenon and explores dollarization by tracing its roots in the emergence and development of the Georgian state. This study offers a historical analysis and takes into consideration political, economic, social, and cultural aspects. Furthermore, the research contributes to the development of theories of dollarization, as well as to the debate about peripheral states within critical political economy and post-positivist theories. This chapter deals with the main methodological questions, sheds light on the ontological and epistemological foundations of the research, agency-structure relations, research strategies and methods, as well as research limitations.

Ontological and epistemological foundations

The foundations of this research lie in postpositivist theories that reject the idea of objectivity and argue that the social sciences cannot be seen as natural sciences (Wullweber, 2014, p. Introduction section). These approaches are problem driven, focusing on the reasons of the *problématique*, examining power relations, and questioning social conditions (Wullweber, 2014, p. The Primacy of Politics section). Therefore, research does not begin with an objective problem, but it is rather up to a researcher to analyse why certain processes are perceived as a problem, which then become objects of analysis (Wullweber, 2014, p. Postfoundational Ontology section).

Postpositivist theories do not make a clear-cut distinction between ontological and epistemological premises, as these categories are intertwined with one another (Wullweber, 2014, p. Introduction section). Foundationalists or essentialists claim that social life is based on certain foundations, which is made up of 'essential differences of "being"' (Marsh & Furlong, 2002, p. 18), while for anti-foundationalists such differences are a product of social construction, as the 'real' world does not exist without actors giving meaning to

DOI: 10.4324/9781003240174-15

it (Marsh & Furlong, 2002, pp. 18–19). Nevertheless, as Wullweber argues, postpositivism is postfoundationalist and not antifoundationalist, which means that there are certain foundations of the society but they are constantly changing (Wullweber, 2014, p. Post-foundational Ontology section). If foundationalists argue that they can observe the 'real' world and come up with universal laws as in natural science (Marsh & Furlong, 2002, p. 19), postpositivist approaches share a basic assumption that the understanding of meaning is crucial for any analysis. Thus, beliefs, ideas, and discourses matter, and it is impossible to gain objective knowledge (Bevir & Rhodes, 2002, pp. 131–133).

Structure and agency

Debate on the role of structure and agency has a long history in social sciences. However, as McAnnulla argues, this debate should not be oriented on finding a solution, but should be seen as 'an *unavoidable problem*. [...] an issue [on which] we cannot avoid adopting a position' (McAnulla, 2002, p. 273) italics original). Indeed, the meaning that is attributed to structure or agency is the core of social science theories. On the one hand, this defines the sources of power and, on the other hand, it displays power relations and defines the vectors of analysis.

Structuralists are criticized for lacking a theory of subject. On the other hand, intentionalists assign all the power to agents and structures do not play an important role for them (McAnulla, 2002, pp. 276–277). However, not all theories tend to choose either structure or agency; there are also dialectical approaches, where agency and structure both affect one another (McAnulla, 2002, p. 278). Regulationists try to explain agency structure relations through a conceptualization of different levels of abstraction, where structure can be defined as 'basic, long term stabilized and internalized forms of social relations with special positions of action' (Becker, 2002, p. 13). However, specific accumulation strategies, as well as regulation-related political strategies cannot be derived simply from structures. Capitalist structures give actors certain strategies, but also limit them (Becker, 2002, p. 273). It is important to analyse 'hegemonic articulation in discourse formation' while referring to capital accumulation (Scherrer, 1995, p. 475). Structures are not closed totalities, but rather dislocated that produce partial 'free' subjects (drawing on the ideas of Laclau, 1990). The accumulation regime depends on discourses based on relations between these subjects (Scherrer, 1995, p. 476).

A dislocation of structures shall not be interpreted as meaning that everything is possible, or that one could convert metal into gold in Jessop's terms (Bieler & Morton, 2008, p. 114). The structure is not able to fully shape the actions of the subject and the dislocation of the structure enables the subject to act (Wullweber & Scherrer, 2010). Thus, the subject is neither autonomous or rational, nor completely free. Agents are embraced in social discourses (Wullweber, 2014, De-centered Subject section). Furthermore, it is important to note that structures and agents are not dislocated from each other, they produce and reproduce each other constantly. The idea of discourse helps to explain these relations (Wullweber & Scherrer, 2010).

Thus, here it is important to grasp the meaning of discourse in order to understand structure–agency relations. The introduction of concepts – discourse and dispositive – avoids the only focus on structural aspects. Furthermore, the concept of hegemony, which has been introduced in this chapter, offers an analytical tool to focus on subjects and struggles. In this way, structures do not appear as being deterministic, but rather undergo the shaping and reshaping of one another through constant dialogue between agency and structure.

Discourse

The importance of discourse in postpositivist academic work is crucial, especially in ontological terms. Even though these postpositivist scholars do not accept the notion of social structures as a fixed base of the society, they do not neglect this kind of structure and refer to it as discourse (Wullweber, 2014, p. Postfoundational Ontology section).'Thus, a discourse is a relational structure [...]. [A]n ensemble of signifying sequences, which together constitute a more or less coherent framework of what can be said or done' (Wullweber & Scherrer, 2010). However, one should not equate the meaning of discourse to the structure. One of the main differences is that a discourse is never completed and closed; something always escapes (Wullweber & Scherrer, 2010). The understanding of discourse in this research is not limited to linguistic practices only, but 'It contains the sum of all verbal and nonverbal articulations on a particular topic, shaping the perception, thinking, and action of individuals' (Wullweber & Scherrer, 2010).

Discourse cannot be understood without the notion of power. Discourse creation is not only based on power struggles, but also produces new power relations. The understanding of power in this book is based on Foucaldian power relations, where power does not mean that A forces B to act, but it is rather a relation between A and B running both ways; thus, power circulates (see De Goede, 2005, pp. 151–152; Foucault, 1980a, pp. 200–201; Lemke, 2012, p. 10). Knowledge and truth production are strongly connected with the notion of power. As Foucault argued: 'We are subjected to the production of truth through power and we cannot exercise power except through the production of knowledge' (Foucault, 1980b, p. 93).

The idea of discourse leads to the debate on truth – is there truth and what is truth? There is neither neutrality, nor one reality; instead, there are various ideas on realities. These different discourses have a different place and credibility as they are competing against each other for domination (Dzudzek et al., 2012, p. 16). The above-mentioned competition and its outcomes produce truth and it does not exist outside the discourse.

> The idea of 'objective' in metaphysical materialism would appear to mean an objectivity that exists even apart from man [...]. We know reality only in relation to man, and since man is historical becoming, knowledge and reality are also a becoming and so is objectivity.
>
> (Gramsci, 1992, 1049, cited in Wullweber & Scherrer, 2010)

Yet, the process of truth production is shaped by struggles. However, these claims should not be interpreted as an absolute rejection of the existence of truth. This kind of understanding of objectivity opens a space for plausible theoretical explanations and further theorization based on empirics, instead of locking and taming empirics within a given theoretical framework. Furthermore, the research and its findings do not raise a claim for objectivity or truth, but rather for plausibility.

Research methods

The book is a case study of the persistence of dollarization in a small transition economy that has undergone waves of liberalization and neo liberalization in the last three decades. The aim is to generalize major explanations and contributions to the literature of dollarization, as well as to state theory building for transition countries. The research is mostly qualitative, based on in-depth interviews and content analysis of official documents, reports, and news. In addition, secondary quantitative data has been analysed and used for the visual presentation of relevant trends and changes in dollarization-related areas. The qualitative character of the research allows the study of ideas, discourses, perceptions, culture and history, social process and change to unravel the social reality. Furthermore, thick descriptions are possible that are crucial for describing actions. However, analysis does not stop at this level but also provides explanations.

Within the study, 27 in-depth interviews were conducted in two time periods – April 2016 and April–June 2017 (see Appendix 1). Respondents were chosen across various professions, places of work, and positions. Amongst others, these included policy experts, policymakers (at the ministry of economy, the office of the president, the central bank), representatives of NGOs, IOs and international financial institutions, a lawyer, and staff of a commercial bank and microfinance organization. As most of the interviewees preferred to stay anonymous due to the high sensitivity of the research topic in Georgia, the names of respondents have not been mentioned in this work; only a reference to their workplace has been made to provide a context for opinions. All interviews were conducted in person, in face-to-face conversation. The language of interviews was Georgian with very few exceptions.

The year 2017 was especially important in the discourse of dollarization in Georgia as this was when new de-dollarization laws and regulations were introduced. I had the possibility of attending public discussions on the new regulations and these experiences are directly or indirectly reflected in the research. Having witnessed dollarization-related discussions in Georgia personally has inspired this research and helped me to identify the narratives.

This monograph focuses on household debt held in foreign currency rather than the dollarization of corporate debt. Household loans in foreign currency (50% share) (National Bank of Georgia, 2016c, p. 88) are the focus of this analysis for two reasons. The problematization and politicization of dollarization, in the aftermath of the currency crisis (2015), were driven by household indebtedness. Moreover, households as unhedged borrowers have been most vulnerable to exchange-rate fluctuations.

The research has focused on a macro-level and most of the interviewees were conducted with decision makers, experts, or the staff of financial institutions. A closer look at the perspectives of households and especially of indebted households would have been of added value. However, due to time constraints and the limited scale of research, no interviews were conducted with households. This 'gap' was partially made up by the results of different studies and household surveys, focusing on research relevant themes. Furthermore, the challenging aim of theorizing Georgia beyond existing or already applied theoretical frames (that prove to be shorthanded) is not fully achieved in this work. Although the study has identified important gaps in the literature, acknowledged the need for theorizing the post-colonial transition state, and developed trajectories of new conceptualization such as the hybrid state, much more work has to be done in future in this regard.

Appendix I

Table 11.1 List of Interviewees

Nr.	*Year*	*Organization/Department/Position*
1	2017	Association of young businessmen and financiers, NGO
2	2017	NBG, Department of Macroeconomic Policy
3	2017	NBG, Department of Macroeconomics and Statistics
4	2017	NBG, Department of Banking Supervision
5	2017	NBG, former president
6	2017	Banking Association
7	2017	IMF representation in Georgia
8	2017	ISET Policy Institute
9	2017	KfW representation in Georgia
10	2017	NBG, Department of Consumer Protection and Financial Education
11	2017	Advisor of the president of Georgia in economic affairs
12	2017	Sparkasse Stiftung representation, Georgia
13	2017	Ministry of Economy, Department of Macroeconomic Analysis
14	2017	Former minister of economy, under Shevardnadze
15	2017	WB representation in Georgia
16	2017	TBC Bank, credit expert
17	2017	Society and Banks, NGO
18	2017	Urban Reactor, NGO[1]
19	2017	NBG, former president
20	2016	Society and Banks, NGO
21	2016	NBG, Department of Macroeconomics and Statistics
22	2016	Economic Policy Research Centre, NGO
23	2016	TBC Bank, Department of Credit Risks
24	2016	Microfinance organisation Credo[2]
25	2016	Independent lawyer
26	2016	Microfinance organization NCA Group
27	2017	Association for debtors' rights

Notes

1 Urban Reactor is a non-profit organization, which was established by Georgian architects with the main aim of studying urban planning and architecture.
2 Credo acquired a banking license in 2017.

References

Becker, J. (2002). *Akkumulation, Regulation, Territorium: Zur kritischen Rekonstruktion der französischen Regulationstheorie.* Metropolis Verlag.

Bevir, M., & Rhodes, R. A. W. (2002). Interpretive Theory. In D. Marsh & G. Stoker (Eds.), *Theory and Methods in Political Science* (2nd ed., pp. 131–152). Palgrave Macmillan.

Bieler, A., & Morton, A. D. (2008). The Deficits of Discourse in IPE: Turning Base Metal into Gold? *International Studies Quarterly*, 52, 103–128.

De Goede, M. (2005). *A Genealogy of Finance Virtue, Fortune, and Faith.* University of Minnesota Press.

Dzudzek, I., Kunze, C., & Wullweber, J. (2012). Einleitung: Poststrukturalistische Hegemonietheorien als Gesellschaftskritik. In I. Dzudzek, C. Kunze, & J. Wullweber (Eds.), *Diskurs und Hegemonie: Geselschaftskritische Perspektiven* (pp. 7–29). transcript Verlag.

Foucault, M. (1980a). The Confession of the Flesh. In C. Gordon (Ed.), *Power/Knowledge: Selected Interviews and Other Writings 1972–1977* (pp. 194–229). Pantheon Books.

Foucault, M. (1980b). Two Lectures. In C. Gordon (Ed.), *Power/Knowledge: Selected Interviews and Other Writings 1972–1977* (pp. 78–109). Pantheon Books.

Gramsci, A. (1992) *Prison Notebooks.* Colombia University Press.

Laclau, E. (1990). *New Reflections on the Revolution of Our Time.* Verso.

Lemke, T. (2012). *Foucault, Governmentality, and Critique.* Routledge Taylor & Francis Group.

Marsh, D., & Furlong, P. (2002). A Skin not a Sweater: Ontology and Epistemology in Political Science. In D. Marsh & G. Stoker (Eds.), *Theory and Methods in Political Science* (2nd ed., pp. 17–41). Palgrave Macmillan.

McAnulla, S. (2002). Structure and Agency. In D. Marsh & G. Stoker (Eds.), *Theory and Methods in Political Science* (2nd ed., pp. 271–292). Palgrave Macmillan.

Scherrer, C. (1995). Eine diskursanalytische Kritik der Regulationstheorie. *Prokla*, 25 (3), 457–482.

Wullweber, J. (2014). Postpositivist Political Theory. In M. T. Gibbons (Ed.), *The Encyclopedia of Politcal Thought.* Wiley.

Wullweber, J., & Scherrer, C. (2010). Post-Modern and Post-Structural Intenational Economy. In R. A. Denemark & R. Marlin-Bennett (Eds.), *The International Studies Encyclopedia.* Wiley-Blackwell.

Index

Page numbers in italics refer to figures. Page numbers in bold refer to tables. Page numbers followed by 'n' refer to notes.